ACCOUNTABILITY AND QUALITY IN HEALTH CARE
THE NEW RESPONSIBILITY

Edited by

Leona E. Markson, ScD

David B. Nash, MD, MBA

JOINT COMMISSION MISSION

The mission of the Joint Commission on Accreditation of Healthcare Organizations is to improve the quality of care provided to the public.

Printed in the U.S.A.

ISBN Number: 0-86688-431-9
Library of Congress Catalog Number: 94-73069

Contributors

Carol A. Cronin, MSW, MSG
Senior Vice President, *Health Pages Magazine*, New York, New York

Mark H. Epstein, ScD
Executive Director, National Association of Health Data Organizations, Falls Church, Virginia

J. Richard Gaintner, MD
President and Chief Executive Officer, New England Deaconess Hospital Corporation; Professor of Medicine, Harvard Medical School, Boston, Massachusetts

Susan Koskoff Glazer, MBA
Vice President, Planning, New England Deaconess Hospital, Boston, Massachusetts

Joseph S. Gonnella, MD
Senior Vice President for Academic Affairs and Dean, Jefferson Medical College, Thomas Jefferson University, Philadelphia, Pennsylvania

Robert W. Hungate, MBA
President, Physician/Patient Partnerships for Health, Wellesley, Massachusetts

Stephen F. Jencks, MD
Senior Clinical Advisor, Health Standards and Quality Bureau, Health Care Financing Administration, Baltimore, Maryland

Catherine M. Kunkle, BSN
Vice President, Operations and Information Services, National Business Coalition on Health, Washington DC

Barbara S. Kurtzig, MA
Associate Director, National Association of Health Data Organizations, Falls Church, Virginia

Daniel Z. Louis, MS
Managing Director, Center for Research in Medical Education and Health Care, Jefferson Medical College, Philadelphia, Pennsylvania

Leona E. Markson, ScD
Associate Director, Clinical Outcomes Research, and Research Assistant Professor of Medicine, Center for Research in Medical Education and Health Care, and the Office of Health Policy and Clinical Outcomes, Jefferson Medical College, Philadelphia, Pennsylvania

David B. Nash, MD, MBA
Director, Office of Health Policy and Clinical Outcomes, and Associate Professor of Medicine, Jefferson Medical College and Thomas Jefferson University Hospital, Philadelphia, Pennsylvania

Robert J. Panzer, MD
Associate Medical Director, Quality Improvement; Director, Office of Clinical Practice Evaluation; and Associate Professor of Medicine, Strong Memorial Hospital/University of Rochester Medical Center, Rochester, New York

Haya R. Rubin, MD, PhD
Director, Quality of Care Research, and Assistant Professor of Medicine, Departments of Medicine and of Health Policy and Management, Johns Hopkins University, Baltimore, Maryland

Contents

Dedication

To Zachary Alan Markson who, at eight years old, defined a balance between quality of life and aggressive medical care.

Preface

Over the past decade, we have witnessed a transformation in health care quality measurement—from a perception that "quality is impossible to define" to "quality can be graded and reported on the front pages of newspapers." This volume on quality and accountability in health care takes a broad perspective on the forces driving the general expectation for health care institutions to be more accountable for the quality of the care they deliver. Opinions on this subject are diverse and the authors of this volume neither share a common goal nor vision for future accountability systems. Instead, this book highlights the major forces that will shape health care accountability through the next decade and will help the reader understand the complexity of issues that surrounds attempts to make our health care system more publicly accountable for quality of care.

This volume is an outgrowth of a national workshop funded by the Agency for Health Care Policy and Research (AHCPR) that we hosted on *Public Accountability of Hospitals Regarding Quality.* Papers from the workshop were published in the July 1994 issue of *The Joint Commission Journal on Quality Improvement.* Recognizing the importance and timeliness of the topic, the Joint Commission asked us to expand this work into a book that would reach a wider audience.

In this book, we first provide an extensive introduction to the topic of accountability in health care to set the stage for the growth, interest, and demand for information on quality of medical care. The chapters that follow our introduction are dedicated to issues surrounding (1) the federal government's influence on quality of care initiatives; (2) the contributions of state data organizations; (3) the information demands from business coalitions on health; (4) the information needs of health care purchasers; (5) the impact of accountability demands on hospitals; (6) the compatibility of public accountability efforts with quality improvement programs; (7) the responsibility of physicians for outcomes of medical care; and (8) perspectives on future directions in health care accountability. We looked to health and business leaders across the country to shape this book. We are indebted to the authors: Carol A. Cronin, MSW, MSG; Mark H. Epstein, ScD; J. Richard Gaintner, MD; Susan Koskoff Glazer, MBA; Joseph S. Gonnella, MD; Robert W. Hungate, MBA; Stephen F. Jencks, MD; Catherine M. Kunkle, BSN; Barbara S. Kurtzig, MA; Daniel Z. Louis, MS; Robert J. Panzer, MD; and Haya R. Rubin, MD, PhD. The unique views and experiences of these authors and their willingness to relay their insights on paper allowed us to assemble in one volume the forces that are driving accountability in health care, and that will ultimately influence any health care reform effort that will come to pass.

In addition to the authors, many individuals shaped this volume. First, we would like to thank the excellent staff at the Joint Commission. They critiqued our work, but allowed us to produce a book that reflects the opinions and views of the authors. At its inception, we were encouraged to craft a book that would help to define the state of the art of public accountability without taking on any given institution's agenda. The Joint Commission is to be commended for its interest in furthering the field beyond what it accomplishes through the important work of accreditation. While the AHCPR did not directly fund this volume, we wish to thank the AHCPR since its funding was the basis for much of our previous work from which this volume has evolved. At Jefferson Medical College and Thomas Jefferson University, we could not have completed this book without the ongoing support from Dr Joseph S. Gonnella, the Dean of the Medical College and Senior Vice President for Academic Affairs, and Thomas J. Lewis, the Chief Executive Officer of the Hospital and Senior Vice President for Healthcare Administration. Much of the day-to-day legwork was handled superbly by Susan Howell, Project Coordinator, and our administrative assistants, Karen Jordan and Elizabeth Brown. Finally, we wish to thank our families who know all too well the value of high quality medical care.

Almost everyone will ultimately need to contend with a serious health care problem either for themselves or a loved one. When this occurs, some level of trust will be required to feel assured that quality-of-care systems are working in our favor. We may be foremost concerned about sustaining life over death, but also know that quality has more than a single attribute. Packaging information on quality in a way that conveys the information needed so that we can make informed choices and have no regrets about our health care decisions will undoubtedly remain a challenge into the next century. This volume helps to define how public accountability for quality of medical care has become a new field of investigation that has many stake-holders who will all try to guide us in our medical decision making.

Leona E. Markson, ScD

David B. Nash, MD, MBA

Foreword

In this country, we often use fine sounding terms to frame concepts that we know are right but not fully understood. "Accountability" is such a term, and "public accountability in health care" is such a concept.

Accountability is set upon the foundation of public disclosure—the willingness of providers to share information about their performance with those having a "need to know" or simply an interest in this information. But are the providers ready? What information should be shared? How do we determine the accuracy and validity of the information? And how do we ensure that the information is useful and understandable to a wide variety of audiences?

As readers of *Accountability and Quality in Health Care: The New Responsibility* will come to understand, these are not idle questions. Those providers who believe they will be able to compare effectively in an information-driven marketplace are more ready for public disclosure than providers who see themselves at a competitive disadvantage. The combination of measurement and disclosure is like a loaded gun—dangerous if misused or pointed in the wrong direction. In the volatile health care arena, performance information hastens the distinctions between winners and losers. There will be happy success stories, to be sure, but hospitals will close and professional careers will founder. For many, professional readiness for public disclosure is a state of courage.

What information should be made available? This is not a question of whether anything should be kept hidden; it is rather the converse difficulty of choosing carefully from the rapidly burgeoning mass of performance measurement data. When the grand national debate on health care reform began, America fell in love with the simple idea of report cards on providers. Now, many months and one failed reform initiative later, there is no agreement on the format or broad content areas for report cards, or even whether report cards *per se* are a good idea. Assuming that there is broad public interest in performance information in health care (which has not been established), what information is most meaningful? Are we talking about measuring health promotion efforts, clinical outcomes, patient satisfaction, individual functional status, standards compliance (i.e., whether health care organizations are doing the right things, right), or some combination thereof? In making this judgment, we must remember that the user will have a finite capacity to grasp and use the information that we do provide.

The effectiveness and credibility of any public disclosure initiative depends upon the strength of its underpinnings—the quality of the data gathered through the performance measurement process. In this book, you will hear from many of the cutting-edge brokers of performance measurement in this country. Suffice to say, performance measurement in health care is a new and evolving science. . .and an art form as well. We need to design measures that truly measure what we intended to measure, and we need to evaluate these measures to be sure that they have met this objective. There are needs as well to standardize the definitions of data elements and to agree upon a measure specific approach to risk adjustment so that the resulting measurement data are actually comparable. And there are issues of data integrity. How do we establish cross-checks to ensure that the data reported are the real results? These are all solvable challenges which will be addressed over time. Today, however, the public foundations and provider anxieties come in part from the realization that the underpinnings of accountability are not as strong as we would like them to be.

Finally, let us not underestimate the vast chasm between performance data and understandable and useful information. Providers have long questioned the ability of lay persons to interpret and understand health care performance data. The providers are probably right, but whose problem is this? Today's dawning honesty tells us that *we in health care* have only rudimentary understandings of what our performance data mean. This will turn out to be one of the major challenges in health care for the remainder of this century. The basic obligation encompassed within public accountability is not simply disclosure. It is the responsibility to translate data into information through objective, well-informed interpretation, and to portray this information in ways that it can be understood and used by various audiences.

Are we in health care up to these challenges? Leona Markson, ScD, and David Nash, MD, MBA, have for several years led efforts to define the field of outcomes research and its implications for accountability in the delivery of health care. In *Accountability and Quality in Health Care: The New Responsibility,* they bring together a diverse group of leaders in business, hospital administration, clinical medicine, government, and health services research to critically review the issues and implications of disclosing performance data and information. This important new book will stimulate those engaged in this exciting new area of health services research and provide reassurance to those who have steadily pushed toward a fully accountable health care system.

Meeting the public accountability imperative in health care will be an incremental process. Good data and information will give way over time to better data and information, and pioneers like Markson and Nash will make this happen.

Dennis S. O'Leary, MD
President

Chapter One

ACCOUNTABILITY AND QUALITY IN HEALTH CARE
An Introduction

Leona E. Markson, ScD

David B. Nash, MD, MBA

Medicine is no longer solely within the purview of the professionals who have been granted a license to practice. Discussions of complicated medical procedures and clinical decisions are the focus of television broadcasts and general readership magazines. Patients with chronic diseases are increasingly being educated about the implications of their conditions, the complications they need to be wary of, and the life-style changes that may result in improved health. The high costs associated with the delivery of medical care appear to be a regular focus of congressional debate and state legislative initiatives. Variations in how care is delivered by different health care providers is viewed as worrisome, and business people, always interested in the bottom line, are determined to control health care spending and make sure they are receiving value for the high costs expended on employee health benefits. There is a general feeling on the part of elected officials, business groups, providers, and consumers that we need to do something to feel that we are controlling health care, and not that health care is controlling us. The theme of *accountability* has become the vision that will put all who are concerned—patients, payers, and providers—back in control.

For patients, accountability brings a promise of control in the selection of effective health care services, and knowledge that may facilitate medical decision making. For payers, accountability may produce information that can be used in contract negotiations to put cost-control mechanisms into place. For health care providers, accountability may define the scope of professional responsibility, perhaps lessen liability if parameters for practice are established, and provide a negotiating tool with health care administrators if additional resources seem warranted to meet the practice standards recorded at other institutions. At first glance, health care accountability should be a win-win situation for all involved.

Currently, the field of hospital accountability is caught in a struggle between the demands by many interest groups to immediately release data on quality of care to the public and the reality that much of the available information on hospital quality is poorly specified, often misleading, and potentially dangerous when misinterpreted. Health care reform initiatives have further sparked interest in hospital quality information to facilitate the purchasing of health care benefits as well as the marketing of services by providers. The motivation for seeking data on hospital quality varies depending on whether the user of the data is a benefits administrator aiming to buy the most cost-effective plan; an executive of a managed care plan forming provider networks; a clinician who is a member of a quality improvement team; a newspaper reporter covering health care reform issues; or a patient considering treatment for a life-threatening illness.

Accountability is being promoted not only because, philosophically, the public is entitled to have information on quality, but because demands for information on hospital quality are being generated from many diverse groups. As pointed out in this book, accountability in health care is attempted through numerous avenues. There are licensing and accreditation processes that attempt to serve quality-of-care functions; state and federal efforts to construct health care "report cards" for hospitals and insurance plans; some HMOs that are producing their own quality-of-care report cards; business coalitions that have developed consumer guides to health care; and statistical reports on hospital and physician care have been issued by the Health Care Financing Administration (HCFA), as well as state data organizations. Hospitals participate with other institutions to identify benchmarks for selected processes of care, and foster accountability by sponsoring continuous quality improvement programs. In addition, accountability is facilitated by carefully designed research projects that are reported in peer-reviewed journals and are further disseminated through press releases. The media has tapped into all of these efforts and generated a demand for additional information on quality of health care by developing news stories on health care information obtained from any of these sources.

As dissemination of information on health care quality escalates from any of a number of sources, it is important to begin to set goals for accountability systems. Accountability in health care should, at a minimum, accomplish the following: (1) comprise the documentation of the use of health care services; (2) summarize the rationale for the critical actions taken; (3) assess differences in outcomes; and (4) produce an information base that supports health care decision making. Health care accountability will grant different types of controls to the various participants in the health care field. The perspectives about health care accountability are diverse among clinicians, health care administrators, business groups, and elected officials. The goal of this book is to convey the diversity of opinions on hospital accountability from leaders in the health care field to develop an appreciation for the demand for information, as well as the complexity of attempts to make our health care system more accountable for its actions.

This chapter provides background information about developments in health care assessment to establish the context for current accountability efforts, and to better understand the fundamental components of accountability. Quality of care can be influenced by factors related to patients, providers, organizations, and insurance arrangements. The elements of quality that should be attributable to each of these dimensions deserve careful attention. The background section of this chapter is divided into the following sections. First, we think it is important to acknowledge the information base that has been generated through population-based studies of the delivery of health care services. Second, the extension of health services research techniques outside of academic settings is described. Third, we address the controversial topic of the influence of payment mechanisms on the agenda for measuring quality of care. Since the financial arrangements for paying for health care will evolve over time, it is important to consider quality measurement under different financial arrangements, especially since quality of care measurement may increasingly be used to reshape market forces in health care. This third section describes some of the larger general issues related to payment for care that need to be considered in the quality and accountability agendas of policymakers. Our fourth section moves from the general level of payment mechanisms to the organizational level to briefly explore the institutional role in quality and accountability. The specific issues related to physicians and individual provider accountability are addressed in later chapters and are not the focus of this introduction. Finally, we believe it is important to lay out from the outset what we believe are some of the misconceptions about the field, and issues that stand in the way of implementing the field of health care accountability. We conclude with a brief overview of the chapters that follow.

Background

Population Medicine and Health Care Accountability—Setting the Context

Information on quality of health care varies tremendously in terms of the rigor that has been used to define patient populations, analyze patterns of care, and interpret the findings. Solid health services research lies at the heart of good accountability approaches. We believe some background is warranted on the contributions of health services research to the current efforts aimed at improving health care accountability systems. Population medicine and health services research efforts have helped to define gaps and inconsistencies in the delivery of care, and can at least partially be given credit, along with escalating health care expenditures, for the heightened demand for accountability in health care.

A number of population-based approaches have been used to generate information that evaluates the health care delivery system. For over 20 years, extreme variation in the practice of medicine has been well documented. Early studies by Wennberg[1] indicated that the rate of certain surgical procedures varied widely within the same state, showing for instance, that the rate of cholecystectomies per 10,000 women in certain Vermont areas ranged from a low of 17 per 10,000 to a high of 57 per 10,000. Similar variation in practice has been documented for prostatectomy rates,[2] cesarean section rates,[3] and other medical and surgical services.[4–6] These and other landmark studies on practice pattern variation applied certain principles of epidemiology—the study of disease in population groups—to the study of health care delivery in population groups. Among the most disturbing findings associated with population-based studies of health care use were the results which suggested that illness rates in the population did not explain service utilization rates.[7] Evidence of wide variation in the use of medical services gave rise to a number of important questions. Was the care being provided in some areas excessive? Were there serious problems with underutilization occurring in other areas? Practice pattern-variation studies have not defined appropriateness of care; however, these studies generally led to the perception that the degree of variation in the use of medical services was too high. There seemed to be a lack of control in how medical decisions were being made, and a perceived sense of urgency to begin to address these issues.[8]

A series of studies that followed in the late 1970s and are continuing today have focused on reasons for variations in practice. Many of these studies focused on physician influences on practice pattern variation. Eisenberg and Nicklin[9] studied whether the use of medical tests among generalists varied with the experience level of the physician. They found that in a study population of generalist physicians, the physicians who had been out of medical school for longer periods of time had lower test order rates than physicians recently completing their training. Physician attitude toward risk,[10–12] as well as attitudes toward the role of cost-effectiveness of care in recommending treatment options[13] also may have a substantial influence on practice pattern variation. In addition, a series of studies[14] explored whether the use of medical services was "physician generated." There was some evidence that higher rates of surgery occurred in regions with a higher rate of surgeons per 10,000 population, leading to a concern that physicians can create their own demand for medical care.[15, 16]

Practice pattern variation also appears to be closely linked to certain patient characteristics. There have been reports of inequities in the availability and use of certain procedures across different population groups. For instance, women hospitalized for coronary heart disease may be less likely than men to be offered angiography or revascularization.[17] The likelihood of having coronary artery bypass graft (CABG) surgery appears to be four to five times higher in men, and this variance does not seem to be explained by differences in the rate of coronary artery disease by gender.[18,19]

There is also evidence that the rate of CABG surgery is proportionally lower among blacks than whites.[20–24] Among white populations, women appear to have higher operative mortality for coronary procedures than men,[25–27] although body surface area between women and men may be a contributing factor.[28] In contrast, cardiac mortality from all causes did not appear to vary by gender in an inner-city black population.[29] It is difficult to tell from many of these studies whether differences in outcomes by gender are due to factors that can be modified through improved clinical practice, or whether predisposing factors exist that place one gender at higher operative risk.

Racial differences in the receipt of health care services have been reported among other types of patients, such as breast cancer patients,[30] although it is not clear whether these differences are due to problems with access to care, or racial differences in attitudes toward care. There is some evidence that race is associated with the overall intensity of care for hospitalized patients,[31] and at least one study suggested that patients who are black or from poor neighborhoods have worse processes of care while they are hospitalized.[32]

In addition to gender and racial influences on care patterns, access to care may vary by type of medical condition. A study showed that "do not resuscitate" orders are greater among patients with acquired immunodeficiency syndrome and lung cancer than among patients with cirrhosis or severe congestive heart failure regardless of the similar prognoses among these groups of patients.[33]

Patient preferences and psychosocial characteristics of patients can also influence patterns of disease and health care utilization. Data from the Framingham study found that women of lower educational levels, those with symptoms of tension, and women who lacked vacation time were more prone to myocardial infarctions.[34] Variations in the recognition of important symptoms and subsequent use of health services also may be related to educational levels and other "nonmedical" factors.

Data from a survey comparing the association of income and education with breast cancer and cervical screening in Ontario, Canada, with those in the United States found that despite the long-established presence of universal insurance coverage in Canada, the low use of cancer screening procedures by the poor in Canada was similar to that prevalent among the poor in the United States. Universal coverage does not appear to be sufficient to counteract the effect of low socioeconomic status.[35]

It is important to note that some element of variation in practice when caring for patients with similar conditions should be regarded as desirable. For instance, respect of patient preferences for type of treatment is being encouraged by the medical community when treatment options are available.[36,37] Therefore, variation in the use of mastectomy versus lumpectomy followed by radiation or chemotherapy for breast cancer may be partially a patient preference issue.

Health services research studies provide a level of accountability by highlighting issues related to the delivery of health care services that deserve public attention. The cumulative knowledge over the past 20 to 25 years obtained from health services research studies helps define the complex culture and circumstances that influence outcomes of care. As shown in Table 1, the provider and patient factors contributing to practice pattern variation, and hence control of health care delivery, are quite diverse. The Agency for Health Care Policy and Research (AHCPR), an agency of the Public Health Service, is dedicated to studying medical effectiveness, appropriateness, and outcomes of care in order to determine the most effective ways to prevent, diagnose, treat, and manage clinical conditions (Omnibus Budget Reconciliation Act of 1989). Funding provided by AHCPR, a number of private foundations, and other federal and state agencies has produced a sizable funding base for conducting rigorous assessment of health service utilization and the influence of care on patient outcomes, demonstrating that there is a common purpose to health services research. As described by Dr Rohrer from the Graduate Program in Hospital and Health Administration at the University of Iowa:[38]

> *". . .health services research can be defined as efforts to determine how the health system functions so that its performance can be improved. This definition makes the field essentially activist in nature."*

It is the activist nature of the work of evaluating health services that perhaps explains why much of the accountability work is conducted outside of academic centers. The information produced in the context of accountability is frequently not produced using the academic model of designing protocols, submitting these protocols for review by funding agencies, obtaining funding, and then submitting findings to peer-reviewed journals. In fact, for many proponents of improved systems of health care accountability, the pace of receiving information through health services research programs has been too slow to meet business and other needs. In addition, academic research projects are less likely to provide information on individual doctors and hospitals, the type of information that makes up consumer report cards.

TABLE 1

Examples of Provider, Patient, Organization, and Payment Mechanism Factors Contributing to Variation in Health Care Delivery

Provider-Related Factors

- Experience level of providers
- Attitudes toward risk
- Availability of specialists in the community
- Attitudes toward cost-effectiveness as a criteria for recommending care
- Poor quality of the medical evidence

Patient-Related Factors

- Severity of illness
  - Gender
  - Race
  - Type of disease
- Inequities in availability or use of services among special populations
- Patient risk-taking preferences in selecting treatments
- Patient tolerance for pain or discomfort
- Psychosocial issues

Organizational Factors

- Style of medical and administrative leadership
- Role ambiguity
- Staff education
- Coordination between departments
- Availability of technology

Payment Mechanism Factors

- Restrictions on access to specialists and providers
- Level of copayments and deductibles
- Services covered
- Incentives to reduce resources consumed
- Freedom of patients to change coverage

Measuring Quality of Care—Beyond Academic Studies

HCFA, in an attempt to understand quality of care in the Medicare program, began to produce hospital-specific mortality rates that the agency published directly rather than through peer-reviewed journals. The release of hospital mortality data caused a great stir of emotions,[39] the type of reaction that often accompanies cultural changes. In this instance the cultural change was to discuss potential hospital quality-of-care problems in a public forum. Leaders of medical and hospital associations were quick to respond to the bold step taken by HCFA. Dr John Kelly, Director of the American Medical Association's Office of Quality Assurance, is quoted as saying "mortality data are an inadequate measure of the quality of care."[40] As president of the American Hospital Association, Dr Carol McCarthy had the following remarks: "We continue to believe that an analysis this complex and difficult to interpret is not an appropriate basis for public disclosure."[40] Leaders of public hospitals were particularly critical of HCFA's mortality statistics. "...hospital industry leaders criticized HCFA's dissemination of mortality information charging that the list, even with its cautionary language, targeted public hospitals without placing their mortality statistics in a broader context."[41] Dr Dennis Andrulis of the National Association of Public Hospitals stated: "...implicitly or explicitly certainly public hospitals are being singled out."[41] The public distribution of statistical data on hospital performance is no longer an exclusive activity of HCFA. A number of states have initiated statewide reports on hospital-specific mortality rates and other statistical measures of hospital performance. Now, information of this type is available in public libraries across the country.

The holders of insurance data have a valuable asset of population-based information on the delivery of medical care. Contractual arrangements and negotiations between providers and insurers have traditionally focused on payment arrangement, and not on quality-of-care assessments and rights to public release of data. The confidentiality of patient data is held sacred, but the same does not hold true for organizational identities in our pursuit of an accountable health care system. It is hoped that the population-based analyses generated to evaluate the health care system, whether conducted by researchers or by insurance companies, have the goal of improving the quality of care provided to the population studied. For the health care community this self-assessment process can be painful. As so eloquently stated by Dr Donald Berwick:[42]

> *"Sometimes learning requires courage. It can be difficult for experts, especially, to admit candidly that they could be better at what they do if only they knew more. To become a learner is to become vulnerable."*

However, accountability, as it is viewed today, appears to have cost-control as the driving force, with quality improvement as a secondary goal. As the inflation rate for health care costs has far exceeded the consumer price index over the past two decades, there is the perception that "U.S. companies are losing the war on health care costs."[43] Unfortunately, this overwhelming concern about health care costs has perhaps inadvertently placed the health care industry in the perceived position of enemy of American business, and has provided an excuse for poor business performance in international markets. Assessment and accountability in health care are increasingly being viewed with financial implications. Dr Stephen Shortell and Dr Walter McNerney have advocated the following five criteria for health care assessment and accountability:[44]

> *"A set of benefits mandated for all; the allocation of resources on the basis of defined needs; the payment of providers on the basis of performance; the establishment of clinical and fiscal responsibility at the level closest to that of care delivery; and an establishment of a global cap on expenditures based on the needs of the population and the capabilities of the providers in the area."*

As the goals of health care are defined in this manner, accountability and outcomes assessment will be used not only to assist with medical decision making, but also to define medical necessity in contractual arrangements between patients, insurers, and providers.[45] Since financial implications are starting to drive the health care accountability agenda, we will now turn our attention to issues that should not be overlooked about the influence of financial arrangements on quality-of-care assessments.

Payment Mechanisms—The Financial Link in Accountability

An interesting essay on financial incentives in health care appeared in the July 1993 issue of *Scientific American*. The article began with the following description of our health care system:[46]

> *"To traditional economists, the U.S. health care system looks as if it had been designed to produce market failure. Customers have relatively little information about the product they are buying and must rely largely on sellers for advice. Sellers are paid according to how many procedures they perform regardless of their effectiveness."*

The article goes on to describe why payment mechanisms will have unintended and often negative effects regardless of reform efforts. Under fee-for-service systems there is an incentive (or no disincentive) for overtreating. When higher out-of-pocket costs are used to control patient use of services, patients have a financial incentive to put off preventive or health maintenance services, and may only seek care when serious problems result, a time when symptoms have developed to a point that they cannot be ignored. Results from the Medical Outcomes Study, a longitudinal study of patient care and insurance coverage conducted by the RAND Corporation, provides some evidence that out-of-pocket expenses represent substantial access barriers to primary care in fee-for-service systems.[47]

When prospective payment systems are employed to control costs, there is an incentive to deliver care with less resources. In the hospital setting, prospective payment encourages early discharge of patients. If this push for early discharge is pursued too vigorously, the health of patients may be compromised, ultimately leading to higher rehospitalization rates. In fact, the results of one study suggest that the prospective payment system has increased the likelihood that patients will be discharged in an unstable condition,[48] although the general conclusion from a series of studies on the influence of the Medicare prospective payment system did not find any convincing evidence that the payment system caused direct harm to patients within the first two years after implementation, despite an observed decline in length of stay.[49]

With HMO or other capitated arrangements, physicians receive a fixed sum of money to care for their patients, and the provider stands to lose income if too much care is delivered. An added problem is that providers have little fear of losing patients since preenrollment has been determined in advance. Patients in HMOs may demand more care because out-of-pocket payment is not of consequential amounts. When HMO patients are dissatisfied with care or feel they have been undertreated (e.g., not given access to specialists), they may have to wait until the next enrollment period to switch providers.

Other payment structures include selective contracting. This payment structure can be used for certain high technology procedures, but there is no mechanism in place to guarantee that these contracts will be given to the highest quality provider versus the lowest cost provider. For patients receiving care under selective contracts, the choice to go elsewhere when dissatisfied with care does not become a threat to the selected provider because this option has been removed from the patient.

The position maintained by Dr Uwe Reinhardt of Princeton University is that:[50]

> *"There is no way of arranging health care financing that does not lead to perverse incentives...We proved that years ago."*

It is quality assessment methods and public information on quality that are now being viewed as a way to reshape the market forces in health care.[50] It is the purchaser demand for information on value that seems to be driving the health care markets to develop assessment and accountability systems.[51,52]

Since there does not appear to be one financing approach that is totally free of "perverse incentives," one approach to accountability is to measure the influence of the anticipated perverse incentive under a particular financing arrangement. As a result, the informed purchaser should be concerned about measures of overutilization for patients who are insured by fee-for-service mechanisms, and in contrast, these purchasers should insist on having measures of the use of appropriate specialist care for patients covered by HMO plans. In a national study of Medicare patients having symptoms of either joint pain or chest pain, Medicare patients enrolled in HMOs were less likely to report seeing specialists for care, and less likely to report that their symptoms had been monitored, which may have led to less satisfactory outcomes for some HMO patients compared to similar Medicare patients enrolled in the traditional fee-for-service plan.[53]

Problems in care patterns identified through health services research projects could provide guides to selecting measures that assess the undesirable consequences that can be anticipated from a particular financing mechanism. When prospective payment is used with traditional indemnity insurance (as Medicare has done for inpatient reimbursement), measures should be available for early hospital discharges and readmission rates. The concern in HMO settings may be on the timeliness of hospital care, a measure developed by Gonnella,[54] since there is an incentive to avoid expensive care under HMO arrangements. It should be noted that information on services utilization is sometimes lost through capitated programs. For instance, some Medicaid programs that have used capitation for prenatal care do not receive information on the individual services received by women in the capitated plans. The promise of less paperwork through a capitated system may eliminate the possibility of ever evaluating whether care was adequate.

It is important to consider that the ease of measuring quality-of-care indicators varies by type of financial arrangement. One of the great advantages HMOs have in outcomes assessment and marketing outcomes data to the public, is that the denominator for population-based analyses can be defined as their enrolled population. The database developed from insurance information on the enrolled population allows HMOs to assess the use of certain preventive services such as mammography screening rates for women. These rates of the use of preventive services can then be compared to benchmark data when comparison points have been established.

This was the approach taken by Kaiser Permanente when preparing a public document on their performance, referred to as a "Quality Report Card," for the Northern California Region of Kaiser Permanente.[55] It was interesting to note the number of rate-based measures of performance in which a benchmark was not available, although over time Kaiser and other HMOs could benchmark current performance against past performance. What is not apparent from Kaiser's first report card is the level of performance that should be attributable to the HMO versus the amount of the performance that should be attributed to the selective population who chose to enroll in the HMO. For instance, the HMO had a 22 percent favorable rating on the percentage of patients receiving first trimester maternity care, compared to an overall report on maternal and child health produced by the Department of Health Services in the state of California. It is possible that the patients in the Kaiser plan are at higher socioeconomic status than the entire California population. This leads to questions about whether good performance based on these kinds of measures are directly attributable to the health care plan. In other words, will the results be reproducible in other population groups that may use this data to select a health plan?[56,57] A common response of HMOs when issuing this type of data is to suggest that they at least know the rate of certain preventive services, while these rates are not known in other health care settings.

Assessments of care within health plans such as HMOs are usually aggregated across providers, so that differences in care received in one hospital are not evident from the data. The plan should be held accountable for decisions made about medical necessity in distinguishing between covered and not covered services. The outcomes of care are more reasonably associated with the providers of care, and not the health plans, assuming that the perverse incentives of a health plan did not erode the quality of care delivered by providers. Large hospitals, such as tertiary centers, may want to produce report cards similar to those produced by HMOs, but the way services are used in major hospital centers does not lend itself to the same type of analyses. The population served by the hospital is not readily known, or the patients may use the center for only certain aspects of care. Within a hospital, the denominator of rate-based measures is more easily obtained for acute events, such as outcomes associated with specific surgical procedures. Preventive services or episodes of care may be more difficult for hospital providers to track when patients use multiple providers for these services. It may be necessary for hospitals to work with insurers in order to obtain data that span across organizations as well as inpatient and outpatient settings, although questions still remain as to the aspects of quality that should be attributable to health plans, hospitals, physicians, and patients.

Care Within Organizations

The organizational context of care is an important area of investigation that can facilitate accountability efforts. Organizational differences in the quality of care may largely be a function of variations in the processes and structure of care across institutional settings, such as the composition of the senior leadership or ongoing educational programs. Information on organizational characteristics is typically lacking in data on hospital quality that are made publicly available.

A series of studies highlighting the importance of the organizational context of care on patient outcomes have been appearing in the health services research literature at least as long as practice pattern-variation studies.[58] While we previously described the application of population medicine and epidemiology to the study of health care delivery, the health care industry has also been highly influenced by business school methods of organizational management, and the social science disciplines focused on organizational behavior.

Organizational diversity observed among health care institutions has been linked with outcomes of care. Variations in the delivery of high cost services, such as intensive care units (ICUs), have been a particular focus of attention. Reported differences in average length of stay across 42 units ranged from 3.3 to 7.3 days, and 78% of the length of stay variation has been attributed to patient and selected organizational variables.[59] In a study of over 17,000 intensive care patients, Shortell and colleagues[60] found that the availability of technology within ICUs was significantly associated with lower risk-adjusted mortality. In addition, caregiver interaction, leadership, and conflict management abilities were associated with lower lengths of stay, lower nursing turnover, and greater ability of the ICU to meet the needs of family members.

Analysis of the patterns of hospital length of stay were analyzed for 2,484 patients hospitalized at six teaching hospitals in California and Massachusetts for acute myocardial infarction (AMI), rule out AMI, coronary artery bypass graft surgery, total hip replacement, cholecystectomy, or transurethral prostatectomy revealed significant interinstitutional differences for all conditions studied except rule out AMI.[61] Institutional differences may reflect problems related to role conflict and job ambiguity that have been associated with stress, job satisfaction, and absenteeism.[62] These organizational issues may influence quality of care as much as the technical proficiency of the medical team.

Outcomes of care attributable to an organization may be influenced by the availability of technology, management style of key leaders, experience level of clinicians with certain procedures, coordination of care between departments, as well as the degree to which processes of care have been examined, streamlined, and formalized by health care teams. How accountability systems will relay these complex organizational issues to consumers and purchasing groups has yet to be determined. Continuing quality improvement efforts, the formation of critical pathways, and some guidelines are largely focused on the organizational context of the delivery of health care services.

Misconceptions About Outcomes Assessment and Accountability

The success of health care accountability efforts will be as much a function of the soundness of our methods as of the expectations placed upon these efforts. The list of misconceptions about the field outlined below should be considered in order to set realistic expectations of what accountability systems can accomplish.

Misconception 1: Outcomes Data Will Be Immediately Useful to Clinicians

Research knowledge, whether conducted in a laboratory with test tubes or conducted by teams of statisticians and clinicians working over computer printouts, provides information that becomes cumulative over time. When the results of one study are combined with findings obtained from other studies, the resulting knowledge base will improve clinical decision making. Through interviews on outcomes analyses with physicians, Tanenbaum[63] suggests that the utility of outcomes research to practicing physicians is not immediately apparent. In Tanenbaum's words:

> *"Perhaps they (i.e., physicians) misunderstood statistical probability or were professionally threatened by the possibility*

that medical uncertainty would issue not from the physician but from the statistician. More likely, they were grappling with real discontinuities—between probability and the treatment of individual patients, between the usefulness of outcomes data and the claims being made for them."

The field of outcomes research is still relatively new, and the cumulative benefit that can accrue from these efforts cannot fully be assessed at this time, although at least one study contends that dissemination of risk-adjusted mortality data for CABG surgery played a significant role in the decline of CABG-related mortality in New York State.[64] Despite some early reports of the success of public release of outcomes data, strategies need to be developed to improve the collection, dissemination, and usefulness of quality of care data.[65] This will involve a substantial investment of resources to transform population-based statistics on health care delivery into clinical decision-making and policy relevant tools.

Misconception 2: Outcomes Research Can Replace Clinical Trials

It was surprising to see the following subheading in a February 1994 article in *Science*:[66]

> *"Using health care records to measure outcomes was supposed to provide a quick and cheap alternative to clinical trials. But 5 years and $200 million later, critics are asking: Where's the beef?"*

Outcomes research is a relatively new discipline, but measuring patient outcomes is not new; this has been the focus of clinical trials since their inception. Clinical trials are the essential first step in assessing outcomes of medical care.[67] The clinical trial takes a population of patients with a condition and then randomly assigns them to an intervention or control group. Differences in outcomes are compared between the experimental and control group to determine the efficacy of the medical intervention. Efficacy tells us what works under ideal conditions and a controlled setting of a selected group of patients cared for by a selected group of providers. Outcomes research focuses on what works under ordinary conditions, how medical practice is carried out in everyday practice. It studies the natural practice pattern variation that was described earlier in this chapter. The following definition is offered for outcomes research:

*Clinical and epidemiological investigations designed to assist with medical decision making, by analyzing the degree to which health care services delivered to individuals and populations produce desired outcomes.**

Outcomes research should not be viewed as a competitor to clinical trials. In fact, outcomes research studies may identify areas of study in which additional clinical trials are needed in order to fill in gaps in medical knowledge.

Misconception 3: Patients Are Demanding Quality-of-Care Reports

While outcomes research and data produced from these efforts often have a patient-centered focus (i.e., measure the outcomes that are important to patients), the demand for quality of care report cards is primarily coming from policy and business leaders who want to make sure that they are allocating health care dollars in appropriate ways. A survey conducted by the Harvard Community Health Plan, an HMO in the Boston area, found that consumers were less interested in report card type measures, and generally favored additional information on the doctors who belonged to a health plan, and the reputation of an insurance plan among friends and coworkers.[70] If this is true, the surveys of provider reputation, such as the one conducted for the past several years by *Philadelphia* magazine,[71] may receive more attention from consumers than detailed report card systems of outcomes statistics produced by health care plans. When the focus is on health care plans, the most important information for consumers may be a detailed description of covered services, as well as a detailed examination of the type of claims rejected by the plan over the past year.

The issues that confront us about how to make our health care system more accountable to the public are difficult and will be with us for some time. We believe it is timely to take a critical look at the state-of-the-art of hospital accountability. This book contains the insights of a diverse group of leaders in business, hospital administration, clinical medicine, and health services research on future directions for hospital accountability. The following is a brief overview of the topics addressed in the remaining chapters of this book.

---

* This definition of outcomes research is a combination of Dr Paul Ellwood's definition of outcomes management[68] and the Institute of Medicine's definition of quality of care.[69]

About This Book

Federal Government's Role

The second chapter, by **Stephen F. Jencks, MD**, from HCFA, reviews the US federal government's influence on hospital quality initiatives. As a major payer of health care services, the federal government has a natural role in, and responsibility for, the assessment of care delivered through the Medicare and Medicaid programs, as well as the Department of Defense, the Department of Veterans Affairs, and the Indian Health Service. The release of the HCFA hospital mortality data demonstrated early on to the hospital industry that the federal government, as the holder of a large pocketbook for health care expenditures, can collect data not only to pay medical bills, but also to assess quality.

However, the federal government's role goes beyond that of a direct evaluator of health care services. Through its actions the federal government also defines paradigm shifts in how the quality-of-care "industry" is viewed. One example is the shift in emphasis associated with the transformation of the PSRO (Professional Standard Review Organization) to the PRO (Peer Review Organization) program and the corresponding change in emphasis from standard setting and quality assurance in the Medicare program to review functions and quality assessments.

Although the PRO program was designed to facilitate the Medicare and Medicaid programs, the federal role in hospital accountability also extends beyond direct regulation and data collection that are attached to the receipt of federal funds. Federal initiatives can drive the national research agendas related to the design and development of quality-of-care systems, and can provide guidelines for developing a more uniform approach for assessing hospital care across diverse treatment settings. With health care reform still a subject of debate, it is important to consider the quality-of-care assessment activities that can best be met at the federal level versus those that should be delegated to the individual states or assumed directly by hospitals.

State-Level Programs

A number of states, such as Pennsylvania, have instituted their own programs to assess hospital quality. We need to ask whether state-level programs duplicate or complement federal initiatives. Alternatively, should the states be assuming more of the roles currently held by federal agencies? Legislative initiatives to form state data-collection organizations may create unrealistic expectations—namely, that within a few years these often poorly funded agencies can produce rigorous assessments of hospital quality and cost that can be interpreted by prospective users, consumers, and business leaders alike. In some states these organizations have been handed a remarkable amount of power to either enhance or damage the reputations of hospitals through the release of information on the cost or quality of care. **Mark H. Epstein, ScD,** and **Barbara S. Kurtzig, MA,** of the National Association of Health Data Organizations, review hospital quality initiatives at the state level.

Business Coalitions

Control over health care data is not just in the hands of hospitals and state and federal regulators. A growing number of businesses are participating in coalitions to become more effective purchasers of health care coverage for their employees. The demand for information on the value of the health care services purchased, as voiced by employers and business groups, has provided an important "wake-up call" for the hospital community to scrutinize the way they provide care. However, some business groups believe they can generate information that will enable them to negotiate health care not only on the basis of cost, but also on the basis of quality. This in many ways is a disturbing concept. Since many quality of care measures are still in their infancy, it is difficult to know if these measures are sensitive enough to detect "true" differences in quality. The measures may simply provide an excuse for businesses to insist on selecting the lowest cost provider. **Carol A. Cronin, MSW, MSG,** of *Health Pages Magazine*, and **Catherine M. Kunkle, BSN,** of the National Business Coalition on Health, provide an assessment of the role of business coalitions in public accountability.

Purchaser Information Needs

Because the health care industry is obligated to many different "constituencies," it is important to identify the critical information that needs to be collected and disseminated. The chapter by **Robert W. Hungate, MBA,** of Physician/Patient Partnerships for Health, is based on the premise that the information that purchasers say they want can be endless. For data to be collected in a meaningful fashion, it is essential to define the quality of care measures that purchasers actually need. Data generated on specific diseases, clinical conditions, or procedures are likely to yield the most informative quality-of-care statistics. This creates another conflict in handling hospital accountability systems. Purchasers may desire a short report card that assesses overall quality, but this generic information may have limited value for health care decision making. Hundreds of clinical conditions could be assessed, and developing accountability measures for each condition that a hospital treats would entail an overwhelming amount of work. If hospitals and their clinicians do not take the lead in helping the public prioritize quality-of-care information needs, these institutions will be constantly trying to satisfy every information whim that any number of the many inquirers may request.

Hospital-Based Programs

Susan Koskoff Glazer, MBA, and **J. Richard Gaintner, MD,** of the New England Deaconess Hospital, describe the challenges faced by hospital administrators in meeting the information demands from insurance companies, regulatory agencies, the press, their clinical staff, and others.

The US government is built on a system of checks and balances, and it is quite likely that the hospital industry will need to be tolerant of multiple oversight roles among government and regulatory agencies. At the same time, hospitals need to demonstrate leadership in setting the quality-of-care agenda. This is in contrast to the relatively passive and reactive role many hospitals have played in responding to managed care contracts, state data organizations, and other groups that have requested information on the quality of hospital care.

Some physicians and health care providers may argue that we could do more to improve quality of care if we let hospital providers tackle these issues on their own. A number of cooperative arrangements have been formed among hospitals to assess and improve quality of care on a voluntary, rather than a regulated basis. **Robert J. Panzer, MD,** from the University of Rochester Medical Center, and a leader within the Academic Medical Center Consortium, considers the possible compatibility between hospital quality improvement and public accountability. Although there are many approaches for assessing hospital quality, the "report card movement," which focuses on public release of outcomes data, has some fundamental differences from the continuing quality improvement (CQI) "movement," which focuses on the internal assessment and development of cooperation between various members of the health care team. What type of marriage these two movements form will be part of the quality-of-care evolution that is bound to unfold over the next few years.

Clinical quality improvement efforts are difficult even when they are strongly endorsed by the hospital's chief executive officer (CEO). Clinical leaders need to help design and develop initiatives and to believe that the project is worthy of their time and attention. The report card approach can either be used to shock clinical leaders by publicly displaying outcomes information that they have never seen before, or, report card initiatives can be developed through an interactive process with clinicians using some of the very methods of continuing quality improvement that build trust among team members.

Physicians' Responsibilities

Hospitals are composed of a large number of clinical, technical, and administrative personnel, all of whom shape quality of care. Some outcomes-based assessment systems, such as reports of hospital mortality rates, have not only aimed to identify good and bad hospitals but have also attempted to define good and bad physicians. Given current approaches to hospital accountability, it may not be feasible (much less helpful) to use our relatively primitive assessment methods to assign individual blame, especially if early attempts to make sense of the data are carried out in the media and other public forums. Given the fact that health care is often delivered by teams of providers, it is not clear how outcomes are influenced by physician decision making, patient compliance with medical recommendations, systems of nursing care, or organization of the diverse set of laboratory, pharmacy, physical therapy, and other support services.

Joseph S. Gonnella, MD, and **Daniel Z. Louis, MS,** of Jefferson Medical College, provide their perspectives on physicians' responsibilities for outcomes of medical care. We need to recognize, the authors argue, that critical aspects of the clinical process are not measured in most hospital accountability systems. For example, it is a fundamental concept of clinical medicine that the physician, as the leader of the clinical team within a hospital, must first arrive at a correct diagnosis of the patient's symptoms. However, identifying the correct diagnosis is rarely the subject of current quality-of-care assessment. In addition, quality-of-care data need to be meaningful to clinicians. Dr Gonnella and colleagues highlight why disease-specific measurement of the severity of patient illness is fundamental to most quality-assessment systems.

Future Directions

In responding to the question "For what should hospitals be accountable?" **Haya R. Rubin, MD, PhD,** of Johns Hopkins University, comments on both the responsibilities of hospitals and those of the evaluators of hospital quality. Given the considerable costs associated with collecting data on hospital quality, the *evaluators* of hospital quality and the processes used to make quality-of-care assessments must also be evaluated.

Researchers need to critically examine the available measures of hospital quality. In a workshop that we conducted on this topic, one of the participants referred to the "SAT phenomenon." In the educational field, the Scholastic Aptitude Test (SAT) was developed as an indicator of academic potential. This simple score of a person's performance in a one-day test situation are often used to screen applicants in many college programs, despite documented evidence that the test can contain cultural biases. Johns Hopkins University was among the first medical schools to abandon the requirement for the standardized medical school admission test (MCAT), largely because the University believed that the criteria for determining whether or not a student would make a good physician could not adequately be summarized in a single score.

The problems associated with using relatively few indicators of performance in the educational field should raise some questions about similar attempts in the health care industry to summarize performance using a relatively small set of measures.

At the same time, we must be cautious of the two extreme perspectives that can be evoked by the release of data on hospital quality, "any data on hospital quality are better than no information," and "unless the data are known to meet the highest scientific standards they should not be released." As Dr Rubin argues, an acceptable level of rigor for data-collection initiatives needs to be established. Still, quality-of-care initiatives are unlikely to undergo processes that parallel the developmental phases used to approve new drugs for clinical practice.

Regardless of how quality-of-care measures are developed and tested, some level of public trust is essential for the soundness of hospital accountability systems, since it is impossible to measure every aspect of hospital quality.

In Summary

Public accountability for hospital care—and health care in general—is now firmly on the agenda of the highest level of the government. Yet the measurement of hospital quality is far from an exact science. There are many methodological challenges for the health services research community, as well as challenges for those who wish to make decisions from available data. Researchers debate the appropriate way to adjust for the severity of illness of our patient population. Improved methods are also needed to assess quality of care for less common medical events for which sample sizes are small. We can measure outcomes such as patient satisfaction, but it is not clear whether it varies with diagnosis. It is difficult to link processes of care to specific patient outcomes. Even when we are able to link certain practice patterns to improved outcomes, we do not know the best ways to persuade health care providers to change their practices.

There are also ethical concerns related to hospital accountability. For example, should hospitals advertise that they have the lowest severity-adjusted mortality rate on the basis of studies conducted by federal and state agencies? Should the "successful" ways of practicing medicine be proprietary secrets that some institutions hold as a way to increase market share? Will systems of public accountability facilitate collaboration to improve the standards of care across all hospital providers?

Our hospitals and other health care institutions cannot be accountable for the care they provide if each and every clinician operates with complete autonomy. As a result, the balance between autonomy and accountability will be a delicate one, since it is impossible and highly undesirable to micromanage the health care industry. As efforts continue to increase accountability in health care, policy analysts need to consider whether the balance between autonomy and accountability is a zero sum game.

We need to ensure that hospital accountability produces positive change. As we work to accomplish this, it may be helpful to consider these words of Thomas Jefferson: "Only aim to do your duty, and mankind will give you credit where you fail." We know that the health care industry is filled with devoted clinicians and support personnel who have the patient's best interest as their highest priority. Public accountability should do more than simply assign blame when health care services fail—it should be the basis for improving the way care is delivered.

It is our hope that this book will help further discussion on developing and refining approaches to public accountability.

References

1. Wennberg JE, Gittelsohn: Small area variations in health care. *Science* 182(117): 1102–08, 1973.

2. Wennberg JE, et al: An assessment of prostatectomy for benign urinary tract obstruction: Geographic variations and the evaluations of medical care outcomes. *JAMA* 259:3027–30, 1988.

3. Goyert GL, et al: The physician factor in caesarean birth rates. *N Engl J Med* 320:706–09, 1989.

4. Chassin MR, et al: Variations in the use of medical and surgical services by the Medicare population. *N Engl J Med* 314:285–90, 1986.

5. Perrin JM, et al: Variations in the rates of hospitalization of children in three urban communities. *N Engl J Med* 320:1183–87, 1989.

6. Wennberg JE, Freeman JL, Culp WJ: Are hospital services rationed in New Haven or overutilized in Boston? *Lancet* 1:1185–89, 1987.

7. Wennberg JE: Population illness rates do not explain population hospitalization rates. *Med Care* 25:354–59, 1987.

8. Wennberg JE: Dealing with medical practice variations: A proposal for action. *Health Affairs* 7:6–32, 1988.

9. Eisenberg JM, Nicklin D: Use of diagnostic services by physicians in community practice. *Med Care* 19:297–309, 1981.

10. Nightingale SD, Grant M: Risk preference and decision-making in critical care situations. *Chest* 93:684–87, 1988.

11. Nightingale SD: Risk preference and admitting rates of emergency room physicians. *Med Care* 26:84–87, 1988.

12. Grol R, et al: Attitudes to risk taking in medical decision making among British, Dutch, and Belgian general practitioners. *Br J Gen Pract* 40(333):134–36, 1990.

13. Williams A: Cost-effectiveness analysis: Is it ethical? *J Med Ethics* 18(1):7–11, 1992.

14. American College of Surgeons and American Surgical Association: *Surgery in the United States: A Summary Report of the Study on Surgical Services for the United States*, Table 11, Chapter 4. Chicago: American College of Surgeons and American Surgical Association, 1975.

15. Wennberg JE, Barnes BA, Zubkoff M: Professional uncertainty and the problem of supplier-induced demand. *Soc Sci Med* 16:811–24, 1982.

16. Evans RG: Supplier-induced demand: Some empirical evidence and implications. In Mark Perlman (ed): *The Economics of Health and Medical Care: Proceedings of a Conference Held by the International Economic Association at Tokyo*. London: Macmillan, 1974.

17. Ayanian JZ, Epstein AM: Differences in the use of procedures between women and men hospitalized for coronary heart disease. *N Engl J Med* 325(4):221–25, 1991.

18. Kennedy RH, et al: Cardiac-catheterization and cardiac-surgical facilities: Use trend and future requirements. *N Engl J Med* 307:986–93, 1982.

19. Gillum RF: Coronary artery bypass surgery and coronary angiography in the United States, 1979-1983. *Am Heart J* 113:1255–60, 1987.

20. Hannon EL, et al: Interracial access to selected cardiac procedures for patients hospitalized with coronary artery disease in New York State. *Med Care* 29:430–41, 1991.

21. Oberman A, Cutter G: Issues in the natural history and treatment of coronary artery disease in black populations: Surgical treatment. *Am Heart J* 108:688–94, 1984.

22. Maynard C, et al: Blacks in the coronary artery surgery study (CASS): Race and clinical decision-making. *Am J Pub Health* 76:1446–48, 1986.

23. Ford E, et al: Coronary arteriography and coronary bypass surgery among whites and other racial groups relative to hospital-based incidence rates for coronary artery disease: Findings from the NHDS. *Am J Pub Health* 79:437–40, 1989.

24. Wenneker M, Epstein AM: Racial inequalities in the use of procedures for patients with ischemic heart disease in Massachusetts. *JAMA* 261:253–57, 1989.

25. Loop FD, et al: Coronary artery surgery in women compared to men: Analysis of risks and long-term results. *J Am Coll Cardiol* 1:383–90, 1983.

26. Killen DA, et al: Coronary artery bypass in women: Long-term survival. *Ann Thorac Surg*. 34:559–63, 1982.

27. Hall RJ, et al: Coronary artery bypass: Long-term follow-up of 22,284 consecutive patients. *Circulation* 68(suppl 2):20–25, 1983.

28. O'Connor GT, et al: Differences between men and women in hospital mortality associated with coronary artery bypass graft surgery. The Northern New England Cardiovascular Disease Study Group. *Circulation* 88(5, Part 1):2104–10, 1993.

29. Liao Y, et al: Survival rates with coronary artery disease for black women compared to black men. *JAMA* 268(4):1867–71, 1992.

30. Diehr P, et al: Treatment modality and quality differences for black and white breast cancer patients treated in community hospitals. *Med Care* 27:942–58, 1989.

31. Yergan J, et al: Relationship between patient race and intensity of hospital services. *Med Care* 25:592–603, 1987.

32. Kahn KL, et al: Health care for black and poor hospitalized Medicare patients. *JAMA* 271(15):1169–74, 1994.

33. Wachter RM, et al: Decisions about resuscitation: Inequities among patients with different diseases but similar prognoses. *Ann Intern Med* 111:525–32, 1989.

34. Eaker ED, Pinsky J, Castelli WP: Myocardial infarction and coronary death among women: Psychosocial predictors from a 20–year follow-up of women in the Framingham study. *Am J Epidemiol* 135(8):854–64, 1992.

35. Katz, SJ and Hofer TP: Socioeconomic disparities in preventative care persist despite universal coverage. *JAMA* 272(7):530–34, 1994.

36. Delbanco TL: Enhancing the doctor-patient relationship by inviting the patient's perspective. *Ann Intern Med* 116(5):414–18, 1992.

37. Barry MJ, et al: Watchful waiting versus immediate transurethral resection for symptomatic prostatism: The importance of patient preferences. *JAMA* 259(2):3010–17, 1988.

38. Rohrer JE: Philosophy of science and health services research: A cross-disciplinary critique and call for action. *J Health Admin Ed* 7(3):543–56, 1989.

39. Berwick D, Wald D: Hospital leaders' opinions of the HCFA mortality data. *JAMA* 263(2):247–49, 1990.

40. McCormick B: HCFA refining hospital mortality data. *Am Med News* January 21:32, 1991.

41. Packer J: HCFA report names 161 'high mortality' hospitals. *Modern Healthcare* 21(18):4, 1991.

42. Berwick D: The double edge of knowledge. *JAMA* 266(6)841–42, 1991.

43. Winslow R: Costs of medical care continue to soar, defying corporate efforts to find cures. *The Wall Street Journal* January 29:B1, 1991.

44. Shortell S, McNerney WJ: Criteria and guidelines for reforming the U.S. health care system. *N Engl J Med* 322(7):463–67, 1990.

45. Anderson GF, Hall MA, Steinberg EP: Medical technology assessment and practice guidelines: Their day in court. *Am J Pub Health* 83(11):1635–39, 1993.

46. Wallich P, Holloway M: Health care without perverse incentives. *Scientific American*, July:109, 1993.

47. Safrin DG, Tarlov AR, Rogers WH: Primary care performance in fee-for-service and prepaid health care systems. *JAMA* 271(20):1579–86, 1994.

48. Rogers WH, Draper D, Kahn KL: Quality of care before and after implementation of the DRG-based prospective payment system: A summary of effects. *JAMA* 264(15):1989–94, 1990.

49. LoGerfo JP: The prospective payment system and quality: No skeletons in the closet. *JAMA* 264(15):1995–96, 1990.

50. Wallich P, Holloway M: Health care without perverse incentives. *Scientific American,* July:109, 1993.

51. Hurley RE: The purchaser-driven reformation in health care: Alternative approaches to leveling our cathedrals. *Frontiers of Health Services Management* 9(4):5–35, 1993.

52. Heinikoff LM: Purchaser-driven reform: Who is at the wheel? *Frontiers of Health Services Management* 9(4):37–41, 1993.

53. Clement DG, et al: Access and outcomes of elderly patients enrolled in managed care. *JAMA* 271(19):1487–92: 1994.

54. Gonnella JS, et al: The problem of late hospitalization: A quality and cost issue. *Academic Medicine* 65(5):314–19, 1990.

55. Kaiser Permanente: *1993 Quality Report Card,* Department of Quality and Utilization, Oakland, California, 1993.

56. Berki SE, Ashcraft M: HMO enrollment: Who joins what and why. A review of the literature. *Milbank Q* 58:588–632, 1980.

57. Hellinger FJ: Selection bias in health maintenance organizations: An analysis of recent evidence. *Health Care Financing Review* 9:55–63, 1987.

58. Flood AB, Scott WR: *Hospital structure and performance*. Baltimore: Johns Hopkins University Press, 1987.

59. Knaus WA, et al: Variations in mortality and length of stay in intensive care units. *Ann Intern Med* 118(10):753–61, 1993.

60. Shortell SM, et al: The performance of intensive care units: Does good management make a difference? *Med Care* 32(5):508–25, 1994.

61. Cleary PD, et al: Variations in length of stay and outcomes for six medical and surgical conditions in Massachusetts and California. *JAMA* 266(1):73–79, 1991.

62. Toft PA, Anderson JG: Organizational stress in the hospital: Development of a model for diagnosis and prediction. In DeFriese GH, Ricketts TC, Stein JS (eds): *Methodological Advances in Health Services Research.* Ann Arbor, MI: Health Administration Press, 1988, pp 119–40.

63. Tanenbaum SJ: Knowing and acting in medical practice: The epistemological politics of outcomes research. *Journal of Health Politics Policy and Law* 19(1):27–44, 1994.

64. Hannon E, et al: Improving the outcomes of coronary artery bypass surgery in New York State. *JAMA* 271(10):761–66, 1994.

65. Kelly JT: Evaluating quality performance in alternative health care delivery systems: A critical challenge. *JAMA* 271(20):1620–21, 1994.

66. Anderson C: Measuring what works in health care. *Science*: 263(25)1080–82, 1994.

67. Berman GD, Kottke TE, Ballard DJ: Effectiveness research and assessment of clinical outcomes: A review of federal government and medical community involvement. *Mayo Clin Proc* 65:657–63, 1990.

68. Ellwood PM: Outcomes management: A technology of patient experience. *N Engl J Med* 318:1549–56, 1988.

69. Lohr K (ed): *Medicare: A Strategy for Quality Assurance*, Vol 1. Washington, DC: National Academy Press, 1990.

70. Winslow R: Health-care report cards are getting low grades from some focus groups. *The Wall Street Journal* May 19:B1, B9, 1994.

71. Saline C: Top Docs: The best in 68 specialties, as chosen by their peers. *Philadelphia* 85(3):64, 1994.

Chapter Two

THE GOVERNMENT ROLE IN HOSPITAL ACCOUNTABILITY FOR QUALITY OF CARE*

Stephen F. Jencks, MD

* This chapter represents the author's views and should not be interpreted as the official position of the Health Care Financing Administration.

This chapter reviews the five government roles in hospital accountability for quality of care: (1) shaping the community of those interested in quality; (2) developing methods and infrastructure; (3) standardizing information (specifying data that must be collected and disclosed); (4) facilitating improvement (by providing information and technical assistance); and (5) enforcing standards (Table 1).

Background

The federal government's role in hospital accountability for quality of care is complex,[1] given its multiple roles and the fact that it is both a payer for Medicare and Medicaid and a general guardian of all citizens. Views vary on federally developed and implemented performance measures, the feasible pace of implementation, the uses of the resulting information, the federal role in quality improvement,[2] and the future form of Medicare- and Medicaid-based federal quality improvement methods.

The government's part in shaping an atmosphere of trust or distrust is critical, although often underestimated. The research and development of methods and infrastructure is widely acknowledged as a government role, and many health system reform proposals emphasize it. Several state governments have begun standardizing and providing quality information, a role also assigned to the federal government in several reform proposals. Enforcing standards, including licensure and certification, is the most widely understood governmental role; states license whereas the federal government certifies compliance with Medicare conditions of participation either directly or through accreditation by the Joint Commission on Accreditation of Healthcare Organizations. These standards are evolving rapidly. Only recently has government taken on the role of providing technical assistance for quality improvement.

What Is Quality?

The Institute of Medicine has defined quality of care as "the degree to which health services for individuals and populations increase the likelihood of desired health outcomes and are consistent with current professional knowledge."[3] In this chapter, five aspects of quality of care are addressed: access, appropriateness, outcomes, satisfaction, and efficiency.

TABLE 1

The Five Government Roles in Hospital Accountability

- Shaping a "Quality Community"
- Developing Methods and Infrastructure
- Standardizing Information
- Facilitating Quality Improvement
- Enforcing Standards

Access

Federal programs such as Medicare and Medicaid are fundamentally access programs. Access to hospital care is likely to be a critical concern in the next few years as budgets become tighter. In the fee-for-service sector, government and private payers are likely to put increasing pressure on payments for hospital care; in the prepaid sector, access barriers (e.g., queues, gatekeepers), and narrow benefit definitions may become more prevalent barriers to hospital care.

The standard approaches to measuring access to hospitals are either surveys of potential patients or studies of treatments that appear to have been delayed. Emergency rooms, where service times and costs may create significant barriers, are a special focus. Antidumping laws,[4] both federal and state, define inappropriate transfers and discharges in a way that also, albeit awkwardly, measures access. Indirect measures, such as whether the surrounding community uses the hospital, are often difficult to interpret.

Appropriate Processes

Although much current discussion suggests that we can make health outcomes our main measure of hospital quality, we will need to focus on processes of care in many areas. Process measures are critical where adverse outcomes are rare, substantially delayed, difficult to adjust for variations in patient risk, hard to collect, or difficult to interpret. In prevention, early detection, and management of chronic disease, outcomes are so delayed that examining appropriateness of processes of care is much more realistic. In addition, some elements of good care have modest effects that are not easily detected among the number of patients treated by most hospitals. For example, it is unlikely that we would be able to detect the impact of failure to use thrombolytic drugs appropriately for heart attack patients in most hospitals over a year or two, even though there is overwhelming evidence that appropriate use results in better outcomes.

Process measures of quality must, above all, be widely accepted as valid *and* be connected to outcomes by strong scientific evidence. The Agency for Health Care Policy and Research (AHCPR)[5] guidelines process establishes the foundations for such measures, as do guidelines produced by the Office of Health Promotion and Disease Prevention and medical specialty groups. Medicare's Health Care Quality Improvement Program[6] (HCQIP), which encompasses what was, until recently, called the Peer Review Organization (PRO) program, focuses primarily on processes of care rather than outcomes.

Outcomes

Despite the limitations described above, outcomes remain the most obvious quality measures; recent technical developments suggest that we may be able to adjust for differences in patients between hospitals so as to validly compare differences in outcomes. At the same time, interest is growing in functional outcomes (e.g., the ability to work or to care for oneself) that are harder to measure and interpret than are traditional outcomes (e.g., mortality, complications, readmissions).

Nonclinicians tend to be more comfortable with using outcomes as measures of quality because clinicians tend to worry more about the problems of adjusting for differences in patient risk and patient preferences. Many commercial and public risk-adjustment systems are available, and some have high clinical credibility, but almost all credible systems impose significant data collection burdens. At this point, studies linking risk-adjusted outcomes to directly observed quality of care have been convincing only across large groups of hospitals, and we do not have evidence as to the sensitivity and specificity of these measures in evaluating individual hospitals. Methods to adjust for differences in patient preferences for different outcomes are rare and generally primitive.

Patient Satisfaction

Methods for measuring patient satisfaction are now well established and widely accepted, but many advocates of market forces have argued that government intervention is not necessary to make this traditional market force effective. However, government surveys of satisfaction may be appropriate, given hospitals' difficulty in collecting satisfaction information and the limited access patients have to data on the inpatient experience of others. While satisfaction questionnaires are fairly well developed, data allowing comparisons among hospitals are rarely available.

Efficiency

Efficiency is an integral part of quality because unnecessary care tends to be inconvenient, hazardous, and expensive to patients, while insufficient care puts patients at risk. The concept of informed choice is critical to efficient care, because one patient may desire what is inconvenient or unreasonably hazardous in the eyes of another. There is a small area of efficiency, care that is medically unnecessary but desired by physician and patient, which indeed represents the traditional "utilization review" problem. However, I will not pursue efficiency as a separate dimension of quality.

Hospital Accountability

Health system reform may shape hospital accountability in numerous ways (Table 2). To consider the government role in hospital accountability we must disentangle several elements.

Hospitals do not exist in isolation. The sociology, power relations, and risk-management responsibilities of hospitals make accountability difficult. Medicare's Peer Review Organization (PRO) program has predominantly held physicians responsible for care in hospitals, whereas the Joint Commission has held the hospital responsible. Each approach had serious limitations. Both Medicare and the Joint Commission are now trying to work with hospitals as if they were corporate entities with a commitment to quality. Realistically, however, few hospitals are yet able to hold up their end of a serious dialog on quality. Hospital quality assurance committees are not the center of power in

TABLE 2

Ways That Health Reform Legislation Might Shape Hospital Accountability

- Mandating uniform quality performance measurement and disclosure
- Emphasizing improvement rather than minimum standards
- Changing the structure of certification requirements
- Mandating participation in quality improvement activities
- Funding of new quality improvement structures

most hospitals, and quality continues to appear unmeasurable and unmanageable to many physicians and executives who hold power.

One purpose of holding hospitals accountable is to force them to develop the capabilities that they lack. Unfortunately, hospitals often respond to outcomes data such as mortality, which they usually do not know how to improve, with perplexity, denial, and finger pointing. Planning must recognize that hospital structures and capabilities influence how the government can hold hospitals accountable.

For What Care?

Hospitals provide far more than care between admission and discharge, but control of the interface between inpatient and outpatient care is even more subtle than control of inpatient care. In general, both hospitals and physicians resist accountability in this area, posing a significant challenge for governments and others who would heighten accountability. Progress is needed to develop measures that examine care across inpatient and outpatient settings, as well as transitions between settings in order to foster continuity of care.

To Whom?

When the federal or state government acts to make hospitals accountable, this does not necessarily make them accountable to the government, which is especially true for public disclosure of quality performance measures.

- *To the public*—The approach to "disclosure" can parallel that of the Securities and Exchange Commission, which is much more concerned with regulating accurate disclosure than with regulating what companies do.

- *To hospital boards and professionals*—Public disclosure is likewise a powerful way for the government to ensure that boards and hospital professionals will be aware of performance information. Both groups may be more aware of what appears in *Consumer Checkbook* or on television than of what appears in committee minutes.

- *Corporate purchasers*—One of the most important functions of government-mandated disclosure is to give purchasers (whether employers or health plans) information with which they can bargain with hospitals. The President's Health Security Act would have required alliances to negotiate with plans on quality issues. Many state health data commissions were created with the same vision. As the market is increasingly dominated by such purchasers, government may have a greater impact on hospitals through the information it requires them to disclose to purchasers than through direct regulation.

- *Government regulators*—In general, government regulators have the least ability to deal flexibly with disclosed performance information because they are operating in the black-and-white arena of allowing the hospital to be licensed, or to participate in Medicare or Medicaid, rather than in the areas of graduated choice, and because every significant action must be defensible in court. This means that government is able to act against egregiously bad performance but is rarely able to discriminate between what is mediocre and what is good.

- *Systems and accountability*—Perhaps the most exciting implication of holding hospitals and physicians mutually accountable for their performance is that it pushes both groups to recognize that they function as part of a system. Physicians are taught to rely on their training and skills rather than on participating in a failure-resistant system. Hospitals have only begun to analyze failure modes and to include physicians in system design.

- *Smaller hospitals*—The problems of accountability escalate in small hospitals; where the infrastructure tends to be weak, critical mass for some quality activities is lacking, and volume is often too small for meaningful analysis. For the moment, it is sufficient to say that holding small hospitals accountable will be even more complicated than doing so with large hospitals. This is especially troubling because there is evidence that outcomes for some conditions are better for hospitals (and practitioners) with larger volumes[7] and because many small hospitals operate in constrained circumstances that aggravate quality problems.

Shaping the Community

As already suggested, government plays a powerful role in structuring the community of professional, industry, purchaser, and consumer groups interested in quality. By promoting and regulating disclosure, government can create dialogs between hospitals and purchasers. Conversely, by overselling performance measures and attributing every difference to quality, governments can poison the atmosphere and promote distrust. A critical governmental role is to create, convene, and mediate public-private partnerships to ensure that decisions represent community consensus rather than the views of government employees.

Status

During the 1980s, Medicare's Peer Review Organizations dominated quality assurance and operated under rules that were abrasive, confrontational, and counterproductive. This not only failed to yield measurable improvements but also gave quality assurance a bad name. Medicare's HCQIP consciously focuses on building community and cooperation, but overcoming the antagonism of the last decade is challenging. In the Public Health Service, careful efforts of AHCPR in working with the medical community to develop practice guidelines illustrate a government effort to build community. The efforts of the Centers for Disease Control and Prevention in hospital infection control and immunization exemplify the same collaborative approach.

Research and Development

The three most important kinds of research and development involve determining what is good care, how to measure it, and how to improve it.

Status

Research and development are not inherently governmental, but the rapid growth in the AHCPR makes the government a dominant player. The key roles of the federal government in building an infrastructure for quality improvement and accountability are development of clinical practice guidelines, research on medical effectiveness and quality improvement methods, and performance measurement. At the same time, specialty groups have published most of the available clinical practice guidelines, and the AHCPR has funded rather than conducted most research.

Measurement

Although private groups such as the Joint Commission and the National Committee for Quality Assurance (NCQA) can establish quality measures and offer accreditation to those who use them, only governments can require hospitals and others to collect data and disclose quality measurements.

Status

So far, only states have chosen mandates to compel data collection and disclosure, but Medicare requires submission of billing data that has been used to compute standardized mortality measures. One part of standardization is identifying both average and benchmark performance levels, which is difficult without data from all hospitals.

Both state and federal governments have selected or are selecting either quality measures or data collection approaches of various kinds. Although many states have focused on basic data, such as all-payer hospital discharge data, others have either mandated collection under commercial systems that adjust for differences (for example, differences in risk in Iowa and Pennsylvania) or have developed and mandated their own systems (for example, New York's cardiovascular program). (Refer to Chapter 3 by Epstein and Kurtzig for a more detailed discussion.) There is no sharp distinction between data developed by governmental initiatives and those developed by "voluntary" purchasing coalitions (such as in Ohio). (Cronin and Kunkle in Chapter 4 describe the numerous national business-led purchasing coalitions and their activities.) In either case, edits and audits to maintain data integrity are part of standardization.

Many states, as well as the Medicare mortality data, treat average performance rather than best achievable performance as a reference standard, and no governmental group has used its data to establish benchmarks, or best achievable performance levels.

Technical Challenges

Finding measures with face validity and adjusting them for differences in patient population between hospitals present serious technical challenges. Improvement activities, such as Medicare's HCQIP, provide empirical validation of performance measures—measures that lead to improvement are more valid than those that do not.

- *Sample size*—Even medium-sized hospitals have limited numbers of patients with individual conditions. Strategies for circumventing this problem, including pooling data across time (years), conditions, or hospitals; each has its special complications. For example, about 50,000 breast surgeries for cancer are performed on Medicare beneficiaries in hospitals each year, which is fewer than 10 in an average-sized hospital. Clearly, there is no chance of distinguishing a complication rate of 5% from one of 10% even over a period of several years.

- *Development cycle*—Developing, field-testing, and implementing data collection for a measure is complex and time consuming. Although the technology of measuring access and satisfaction through surveys is well established and could be put in place rapidly, measures of process and outcomes to compare hospitals meaningfully are more technically complex, require more difficult data collection, and need validation. Very few process and outcomes measures are fully tested today. This means that any program for government-sponsored measurement must include both substantial basic development time and a strategy for further development in later years.

Facilitating Quality Improvement

As the language of quality management has shifted from quality assurance to quality improvement, so has the role of government. The idea that governments should promote quality improvement is relatively new. Although this idea is not

TABLE 3

From Peer Review to the Health Care Quality Improvement Program (HCQIP)

Peer Review Organization (PRO) Program

- ◆ Quality assessment
- ◆ Evaluation by inspection
- ◆ Focus on outliers

Health Care Quality Improvement Program (HCQIP)

- ◆ Continuous quality improvement
- ◆ Performance monitoring of samples
- ◆ Focus on aggregate performance

necessarily a product of the "quality revolution," it reflects a growing understanding that much medical practice is not done as well as might be, and that governments have both a stake in improvement and power to promote it (Table 3). Strategies include not only stimulating a market force for improvement by publishing performance information but also providing technical assistance and nonpublic information.

Status

The change in usage of the term Medicare "PRO program" to the HCQIP reflects a transition in focus from policing quality to improving it. HCQIP supports both information development and collaborative efforts for change.

Prospects

- *Technical assistance*—The major current governmental effort in technical assistance is the Medicare HCQIP, although the future role of HCQIP could be modified by health care reform efforts.

- *Communication*—The federal government's commitment to communicating about quality issues with citizens, and particularly with Medicare beneficiaries, is steadily growing. The publication of hospital mortality data by Medicare was a fitful start in this direction. Although clear in its intent of providing information that had never been available, it was fitful in that the usefulness of the information was never clearly established. Known flaws of the report led to suspension of its publication because its known uses were limited. Nevertheless, the Clinton administration's commitment to communicating useful information is most clearly articulated in the quality performance information that was to be published and interpreted under its proposed health system reform.

Enforcing Standards

Status

States have long licensed hospitals, and the federal government has enforced Medicare conditions of participation for a quarter of a century. In addition, the Medicare PROs have enforced implicit quality standards by reviewing individual cases, and hospitals are accountable for meeting other quality standards set by the Clinical Laboratory Improvement Act, the Occupational Safety and Health Administration, and others. In general, state governments license (determining whether a hospital can do business), whereas the federal government sets standards for Medicare and/or Medicaid program participation. The latter standards are often equivalent to licensing because most hospitals cannot afford to forego Medicare participation. Formally processing consumer complaints (which may be very different from informal approaches) is part of standards because formal resolution of a complaint implies a standard to which the consumer is entitled. State licensure investigations and PRO program investigations tend to seem unresponsive to consumer complaints because they do not give them the detailed explanations of what was found. Health Care Financing Administration (HCFA) investigations of institutional problems tend to suffer the same problem. By contrast, ombudsman programs, which may be government sponsored, often provide much more responsive handling of complaints, even though they may not have the same technical capability to evaluate care or the same power to take actions.

Technical Challenges

Licensing, accreditation, and certification standards usually include requirements for quality assurance or quality improvement, along with requirements for quality of performance. Both Medicare and the Joint Commission have such a requirement, and the Joint Commission has been shifting its hospital requirements from quality assurance to quality improvement. Although quality assurance and improvement standards are difficult to criticize in principle, many critics have wondered whether quality improvement can be imposed from outside.

A second challenge is converting licensing and certification to criteria based on performance rather than hospital organization and administrative structures. As noted previously, performance measures are still in an uneven state of development, and it is not yet clear that the transition can be achieved and validated quickly.

The administration's reform proposal included building new licensure standards that were to be patient-centered and focus on outcomes. Medicare's own hospital conditions of participation are under comprehensive revision with a goal of standards based on performance (and thus analogous to federal nursing home standards). The Joint Commission (which effectively certifies about 75% of hospitals for Medicare participation) is moving toward requiring an effective internal program of quality measurement and improvement.[8] Even advocates of standards based on performance agree that organizational standards in areas such as sanitation, fire safety, and physical safety will remain necessary because adverse outcomes from failures in these areas tend to be rare and catastrophic.

Conclusion

One of the most important aspects of health system reform is how it will shape the community of those interested in quality of care. Because most proposals included increased emphasis on guidelines, effectiveness research, and quality performance measurement, quality issues will probably play a growing role. Whether that community will be essentially contentious or constructive depends on subtleties that, in the absence of legislation, are being played out very rapidly in the marketplace. These include how well measures are tested before use, how much technical assistance is available, and to what degree negotiations focus on improvement rather than on blaming and contract cancellation.

The schedule for implementation of quality initiatives will be critical. If data are published before being validated or shown to be useful, as happened with Medicare's hospital mortality publication,[9] establishing a strong science base will be more difficult.

Almost everyone wants the federal government to declare its hand and explain what approach to standardizing measurements it will support, but they also want the government to work through a public-private consortium that respects and takes advantage of existing nongovernmental efforts such as those of the Joint Commission. Measurement standardization will include developing a health information infrastructure, operational definitions of measures, and standard auditing techniques. There will be considerable debate as to the federal government's role in assuring that measurement data are valid (audited) and properly disseminated. National efforts by voluntary groups such as NCQA and governmental efforts at HCFA are converging toward a set of performance measures for health plans that will probably include some hospital processes and outcomes.

The overlap between Medicare requirements and state licensure is likely to persist. Congress clearly enacted the Medicare hospital requirements because it was not content with state licensure, in the same way it gave Medicare authority to sanction physicians rather than relying on states to revoke licenses and created federal nursing home requirements because it found state licensing insufficient.

Almost certainly, the next few years will see a growing governmental role in standardizing and using quality performance measures. How strong the government's role will be and what form it will take remains to be seen. It is likely that the government's role will involve public-private partnerships as a foundation for quality improvement.

References

1. Roper WL: Seeking effectiveness in health care: The federal perspective. *Internist* 31(1):9–10, 1990.

2. Shortell SM, McNerney WJ: Criteria and guidelines for reforming the U.S. health care system. *N Engl J Med* 322(7):463–67, 1990.

3. Institute of Medicine, Division of Health Care Services. In Lohr K (ed): *Medicare: A Strategy for Quality Assurance*. IOM 1990. Washington, DC: National Academy Press, 1990.

4. Gaddis GM: Substandard care, antidumping, and George Orwell (letter to the editor). *JAMA* 269(11):1384–85, 1993.

5. Anonymous: Bridging the gap between theory and practice: Exploring clinical practice guidelines. National Quality of Care Forum. *Joint Commission Journal on Quality Improvement* 19(9):384–400, 1993.

6. Jencks SF, Wilensky GR: The health care quality improvement initiative: A new approach to quality assurance in Medicare. *JAMA* 268:900–03, 1992.

7. Hannan EL, et al: Investigation of the relationship between volume and mortality for surgical procedures performed in New York State hospitals. *JAMA* 262:503–10, 1989.

8. Brooks DC: The Joint Commission on Accreditation of Healthcare Organizations. In Goldfield N, Nash DB (eds): *Providing Quality Care: The Challenge to Clinicians,* 2nd ed. Ann Arbor, MI: Health Administration Press, 1995, in press.

9. Department of Health and Human Services: *Medicare Hospital Mortality Information 1989.* Washington, DC: Department of Health and Human Services, 1990.

Chapter Three

STATEWIDE HEALTH INFORMATION
A Tool for Improving Hospital Accountability

Mark H. Epstein, ScD

Barbara S. Kurtzig, MA

Health data are needed to better understand our health care system, and to leverage changes, when needed, in the system. Health care reform efforts at the state and national levels point to a need to invest in the development of a national comprehensive, integrated health information infrastructure that will provide comparable data at the local, state, and national levels. These efforts encourage comparisons of provider costs, outcomes, and performance. Provider comparisons can be used to hold providers accountable for their performance, to promote competition in the medical marketplace, and to keep consumers better informed so they can make educated health care purchasing decisions.

Using statewide hospital discharge databases and other statewide databases, state data organizations (SDOs) produce reports, special studies, and pamphlets that provide information on hospital performance and disseminate them in the public domain. SDOs expect that the release of this information to the public will encourage providers to compare their performance to other similar providers and pursue improved performance.

SDOs are valuable, but often overlooked, instruments that help ensure health care providers are held publicly accountable. Several factors influence the capacity of SDOs to analyze and effectively disseminate information they collect. These factors include methodological concerns, financial resources, and legal and political considerations, as well as staff skills and opportunities for staff professional and technical growth. This chapter describes the role SDOs play in the accountability of hospitals and the issues that confront SDOs in meeting their state mandates.

The ability of SDOs and their databases to address issues of quality and accountability can be strengthened by ensuring the stability and growth of statewide health information systems, supporting research on information dissemination techniques, and promoting comparisons among hospitals.

Overview: State Data Organizations

A nationwide health information infrastructure should be built on the experiences and expertise already in place. By 1994, 39 states (Figure 1) mandated the collection, analysis and distribution of data on hospital use, charge or cost of care, effectiveness, and performance. These states are committed to collecting accurate and timely health data and they are using these data as tools to stem rising health costs, promote access to care, and ensure quality.

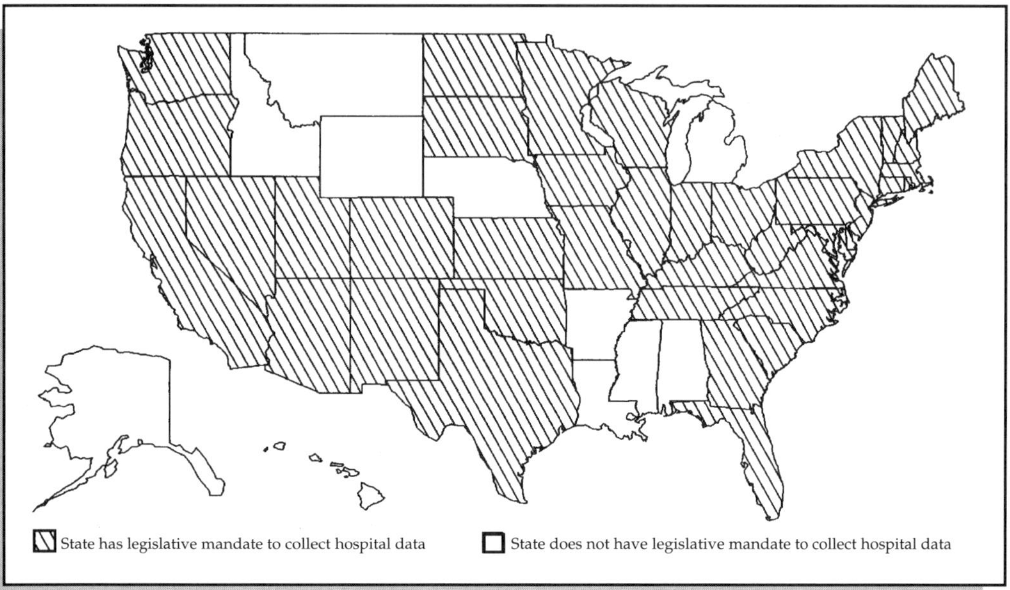

Figure 1. *States with legislative mandates to collect hospital data, 1994. Hospital data include utilization, financial, and effectiveness data. (From National Association of Health Data Organizations, Falls Church, Virginia. Used by permission.)*

While there are other public agencies in states that collect health care information, SDOs are the agencies within the state charged with the responsibilities of collecting, analyzing, and disseminating, at a minimum, hospital discharge information, hospital financial information, or both. In addition to hospital discharge and hospital financial databases, many SDOs maintain nursing home data, hospital-based ambulatory care data, and free-standing surgery center databases. A listing of data sources collected by SDOs has been compiled by the National Association of Health Data Organizations (NAHDO).[1] NAHDO is a not-for-profit national membership association established in 1986 to support SDOs and to promote the development and enhancement of state-level, publicly accessible databases. SDOs in each state perform their duties within the boundaries of their legislative mandate, rules and regulations, and allocated resources.

Legislative Objectives

The development of SDOs parallels trends in the health care system, especially the shift from regulation of hospital rates, budgets, construction, and acquisition of technology to the trends of fostering competition in the medical marketplace as a way to control health care costs. During the 1970s and early 1980s, several states, including Arizona, California, Connecticut, Florida, Maryland, Massachusetts, New Jersey, New York, and Washington, established agencies to regulate hospital rates and budgets. Although the approach to control rising hospital costs changed over time from regulation to competition in several of these states (e.g., Arizona, California, Massachusetts, Washington), the hospital data collection and dissemination function continued.

The SDOs established in the mid-1980s, such as those in Colorado, Illinois, and Pennsylvania, were mandated to collect and place in the public domain data on the use, cost, and in some cases, quality (or effectiveness) of hospital care as a way to encourage and support competition in the market place.

With increased attention on health reform, the need for data to support health policy becomes apparent. Some of the newer data organizations, such as those in Oklahoma and South Dakota were established as part of state-level health reform initiatives.

Regardless of the initial impetus for their creation, SDOs attempt to meet several commonly shared objectives, including assessing the health status of the community, providing information for decision makers, educating the public, containing health care costs, and examining provider delivery systems.

Organizational Setting

SDOs are housed in any of several state agencies or as freestanding commissions or boards. Their position is a function of several factors, which include the perceived role of the agency by policymakers, available resources, existing health data collection and analysis functions, and other indigenous peculiarities of a state.

Reorganization and change in organizational location is common among health data organizations. When the Washington State Hospital Commission was abolished in 1989, its data component was relocated to the newly created

Department of Health. As part of the Health Care Reform Act of 1992, the functions of the Florida Health Care Cost Containment Council were incorporated into the Florida Agency for Health Care Administration. The Wisconsin Office of Health Care Information was relocated from the Department of Health and Social Services to the Office of the Commissioner of Insurance in 1994. The data collection, processing, and dissemination functions continued during these times of organizational change.

Agency Resources

Annual operating budgets and staff size vary considerably among SDOs. Data collection and processing require experienced, qualified staff and computer time to ensure data are submitted and processed in a timely manner and that data submissions meet acceptable standards to ensure data quality. Other operating expenses include the development, production, and dissemination of reports, studies and pamphlets, and other materials to meet the needs of different users and legislative mandates.[2]

SDOs receive their operating funds from three major sources: general revenue funds, assessments of providers, and sales of data products. The stability of data organizations is tied to funding and political support. Several years ago, the budget of the Illinois Health Care Cost Containment Council was cut by 50% as a result of the state's fiscal problems and political infighting. The Council consequently was forced to eliminate its research and public information staff. This severely hindered the Council's information dissemination efforts. The Pennsylvania Health Care Cost Containment Council survived significant budget cuts and the prospect of going out of business before it received a 10-year renewal of its legislative mandate and an increased budget in 1993. During this time, the agency lost several experienced staff, and, more importantly, momentum.

Data Users

Hospitals are the most frequent users of the hospital and ambulatory care information provided by SDOs. Hospitals use the information for strategic planning, facility and program planning, policy development, and marketing. Among other users of these data are consultants, health services and health policy researchers, governmental (federal and state) agencies, health information firms, and software vendors.

State Approaches to Assessing Hospital Care

Health care is one of the largest expenses of a state, and the management of the health care system is one of the most complex issues facing state governments. State and national health care reform efforts are fueling the growing interest in using institutional-level and patient-level data for hospital care to better understand the dynamics of the health care delivery system.[3]

States understand the importance and value of the databases maintained by their SDOs. Hospital discharge databases are the most common type of database maintained by SDOs, and states are exploring new ways to use this rich resource. A hospital discharge database contains information collected on each patient's hospital stay and includes demographic data elements (e.g., patient's age, gender, residence by zip code), clinical data (e.g., diagnoses, procedures), identifier data (e.g., hospital, physician, patient identifier), and billing and payer data (e.g., expected source of payment, total charge).

While hospitals collect these data for administrative purposes such as billing, the data also provide information on service use, charges, and organizational performance. Nevertheless, because these are administrative databases, they do not contain sufficient clinical data to conduct quality-of-care studies.

State Reports and Special Studies

Statewide hospital discharge databases are a source of comparative information on hospitals and they are useful to a variety of audiences. Figure 2 shows the process by which SDOs convert hospital data into information useful to different audiences. State data organizations conduct studies and produce reports using the data they collect and analyze.

A typical report produced and disseminated by an SDO includes hospital-specific experience by diagnosis or diagnosis-related group (DRG) and surgical procedure by volume of services and procedures, and total charge (price). Standard reports include information on:

- charge and volume of services and surgical procedures by hospital;
- patient origin studies by geographic area, i.e., where patients seek hospital care, or where hospitalized patients reside; and

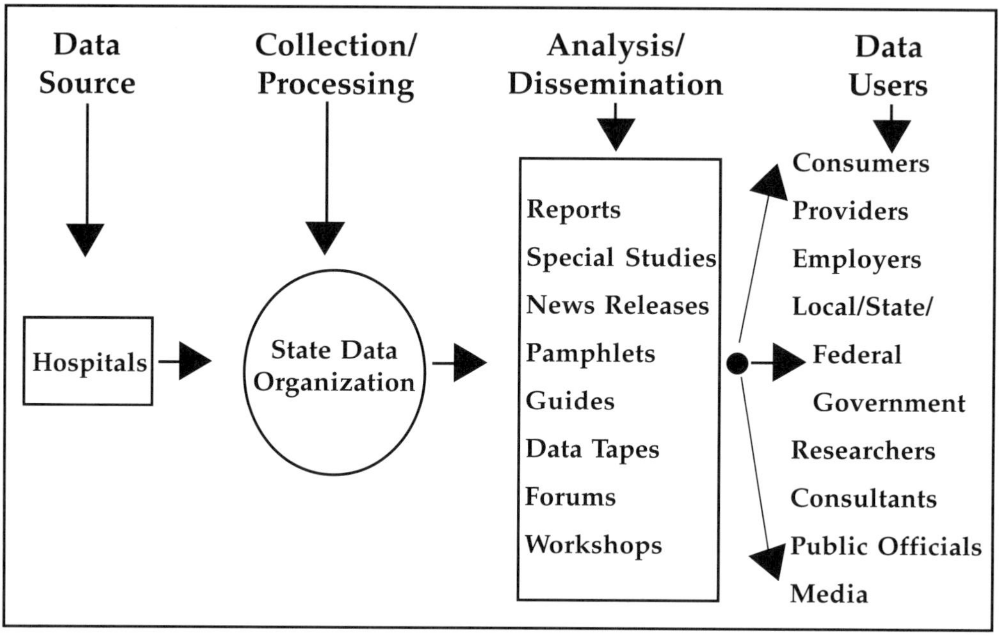

Figure 2. State data organizations collect utilization, financial, and effectiveness data and convert it into useful information. (From National Association of Health Data Organizations, Falls Church, Virginia. Used by permission.)

- length of stay, occupancy and number of admissions, surgical procedures, and average charges.

Special studies may also be conducted by SDOs in keeping with available resources and legislative mandates. Special studies may include information on specific health conditions (e.g., cardiac surgery mortality, obstetrical services, back pain), most frequent DRGs by age and gender, joint ownership of health facilities (such as diagnostic imaging centers or physical rehabilitation centers) by health care providers, public sector purchasing of health care, charity or uncompensated care provided by hospitals, survey of hospital charges, and small-area variation studies.

Several types of SDO studies and reports are summarized in Table 1 and briefly described in the following section. As seen in Table 1, the approaches used to analyze statewide health data vary considerably from report to report. The list of SDO reports in Table 1 is not comprehensive, but it is representative of the diversity of topics and approaches assumed by these organizations.

TABLE 1
State Reports and Special Studies*

Report	Purpose
Small Area Analysis in Wisconsin[4]	To evaluate patterns of care in service areas for 14 major medical and surgical conditions from 58 of the 72 counties in the state
Minority Health in Wisconsin: Toward a Health Diversity[5]	To ensure effective distribution of health care resources among minority populations; to determine which programs will be most successful in improving health status of state residents
Plan for Modification of Cesarean Section Utilization in Dade County (Florida) Hospitals, 1991[6]	To examine reasons for variations in C-section rates in county hospitals
Nursing Home Reporting System: 1992 Annual Report (Florida)[7]	To describe nursing home industry and nursing home resident characteristics
California Hospital Discharge Data for Minorities: Calendar Years 1990 and 1991[8]	To monitor and assess health issues of minority populations
Health Care Costs in Massachusetts, December 1992[9]	To equip providers and purchasers with basic health cost information; explore factors influencing health care spending; identify target areas for cost reduction efforts
State and County Profiles of Hospital Inpatient Utilization: October 1, 1990 through September 30, 1991 (North Carolina)[10]	To provide information for state and local policymakers and planners on patterns of hospital inpatient use and patterns
Buyer's Guides: Outpatient Procedures and Obstetrical Services (Missouri)[11]	To inform consumers when choosing outpatient services
Health Care User's Guide: Hospital Costs by Illness Category (Washington)[12]	To demonstrate differences in health care costs among hospitals for similar illnesses
Health choices: 1992 (South Carolina)[13]	To provide location and medical staff specialty information for each hospital in the state

* From National Association of Health Data Organizations, Falls Church, Virginia. Used by permission.

Small-Area Variation Studies

Variation in care patterns within the state have been an ongoing concern of SDOs. Wisconsin[4] has applied small-area analysis—a method used to compare utilization and charges among population groupings or geographic areas—to stimulate discussion: (1) among stakeholders about the state's health care delivery system; (2) among physicians about different types of medical interventions; and (3) among purchasers and health providers to evaluate the patterns of care in their service area. The analysis will help state analysts evaluate reimbursement or coverage provisions; or in conjunction with other data, to analyze access to, or availability of health care services.

Reports on Special Population Groups

State data reports have also focused on the needs of special population groups[5–8] such as minority populations or care for pregnant women. Some of these reports such as the report on Minority Health in Wisconsin,[5] have combined several data sources to better define the health care needs of the population. To analyze minority health in Wisconsin, the following data sources were used: Wisconsin hospital discharge data from 1990 to 1992, 1990 US Census information for Wisconsin, birth certificates for all live births to Wisconsin residents during 1991, and death certificates for all deaths occurring among Wisconsin residents from 1987 through 1991. A complex set of database construction activities often underlies the production of a SDO report.

In some instances, work groups are formed to study special health care issues. This was the approach taken in Dade County, Florida,[6] when analyzing cesarean section rates. This data collection effort was structured as an educational tool for physicians and others to illustrate variations in medical practice norms for cesarean sections.

Cost Analyses and Pattern of Care

Cost reduction and patterns of care utilization have been the primary focus of a number of SDO reports.[9,10] For example, the Massachusetts Rate Setting Commission[10] produced a report in 1992 that included total private health expenditures, acute hospital inpatient unit costs and use, and information to help explore factors influencing health care spending. This report recommended ways to identify target areas for cost reduction efforts. The purpose of the report is to equip providers and purchasers with basic health cost information, explain the potential uses of the information, highlight areas where more detailed cost-related questions should be asked, and suggest ways in which health providers and purchasers of care can initiate a dialog to address areas of mutual concern.

Consumer Reports

Finally, several SDOs are producing buyers' or consumer guides to health care services. For instance, the Missouri State Department of Health[11] developed detailed reports that consumers can use when choosing outpatient services. These "buyer's guides" to outpatient services contain regional information on facility charges by diagnosis and procedures reported by Missouri hospitals and ambulatory surgery centers. The Department also prepared a guide for obstetric services that includes hospital-specific information on charges, services, volume of deliveries, lengths of stay, rates of cesarean sections, patient satisfaction scores, and out-of-pocket costs to patients. Future plans call for similar reports on other medical conditions and surgical procedures.

The SDO of the Washington State Department of Health[12] has also produced a pamphlet to assist consumers that lists differences in health care costs among hospitals for similar illnesses. Using graphics and easy-to-read charts, the publication defines illness categories and provides healthy life-style suggestions and consumer health care cautions.

In South Carolina,[13] a consumer-oriented report has been published annually since 1988 that contains location and medical staff-specialty information on each hospital in the state. The report also includes charges and length-of-stay data for 25 common diagnoses and procedures listed by hospital, practical information on staying healthy, understanding health benefits, and medical emergency information.

Data Quality and Risk-Adjustment

Releasing health data to the public includes the responsibilities to help ensure data quality and comparability. As noted in *Health Data in the Information Age: Use, Disclosure, and Privacy:*[14]

> *". . . [Database] developers must ensure that the data in their systems are of high enough quality that the descriptive compilations, the effectiveness research, and the comparative*

analyses envisioned can be done in a credible, defensible manner. . .This must be done from the outset so that the long-term integrity and believability of the database. . .will not be undermined irretrievably."

Monitoring data quality is an ongoing effort. Most state data organizations have effective edit systems that validate the accuracy and completeness of the data collected from the hospitals, and offer reporting hospitals an opportunity to review and correct their data before the SDO places the information in the public domain.

In the hospital-level data that are made available to the public, distinctions should be made to account for the severity of illness among patients, the prevalence of disease, and other patient variables, such as differences in age, gender, race, and chronic disease history, which may put a patient at risk for a specific outcome. Adjusting the data to account for these differences is necessary to make meaningful comparisons among hospital performance and outcomes and provide a way to compare what actually happened to patients with what was predicted.[15] SDOs began incorporating severity measures in their public databases in the late 1980s as a means of measuring hospital performance assessment.

Severity adjustment, however, is a difficult, complicated, and often controversial process. Although several approaches, techniques, and software programs for making adjustments are available from both the public and private sectors, each has its strengths and limitations. More research is needed to assess the effectiveness, predictive power, and utility of the various severity-of-illness systems. Each of the severity measurement tools "has its own conceptual framework, approach toward defining severity, data requirements, and method for classifying patients or diseases."[15,16] Each severity measurement may indicate a different approach to quality assessment. However, no objective evidence exists to determine which of these systems, if any, are preferable flags for detecting quality problems.[15]

States must weigh several elements before deciding on an approach to severity adjustment. These include cost, suitability of system to the respective task, predictive power, validity and reliability of methodology, stability of vendor, flexibility of the system for upgrades and enhancements, and availability of technical support. Many commercial severity measure systems are available. Increasingly, organizations are developing their own severity measures using large administrative or clinical databases. The methodologies differ for each severity measure, including, data requirements (e.g., chart review vs. discharge abstract), definition of severity (e.g., "risk of imminent death" vs. resource needs), and whether or not a diagnosis is used. Differences in methodology also apply to scoring systems.

There are generally three ways that states approach severity adjustment of data: (1) developing their own severity system using their unique database(s);[17,18] (2) adopting a commercial severity system;[19–23] (3) or using a number of different systems to determine which fits the state's needs best.

New York and California are using severity systems unique to their states. The New York State Department of Health,[17] using its specialized cardiac care database, applied a severity adjustment formula to provide a comparative hospital and physician-specific picture of performance. The California Office of State Health Planning and Development[18,19] is using its own severity adjustment model to study risk-adjusted measures of patient outcomes in California hospitals. The state's hospital discharge data set is being refined to determine whether additional data elements need to be collected to improve outcomes measurement.

The Pennsylvania Health Care Cost Containment Council has adopted a commercial severity system for all of its reports, including the *Hospital Effectiveness Report*[20] and *Consumer Guide to Coronary Bypass Surgery*, Volumes 1[21] and 2.[22] Included in all three reports was hospital performance in treating a specific medical condition or surgical procedures, mortality and morbidity, and hospital charges. Ratings of individual surgeon performance and surgeon performance in aggregate according to practice group were included in the Consumer Guides. The SDO in Iowa[23] has also adopted a commercial severity system.

Florida is currently in the process of assessing several different severity systems. Florida's Agency for Health Care Administration signed contracts with several firms to provide software to measure the outcomes and prices of hospitals' care. The Agency will compare the products to better determine their usefulness in understanding hospital data during the two-year review period.

Factors Influencing State-Level Quality-Cost Initiatives

State data organizations have experience and expertise in collecting, analyzing, and disseminating health care information. This proficiency comes from an understanding of not only the technical skills required to gather information, but also of the shortcomings or weaknesses of data collection efforts as well as the 'politics' of data collection and dissemination. Several factors may affect the usefulness of the data collection and dissemination efforts of SDOs.

Methodological Factors

Health data should be valid, reliable, comprehensive, comparable, and timely. To ensure the usefulness of information, there must be data quality-improvement measures, and effective efforts toward improving uniformity in data collection methods, definitions, and standardization.

Data may be compromised by inconsistent coding practices, coding errors or omissions, or lack of common definitions for data elements among hospitals. SDOs, however, use data edit checks to help ensure the validity and completeness of the data collected from the hospitals. Most states, however, do not have the resources to perform reabstraction studies that compare the patient's medical record with summary information on the patient reported by the hospital. The California Office of Statewide Health Planning and Development (OSHPD) has performed several reabstraction studies of hospital discharge data. These studies are conducted to improve the quality of hospital submitted data by providing education to hospitals and abstracting organizations; to provide the management of the OSHPD with tools to improve data element definitions, edits, manuals, and data collection systems; and to advise data users of results to ensure appropriate applications of data in health care purchasing, strategic planning, research, and other health policy issues.[24]

There are data elements reported by hospitals that have a greater risk for error than others, such as race/ethnicity information. A critical problem in race/ethnicity data collection centers on who does the reporting. In some hospitals, the information is reported by the patient or the patient's family. In others, the information is reported by the hospital intake interviewer and the information is inferred, not by questioning the patient or the patient's family, but by the patient's surname, appearance, or primary language. Unless there is concurring information collected in the medical record, the hospital (and the SDO) have no way of validating the race/ethnicity information. The data edits for race/ethnicity most often concentrate on whether the information is reported, not whether the information reported is correct.

It is important to remember that discharge databases are administrative databases and hospitals report information for billing purposes. There is little incentive for hospitals to be concerned about the quality of the data reported if the data do not relate directly to reimbursement.

State data systems have been designed to meet the specific information needs of the state. However, health reform efforts have created competing interests for health information. Consumers and providers as well as local, state, and national legislators and public officials are stakeholders in health information and these different users need information in different ways. It is important to recognize the need to strive for data elements that are standard and comparable across settings and over time with uniform definitions and collection formats to meet these different information needs.

Another potential problem is the exchange of hospital discharge data among states. To successfully conduct accurate population-based studies, SDOs may need to acquire hospital discharge data from adjacent states. The lack of data, or problems of comparability and access to the data can distort the findings or otherwise limit the analysis. The Washington, DC, metropolitan area is composed of the District of Columbia and portions of Maryland and Virginia. Hospital discharge data now are available only from Maryland hospitals. Virginia has implemented a statewide hospital discharge data system, but the District does not collected discharge data from its hospitals. The lack of comparable hospital discharge data for this geographic region is a significant limitation when attempting to assess the health status of the population and the use, cost, and effectiveness of its health care system.

The usefulness of the data also may be compromised by the time lag between collection and dissemination. This may occur because the SDO has insufficient resources, inadequate training, time constraints, or a lack of control over how the information will be used.

Another limitation is that hospitals report charges or prices for care received, not the cost of care on standard data collection forms. Because the amount of reimbursement hospitals receive by payer source or cost of care is not collected, comparisons based on charge information are of limited value and may be misleading when compared with actual payment received.

Financial Factors

There is a cost, usually borne by hospitals and the state, to collect, process, and disseminate data. These costs include reporting, processing, analyzing, and disseminating the data in written or electronic formats to various audiences.

Another financial concern centers on requiring hospitals to collect and confirm additional data elements or requiring hospitals or SDOs to implement a risk-adjustment system. Either of these will increase costs to the hospitals. When a state requires hospitals to report more data, the benefit of having the data should exceed the cost of reporting the data.

Dissemination is a major activity of SDOs. The most common form of state-generated reports and studies is hard copy publication. While SDOs would like to take advantage of current technologies for information dissemination, users must be able to receive information in a format that best suits their needs.

States should understand that many users of SDO data may need assistance not only to better understand the information they are receiving from the state, but also to improve its use. As the demand for health information increases, and the circle of users of state data enlarges, educating data users will become a major concern of SDOs and will require significant resources.[25] Without effective dissemination, however, the data and information are of little use.

Legal and Political Factors

Many hospitals may have concerns about the consequences of placing provider information in the public domain. Without caveats and explanations that can be understood by the consumer, releasing comparative hospital information may cause unwarranted hardship on a hospital. Nevertheless, disclosure of hospital information should push providers to measure and improve their performance.

SDOs remain viable as a result of a state's political processes. The mandates, budgets, rules and regulations, and operating environment of SDOs are often affected by state legislative changes and elections, as well as state-determined agency performance and budget reviews and reorganization. The role the SDO is assigned in state health reform efforts also may affect its data collection, analysis, and dissemination procedures.

These organizations must safeguard patient and provider confidentiality and privacy, and monitor data dissemination. There are efficient and effective protection systems in place on the state level, which should serve as models for national confidentiality and privacy standards.

Confidentiality and Privacy

All states gather provider-specific (e.g., hospitals, physician) data, but not all states release or publish these data. There may be significant pressure by providers to prevent public disclosure of their performance. In some states, hospitals and physicians may fear that provider-specific information in the public domain would place them at a competitive disadvantage. Each SDO has policies and procedures in place that are designed to protect the privacy and confidentiality of individuals (i.e., patients). A unique uniform identifier for patients would permit the study of episodes of care while protecting individual privacy and confidentiality. The desire to place health care information in the public domain for informed decision making must be tempered with sensitivity for the need to maintain privacy. Therefore, the assumption that public disclosure of provider information will foster needed change(s) must be carefully examined and several issues must be explored before disclosing provider information:

- Why is the information collected, and can that information be used effectively for purposes other than those for which it was collected?
- What data should be collected and what data should be disclosed?
- Are there proper policies in place to monitor who will have access to what information for which purpose(s)?
- Are there safeguards in place to help ensure the information is properly translated for the intended audience?
- What purpose should disclosure serve?

Educational and Interpretation Factors

Publishing data on hospital charges, outcomes, and performance is an initial step in keeping the public and providers informed about the health care delivery system. To be an effective tool for change, the data must be converted into usable information and presented to consumers, providers, purchasers, and policymakers in clear and useful ways. Experience suggests that not only do SDOs benefit from sharing experiences, information, and methodologies, but also that the quality of their data improves with public disclosure. Public disclosure also often improves the quality of the hospitals' data reporting. How measures of hospital performance and outcomes and comparisons of charges may be interpreted should be considered when placing data into the public domain. Data presentations should be accompanied by appropriate technical and practical assumptions and descriptions, limitations, and cautions that consumers and hospitals need to use the data appropriately. SDOs' reports and studies are valuable sources of information, but some users may need assistance to understand the information gleaned from the data.

Data users, such as hospitals, should find value in participating in and sponsoring educational programs at which information and instruction in using statewide hospital databases and their applications are discussed with the stakeholders.

The Status of Statewide Health Information

When states and their SDOs place comparable hospital data in the public domain, they are encouraging hospitals to continually improve their performance. This same information can influence not only hospitals, but also the behavior of consumers, payers, employers, and physicians.

Several state and federal health reform proposals advocate the collection and publication of comparable data on provider cost and quality of care as a way for consumers to select among health plans and providers.

The following suggestions are offered to strengthen and make more useful the information collected and disseminated by SDOs and by so doing, help ensure the accountability of hospitals.

- Support research on information dissemination and develop effective ways to convert data into useful information targeted to providers, payers, consumers, and policymakers.

  While many SDOs and other state-level agencies gather health data, these agencies often do not have the resources or staff expertise to market their services and generally are not effective at reaching all of the potential audiences for their information. In contrast to direct marketing firms that understand how to reach specific consumers, SDOs often have difficulty communicating their messages. SDOs and others could benefit from learning how to "sell" the stories that lie within the data. SDOs can learn communication and marketing formats and techniques from the private sector to reach consumers, hospitals, public officials, and insurers.

- Promote comparisons among hospitals on the community, state, regional, and national levels.

  Statewide hospital databases facilitate comparisons among hospitals at the community and state levels. But SDOs often lack the time, energy, and finances to better use their information. The federal government can play a leadership role in promoting use of state-level data.

  The Healthcare Cost and Utilization Project, 1988–1994 (HCUP-3), a project funded by the Agency for Health Care Policy and Research (AHCPR), is a federal initiative to build a nationwide hospital database using existing state-level data from public and private data sources. This project will not only provide a comparative database for health services researchers, but also encourage greater uniformity among statewide hospital discharge databases.

- Develop a clearinghouse of information on statewide health data systems.

  A repository of information on statewide health data systems is needed to monitor and improve the health information industry. The clearinghouse should also contain related information on confidentiality and privacy, severity of illness adjustments, data edits, published reports and special studies, and data release requirements. Having a single source for this information would encourage data standardization and uniformity.

- Secure stability and growth of statewide health information systems.

  States have invested in database development, but additional funds are needed to convert data into usable information and to disseminate this information. To be most useful, statewide databases should be adjusted to account for such things as a hospital's patient population as well as the severity of the patients' illness, and efforts should be pursued to promote increased uniformity among states' databases. The federal government should provide leadership in improving data uniformity and quality by encouraging common definitions, reporting formats, coding conventions, and data standards so state-level data may be combined, compared, and used to help improve individual and community health and the health care delivery system.

State-level health data systems would benefit from stable sources of funding. The development, maintenance, and expansion of these data systems is a prudent investment, but these systems may not be sustained if they are dependent completely on state revenues. A secure and committed federal-state partnership for database development, with support from the private sector, is a reasonable approach to ensuring the stability of these systems. Examples of these partnerships include the National Center for Health Statistics' Cooperative Health Statistics System developed in the 1970s, and private foundations such as the John A. Hartford Foundation and the Robert Wood Johnson Foundation underwriting database development and the development of health information systems on state and local levels.

Conclusions

Information to measure provider performance must be placed in the public domain, not only to help ensure prudent and cost effective health care purchasing, but also to give providers comparable information for continued improvement of patient care. State-level health databases are an essential component of the information infrastructure, not only to support health reform efforts, but also to influence provider behavior. SDOs routinely collect, analyze and disseminate information about the use, charges and costs, and quality or effectiveness of hospital care in their states. Their reports and data products are useful tools that hospitals may use to improve their performance and can help stakeholders in the health care system better understand hospital performance.

Health reform proposals on the national and state levels encourage public reporting of hospital charges, costs, outcomes, and performance to monitor the health care delivery system, encourage prudent purchasing of health care, and to improve provider performance and patient care. This suggests that additional resources should be allocated to build a nationwide, integrated, health information infrastructure. The expertise and talent already in place at the state-level are the foundation upon which this information system should be built.

A federal-state-private partnership dedicated to improving the health data systems would help decrease problems of data quality and other methodological issues, support needed database development to acquire a reliable picture of individual and community health over time and setting, and effectively market information to different audiences.

Though the expense of building a nationwide, integrated, health information infrastructure may be daunting, greater long-term costs—not only in dollars, but in time lost in developing an effective, efficient accountability system—would inevitably result without it.

References

1. *State Health Data Resource Manual: Hospital Discharge Data Systems.* National Association of Health Data Organizations, May 1993.

2. *State Health Data: A Tool for Health Care Reform and Consumer Information.* American Association of Retired Persons, Public Policy Institute, May 1993. Prepared by the National Association of Health Data Organizations, 1994.

3. *Statement of Principles on Information for Health System Reform.* National Association of Health Data Organizations, February 1994.

4. *Small Area Analysis in Wisconsin: Selected 1990 Inpatient Medical and Surgical Conditions.* POH 0426. State of Wisconsin, Department of Health and Social Services, Office of Health Care Information, April 1992.

5. *Minority Health in Wisconsin: Toward a Health Diversity.* State of Wisconsin, Department of Health and Social Services, Center for Health Statistics, 1993.

6. *Plan for the Modification of Cesarean Section Utilization in Dade County Hospitals.* State of Florida, Health Care Cost Containment Board, August 1991.

7. *Nursing Home Reporting System: 1992 Annual Report.* Florida Agency for Health Care Administration, December 1992.

8. *California Hospital Discharge Data for Minorities: Calendar Years 1990 and 1991.* Office of Statewide Health Planning and Development, March 1994.

9. *Health Care Costs in Massachusetts.* Massachusetts Rate Setting Commission, December 1992.

10. *State and County Profiles of Hospital Inpatient Utilization: October 1, 1990 through September 30, 1991.* North Carolina Medical Database Commission, Department of Insurance, H911201.

11. *Buyer's Guide: Outpatient Procedures—'92–'93,* Missouri Department of Health, Missouri Center for Health Statistics, Publication No. 17, and *Buyer's Guide: Obstetrical Services.* Missouri Department of Health, Missouri Center for Health Statistics, Publication No. 18.3.

12. *Health Care User's Guide: Hospital Costs by Illness Category: January 1992 to December 1992.* Washington State Department of Health, Office of Hospital and Patient Data, DOH Pub 250–001, Revised 10/93.

13. *Health Choices.* South Carolina State Budget and Control Board, Division of Research and Statistical Services, July 1993.

14. *Health Data in the Information Age: Use, Disclosure, and Privacy.* Institute of Medicine, 1994.

15. Iezzoni LI: Using severity information for quality assessment: A review of three cases by five severity measures. *QRB* December 1989; 376–82.

16. Iezzoni LI, Daly J: A description and clinical assessment of the Computerized Severity Index. *QRB* February 1992;44–52.

17. *Coronary Artery Bypass Graft Surgery in New York State: 1989–1991.* New York State Department of Health, December 1992.

18. *Annual Report of the California Outcomes Project.* California Office of Statewide Health Planning and Development, Vol I: Study Overview and Results Summary and Vol II: Technical Appendix, December 1993.

19. Phillips DK: *Measuring the Clinical Outcomes of Care Delivered in California Hospitals: A Report to the California State Assembly.* Assembly Office of Research, State of California, April 1991.

20. *Hospital Effectiveness Report: Region 5-91,* Vol 6, January 1–December 31, 1991. Pennsylvania Health Care Cost Containment Council, July 1993.

21. *A Consumer Guide to Coronary Artery Bypass Graft Surgery,* Vol I, 1990. Pennsylvania Health Care Cost Containment Council, November 19, 1992.

22. *A Consumer Guide to Coronary Artery Bypass Graft Surgery,* Vol II, 1991. Pennsylvania Health Care Cost Containment Council, February 3, 1994.

23. *Iowa Hospital Resource and Outcome Report, July 1990 through June 1991, DRG Specific Version.* Iowa Health Data Commission, April 1992.

24. *Discharge Data Review.* California Office of Statewide Health Planning and Development, Health Facility Data Division, Patient Discharge Data Section. Selected Issues: March 1990–March 1993.

25. *Linking Health Data Bases: A Blueprint for Action.* Final Report. National Association of Health Data Organizations, March 1993. Submitted to the Office of Science and Data Development, Agency for Health Care Policy and Research, Grant Number #1 R03 HS06639–01.

Chapter Four

BUSINESS COALITIONS ON HEALTH: An Examination of Their Activities and Impact

Carol A. Cronin, MSW, MSG

Catherine M. Kunkle, BSN

Local, state, and regional business health care coalitions have become key elements in efforts to responsibly manage the cost and quality of health care delivered to Americans. While health care coalitions differ substantially in size and focus, they all share an organizing commitment to building cost-effective quality health care systems in their areas. Located in almost every state in both large metropolitan areas and secondary markets, health care coalitions and their employer members have become credible participants in creating community-based change. Employer coalitions are leading a grass roots movement called Community Health Reform. Pooling their purchasing power, employers are seeking value in the care they buy, and are beginning to measure quality and efficiency to compare value and reward superior providers.

This chapter will provide an overview of the history and current status of health care coalitions nationwide. Specific coalition activities involving the quality of health care will be presented, with a focus on coalition legislative support for state public databases, projects using severity-adjusted quality measurement systems, and projects incorporating the principles of continuous quality improvement. Coalition efforts to standardize the collection and presentation of health care information and to develop clinical guidelines are also highlighted. Health care purchasing on behalf of a group of employers is discussed for a number of cities nationwide, as well as projects involving educating consumers about comparative provider performance. Finally, alternative futures are presented with reference to quality-of-care initiatives conducted by health care coalitions.

History of Coalitions

Health care coalitions evolved in the late 1970s and early 1980s in response to growing health care costs. Faced with runaway medical care inflation rates, many large employers realized that a comprehensive cost-management approach must involve strategies that extend beyond their corporate walls and into the community. As not-for-profit community-based membership organizations, health care coalitions provide a vehicle for employers to work both with other employers and with hospitals, physicians, managed care plans, and other health care constituency groups.

A variety of national organizations have been involved in the evolution of the health care coalition movement. The Washington Business Group on Health (WBGH), founded in 1974, provided technical assistance to local coalitions in the late 1970s. The American Hospital Association, the Chamber of

Commerce, the John A. Hartford Foundation, and the Robert Wood Johnson Foundation have all been involved in coalition development and funding activities throughout the 1980s. In 1989 the National Business Coalition on Health (NBCH) was founded as an affiliate of WBGH. NBCH serves as a "coalition of coalitions," with the mission to promote employer-led, market-driven, community-based health care reform. The coalition movement is based on a clear set of principles: purchasing care of the highest value, measuring the quality and efficiency of providers to determine value, rewarding providers who deliver superior value, and working with providers to improve the overall health of the community. In 1992 NBCH became an independent not-for-profit organization with major funding from the John A. Hartford Foundation. Today, NBCH represents more than 85 coalitions, or 6,000 employers, and over 30 million covered individuals.

What Does a Coalition Look Like?

In April 1993 NBCH conducted a survey[1] of 58 members to gain an understanding of the organization and roles of health care coalitions. Results include the following (Table 1):

- Employers clearly dominate coalition membership.
- Almost two-thirds of the total coalition membership are businesses representing 7.7 million employees.
- A number of coalitions limit membership or board service to purchasers only.
- Other constituent groups that participate in health care coalitions include health care providers, health care insurers, organized labor, government, and consumers.
- Most coalitions represent 50 or fewer members.

Health care coalitions are usually modestly run organizations. Half of all responding health care coalitions have one or two paid staff (often a mix of full-time and part-time staff), with the remainder run primarily by corporate or other volunteers within the community. The average coalition budget is $232,000, with the primary source of income derived from membership dues.

With reference to the types of products and services provided by health care coalitions, the top two activities reported by 87% of the coalitions in the NBCH study were data collection and reporting activities and providing information through newsletters. In addition, 77% of the coalitions sponsored seminars on such topics as benefit design, wellness issues, and national health reform; 65% published reports such as HMO buyer's guides, wellness handbooks, and consumer guides to health care; and 46% were involved in selective contracting for hospital, physician, prescription drug, or other ancillary services.

In a follow-up survey on data initiatives, conducted during the summer of 1993 by NBCH and the New York Business Group on Health,[2] a more detailed set of questions was asked. Hospitals were the most frequently cited source of data reported in that survey by 70% of the 45 coalition respondents. All of the data projects involved the use of inpatient hospital data. State, county, and other government agencies were cited as the second most frequently used source (55%), and health plans were the third most frequent source (52%). The least common source of information was the coalition members themselves.

Over 50% of the surveyed coalitions indicated that they had been involved in data initiatives for more than four years, with over three-quarters indicating that the focus of their data initiatives had changed over the years. This often involved movement away from looking exclusively at claims data to examining a broader set of measures to monitor performance and outcome. In response to a question of whether there was any evidence that local cost or quality had been affected by the coalition's data initiatives, 70% said yes.

Another activity conducted by a number of health care coalitions involves group purchasing from a select number of health plans, area hospitals, and other providers. Group purchasing involves the design of health care purchasing specifications on behalf of a group of employers, the identification and selection of health care providers in a community, and ongoing monitoring of provider performance. Participating employers, in turn, agree to offer incentives to their employees to use selected providers. Value-based purchasing has become the primary focus of many employers and coalitions because this is the initiative that most quickly alters the buyer-seller equation. For the first time, the employer is in control of securing reasonably priced, quality health care. Nevertheless, as those who began by placing exclusive emphasis on price have learned, the greatest savings can only be achieved by demanding accountability for provider performance and outcome. Promoting accountability leads to improved efficiency, which translates into long-term cost savings and better results—a benefit to the entire community.

TABLE 1

Coalition	Membership	No. Covered Lives	1992 Growth
Alabama Healthcare Council, Birmingham	32 businesses, 6 insurers, health plans and TPAs	101,000; 6% of state population	7%
Coalition for Health Cost Containment, Erie, PA	18 businesses	55,000; 20% of multicounty region served	2%
Colorado Health Care Purchasing Alliance, Denver	170 businesses	110,000; 3.3% of state population	45%
Employers Health Care Cooperative, Brentwood, TN	187 businesses, 1 provider, 3 labor groups, 2 chambers	50,000; 10% of multicounty region served	15%
Florida Health Coalition, Miami	30 businesses, 5 government groups	650,000; 23% of multicounty region served	8%
Health Action Council of Northeast Ohio, Solon	72 businesses, 37 providers, 31 insurers, health plans or TPAs, 2 colleges	152,000 in cities served	2%
Health Policy Corporation of Iowa, Des Moines	38 businesses, 3 insurers, 3 labor groups, 1 government group, 2 chambers	80,000; 17% to 19% of statewide population	5%
Lehigh Valley Business Conference on Health Care, Bethlehem, PA	4 businesses, 2 providers, 3 insurers, 5 government groups, 1 consumer group	35,000; 17% of multicounty region served	12%
Madison Area Employers Health Care Coalition	66 businesses, 9 providers, 3 insurers	26,090 employees of multicounty region served	26%
Memphis Business Group on Health, Inc.	49 businesses, 1 government group	480,000 nationwide; 128,400 in Memphis (13%)	30%
Midwest Business Group on Health, Chicago	122 businesses, 8 providers, 5 government groups	675,000 employees in multistate area	16%
Ozarks Area Business Group on Health, Springfield, MO	43 businesses, 2 government groups	50,000; 20% of multicounty region served	12%
Richmond Area Business Group on Health	45 businesses, 2 government groups	not available	8.5%
Savannah Business Group	19 businesses, 2 government groups, 1 UR firm	16,481; 19.8% of the city population served	3.6%
Southwest Michigan Health Care Coalition, Kalamazoo	24 businesses, 1 insurer, 3 government groups, 1 chamber, 6 others	24,500; 18% of multicounty region served	0%
Vermont Employers Health Alliance, Burlington	70 businesses, 14 providers, 17 insurers, 3 government groups, 11 chambers	59,249; 29% of state population	16%
West Coast Health Care Coalition, Sarasota	40 businesses, 6 providers, 2 insurers, 8 government groups, 4 others	25,000; 12.5% of multicounty region served	3%

* From the National Business Coalition on Health (NBCH, formerly National Business Coalition Forum on Health). Used by permission. NBCH conducted a survey of its 70-plus members, April 21, 1993. The response rate was 72%.

1993 Survey of Employer Purchasing Coalitions*

Accomplishments in 1992	Priorities for 1993-94	Staff
provided input to draft legislation on workers' compensation	orient employees to be wise purchasers of health care; facilitate creation of meaningful database	3
renewed laboratory and radiology contracts, created pharmacy program	initiate joint venture POS program with tertiary care facilities, strategize ways to stay in game with reform	2
completed abstract of clinical data on 12 cardiac DRGs; implemented a POS program	analyze outpatient claims database, represent business in local health care debate	40
saved 15% to 25% on hospital cost, maintained active claims database of certain hospital claims	expand purchasing group membership and reports on utilization and quality	1
made group purchasing agreement with 3 other business coalitions; expanded wellness council; and doubled membership activities	group purchasing through direct contracting with hospitals; forming PHO network; working with states to develop quality and efficiency data	3
released Cleveland hospital market analysis, initial set of data from Cleveland Health Quality Choice	honor commitment by purchasers to use CHQC data to reward quality, cost-effective providers	2
established community purchasing corporation, did CHMIS feasibility report and obtained foundation grant	community purchasing corporation, establish CHMIS in Iowa, pass enabling legislation, conduct pilots	8
implemented exclusive provider OP laboratory program, preferred provider radiology program with Pennsylvania Blue Shield	develop partnership with insurer in POS managed product, foster coalition growth in PA, develop small employer products	2
outcomes task force released recommendations on improving vaginal birth rate after Cesareans, selected as site for WBGH preventative services project	strategic planning for state and national reform	2
continued to plan implementation of CHMIS; implemented workers' comp/disability, psychiatric/substance abuse case management programs	continue with implementation of CHMIS, remain involved with national reform—Jackson Hole Group HPPC task force	19
completed value-managed health care research project in 3 sites, organized new chapter in Owensboro, KY	develop 2 or 3 more chapters, continue value-managed purchasing and add sites, influence state and federal reform activity	6
created med/surgery and psych. PPO, family practice panel, pharmacy network	implementation of 1992 projects	13
helped pass statewide database initiative, quality measures; small group insurance reform; established provider contracts for charges and data	promote development of partnerships among employers and providers, provide continuing education on purchasing strategies, organize coalitions statewide	2
established primary care facility, increased dialogue with providers	sign agreement on primary care facility, negotiate hospital contracts and single fee schedule for all network physicians	3
shifted consumer focus to value-based purchasing, established common database for hospitals	continue development of common database, contract with providers using professional contracting org., work to enhance access for indigent population	3
took lead in passing Vermont's health reform legislation, secured Hartford Foundation grant to create CHMIS	complete deliberation with VT Health Care Authority for '94 legislation, pursue workers' comp reform	2
initiated selective contracting with preferred rates, began quality assessment project	increase selective contracting, track and influence state reform, conduct another managed care conference	2

*Coalitions described above are purchasing coalitions; NBCH has identified 25 purchasing coalitions and compiled data on the ones above. Key: CHMIS = Community Health Management Information System, an initiative sponsored by the John Hartford Foundation; WBGH= Washington Business Group on Health, NBCH's founding organization; POS = point of service plan; PHO = physician-hospital organization; PPO = preferred provider organization.

Coalition Activities Addressing Public Accountability for Quality of Health Care Delivery

Coalitions are involved in a range of projects which directly address the public accountability of hospitals and health plans for the quality of care delivered. These include activities in the following four areas: (1) legislative efforts in support of state public databases; (2) data projects which address hospital and health plan quality; (3) group purchasing activities; and (4) consumer satisfaction and education projects.

Legislative Activities

Support for health care data legislation was listed as a top legislative activity in the April 1993 NBCH coalition survey,[1] with 95% of the coalitions involved in state legislative advocacy on this issue. Much of the recent legislative activity of coalitions is focused on state reform initiatives, which range from a massive overhaul of the delivery and financing of health care to specific insurance industry reforms. From Washington to California and Vermont to Florida, coalitions have been vigilant in representing purchasers' best interests at the state level.

While managed care proposals are advocated by many groups, antimanaged care proposals will also shape reform efforts. For example, passage into law of "any willing provider" (AWP) legislation has occurred in many states and will restrict managed care plans' ability to determine which providers to allow in their networks. Making the market work is predicated on rewarding the most efficient, quality providers, and creating the right incentives—those that promote cost control and value for the dollars employers spend. Coalitions oppose such proposals whether in the form of AWP, freedom of choice, or patient access proposals.

The Health Policy Corporation of Iowa (HPCI), created in 1982, heralded the signing of the first state-data commission law. Since that time the Iowa Health Data Commission has been publishing reports on cost, utilization, and length of stay, as well as conducting small area variation analysis. The Richmond Area Business Group on Health, a 52-member business-only coalition, was an important supporter of the legislation passed in the 1992 Virginia legislative session that established a patient-level state database. The legislation required the collection of 27 data elements from uniform hospital bills starting July 1, 1993. In addition, the legislation required a study to look at three areas: (1) outpatient information; (2) reimbursement and gross charges, and (3) measures of patient outcome. The Louisiana Health Care Alliance (LHCA) in Baton Rouge and New Orleans has also been extremely active legislatively in support of the establishment of a state data alliance. The Louisiana experience however, is an example of the limitations of business support. While the state data alliance now exists as an entity, it has little funding and no legislative authority to require the collection and reporting of hospital information. In response, the LHCA has been exerting its influence by assisting in the start-up of coalitions in Shreveport, Lafayette, Alexandria, and other cities across the state. In Florida, coalitions have played a visible and influential role in shaping state health care reform legislation, which calls for regional, voluntary purchasing alliances for small employers.

In addition to lobbying to establish public data commissions, business coalitions must also continue to support them in yearly appropriation battles. In Pennsylvania, coalitions have continually fought legislative efforts to underfund or delete the Pennsylvania Health Care Cost Containment Council created in 1986. The Council's annual report lists a number of Pennsylvania employers, including Hershey Foods, Binney & Smith, ALCOA, Bethlehem Steel, and General Electric, that use data to assist in selective contracting with providers. After publication of the Council information, the Erie Coalition for Health Cost Containment saw reductions in open heart surgery charges at one major hospital, resulting in savings to self-insured employers.

Coalitions' Use of Data

Severity-Adjusted Data

Several coalitions are, and have been, involved in efforts to develop comparable *severity-adjusted* information on the quality of care in their community hospitals. HPCI, the Iowa data commission, led an initiative to require all hospitals in Iowa with 100 beds or more to install a severity-adjusted system to measure the cost and outcome of care. A variety of such reports have been generated and are publicly available to all constituency groups. Iowa, along with Vermont and a few other selected states, has been the leading data supplier to Drs Wennberg and Caper in performing small-area variation analysis for over ten years. Employers in the Central Florida Health Care Coalition, an Orlando group representing more than 250,000 employees and their dependents, influenced area hospitals to install a computerized data collection system. The system compares cost and medical outcomes among the hospitals and includes "benchmarks" of the best practices from a national database. Using these measures, the two largest hospitals reduced their average cost per admission for two consecutive years without sacrificing quality. One of the hospitals is now breaking even on Medicare, after losing $12 million annually before, and is no longer shifting costs to the private insurers. One hospital, a regional neonatal center, decreased its cesarean section rate from 32% in 1987 to 21% in 1993. Another hospital decreased its cesarean section rate from 42% in 1989 to 33% in 1992.

Another example, The Cleveland Health Quality Choice Program, was established in 1989 by a coalition of the business and medical communities in Cleveland. It is a voluntary, collaborative effort to measure and improve the quality and affordability of health care services communitywide. The program uses several methods for determining the quality of care in Cleveland area hospitals. The method used to predict surgery and general medicine outcomes, called CHOICE (Cleveland Hospital Outcomes Indicators of Care Evaluations), was developed by an outside consultant. Trained medical abstractors collect data from hospital charts, which are then analyzed using statistical models to determine how each hospital actually performed compared to its expected performance based on the severity of illness of the patients. For intensive care patients, an existing method to predict outcomes, called APACHE, was adapted for use in Cleveland. A final element of measurement included a patient satisfaction survey that contained 69 questions about 11 hospital service areas, including admission procedures, daily care, care by hospitals and nurses, and food quality. Questionnaires were sent to 600 randomly selected patients from each hospital. Two types of reports resulted: the first, published in April 1993, was available to only 187 participating corporate and business subscribers who had received training and education about the project results and included hospital-specific information on each study area using symbols to indicate actual performance compared to predicted performance. The second document, a summary report that was released to the public, included a brief project overview and more gross groupings of the hospitals into three categories of performance: lower than predicted, as predicted, and higher than predicted. Approximately 9,000 copies of the consumer document were distributed. The second round of data was released in December 1993, and a third round in June 1994.

While it is too early to quantify the results of the data released on the overall cost and quality of health care, there are several business activities underway in Cleveland that will eventually help to evaluate the usefulness of the effort. Corporate members of the Health Action Council of Cleveland, a coalition of the area's largest employers and a founding member of Cleveland

Health Quality Choice, have held user group meetings with their managed care plans to monitor the plan's use of the data in their hospital contracting and monitoring. In addition, researchers at Case Western Reserve Business School are monitoring how employers, including Lubrizol and Parker Hannifin, conducted educational activities for their employees on project data.

Recently the Central Illinois Business Group on Health in Peoria announced the creation of a consortium of Illinois coalitions, which embarked on a major initiative to obtain severity-adjusted outcome data for 22 hospitals. The data will provide a means for the 65 involved employers, representing some 600,000 employees and their families, to assess the effectiveness of hospitals and physicians to deliver quality, cost-efficient care.

Soon after the Employer Health Care Alliance in Cincinnati persuaded 14 regional hospitals to use a severity-rating system in 1992, changes were implemented by providers. For example, orthopedic doctors at some institutions are using just one or two brands of artificial hips for hip-replacement surgery, allowing hospitals to save with volume discounts from vendors. Also, the hospitals are setting up 24-hour social service teams to improve discharge planning and facilitating the discharge of patients on the weekend rather than waiting until Monday morning.

In Central Michigan, the Muskegon Area Alliance for Quality Health Care is collaborating with area hospitals on outcomes measurement. The Muskegon Alliance data committee is working with three hospitals that have agreed to use the same criteria for a common database using severity-adjusted data. Along with data for hospital benchmarking, phase two of the project will take a comprehensive look at clinical processes across specific diseases and delivery settings to evaluate clinical outcomes, appropriateness, and resource utilization.

Continuous Quality Improvement

The examination of data by employer-led coalitions has already yielded important benefits and is proving to be important in continuous quality improvement in the clinical setting. Last year, while conducting a routine analysis of data from its hospital providers, the Health Care Network of Greater Milwaukee noted a higher than expected rate of complications for hip and knee replacement patients at a local hospital. The coalition took its findings to the hospital, which responded with its own investigation. Physicians identified postoperative ileus as the primary problem. Shortly thereafter, orthopedic surgeons at the hospital implemented changes in diet and medication procedures for hip and knee replacement patients. Since these changes were implemented, no postoperative ileus has afflicted an orthopedic patient at that facility.

In 1993 the Midwest Business Group on Health (MBGH) completed a three-year project demonstrating a new way for employers to manage health benefits in partnership with hospitals and physicians. Value-Managed Purchasing projects in three cities have shown that health care costs due to waste and inefficiency can be saved by working first to improve the quality of care. In demonstration sites in Kingsport, Tennessee; Chicago; and Milwaukee, a Quality Improvement Council gathered data to select clinical and administrative processes that could be improved through the use of teams trained in continuous quality improvement management techniques. Results included such diverse changes as reducing the number of mothers admitted for false labor, improving smoking cessation programs in public schools in Tennessee, and reducing the length of stay of heart bypass patients in Chicago, resulting in reduced cost and quicker recovery.

In a similar project also sponsored by the MBGH, six medical centers in the Chicago area are engaged in a pilot project aimed at improving the quality of care and reducing costs associated with coronary artery bypass graft (CABG) surgery. The CABG program is the first project of EPIQual (Employers Purchasing Initiative for Quality), created by the MBGH to reduce morbidity and mortality while providing the most efficient care possible. Physicians and nurse clinicians at the hospitals developed a "critical pathway" for CABG surgery—a planned progression of treatments from admission to discharge designed to find the best course of treatment for heart bypass patients. At first, hospitals were reluctant about sharing confidential morbidity and mortality data. Competition, however, was an incentive to overcome this reluctance. The end result has been that patients are ready for discharge on an average of two days earlier, and the cost of the procedure has been reduced by at least $3,000 per procedure at one hospital. The critical pathway is used not only for employees of members of the MBGH, but for all other patients who receive CABG surgery at the participating hospitals. EPIQual may next look at the other high-risk procedures that stand to improve from the process. At the top of the list are coronary angioplasty, treatment of pneumonia, acute myocardial infarction, hip replacement, and congestive heart failure.

In Birmingham, Alabama, purchasers and providers have completed the first phase of the Value Improvement Partnership (VIP), which is working to improve the quality of care and lowering the cost of services for the entire community. The initial six-month phase of the VIP has provided more than ten Birmingham providers and 22 Alabama Healthcare Council member organizations with the first round of data on treatment of pneumonia, heart attacks, and deliveries, with an emphasis on cesarean sections. This first round of data allows participating hospitals to remain anonymous and address their deficiencies for a six-month period. At the end of the second six-month cycle, data identifying hospitals and their performance will be released (targeted for November 1994). Purchasers will then guide their employees accordingly.

Community Health Management Information System

In several communities nationwide, business coalitions are involved in the development of Community Health Management Information Systems (CHMIS), an effort funded by the John A. Hartford Foundation. CHMIS has several components, including electronic transaction systems that link purchasers and payers to speed benefit eligibility and claims payment, as well as electronic highways to foster the rapid dissemination of clinical information and other online communication among health professionals. In addition, CHMIS has established a data repository where employers, providers, insurers, consumers, and the government can all access information on provider performance and other cost, utilization, and public health data.

Implementation of CHMIS varies across the country. In most states, particularly Iowa, Minnesota, New York, Ohio, Vermont, and Washington, CHMIS is part of statewide healthcare system reform strategies being implemented. It is anticipated that many of these states will mandate CHMIS participation on the part of health care providers. While local coalitions have been key players in the legislative push for CHMIS, implementation of CHMIS is often overseen by newly established not-for-profit public and private entities composed of stakeholders representing all of a community's interests. In Memphis the establishment of CHMIS is currently voluntary, although the local business coalition, the Memphis Business Group on Health, requires that any provider under contract with their purchasing group supply information to CHMIS. In addition, other states, including Colorado, Hawaii, Maryland, Michigan, Utah, and West Virginia, are exploring variations on the CHMIS concept as part of their health system reform activities.

Health Plan Employer Data and Information Set 2.0

Under the direction of the National Committee for Quality Assurance (NCQA), coalitions and individual employers worked together with health plans to develop a set of performance measures called the Health Plan Employer Data and Information Set (HEDIS) 2.0. The areas of performance selected for assessment include quality, access, patient satisfaction, membership, utilization, and finance. The measures were developed to respond to a complex but simply defined employer need, namely, to understand what value is being purchased by the health care money spent and how to hold a health plan accountable for its performance.

The HEDIS effort was first organized by The Health Maintenance Organzation (HMO) Group in late 1989 and included representatives from The HMO Group (a coalition of group and staff model HMOs), four large employers (Bull HN Information Systems Inc., Digital Equipment Corporation, GTE, and Xerox Corporation), and Towers Perrin. Representatives of Kaiser Permanente joined the group approximately four months later. Since the release of HEDIS 1.0 in September 1991, further modifications and reporting standards for utilization data resulted in a revised document, HEDIS 2.0, completed in May 1993 and published in November 1993. HEDIS 2.0 is only the beginning of efforts to assess health plan performance. Much work remains to be done in defining comprehensive quality measures that meet external and internal requirements for performance information.

NCQA is sponsoring a Report Card Pilot Project, which includes a total of approximately 30 health plans, employers, and representatives of the National Business Coalition on Health on its advisory steering committee. The purpose of the report card pilot project is to better understand the collection and use of HEDIS 2.0 data and to begin to prepare a useful comparison report of health plans for the public. The report card should be available to the public by the end of 1994.

Guideline Development

The Bay Area Business Group on Health (BBGH) is composed of 19 member employers who cover approximately 2.5 million individuals and spend $3 billion annually on health care. BBGH is dedicated to reducing the cost and improving the quality of health care.

In 1991 BBGH conducted a survey of health plans' preventive care guidelines. The findings indicated that guidelines for preventive services varied significantly across plans. Some plans had no preventive guidelines at all, while others based their guidelines on outdated recommendations. To remedy the problems identified in their survey and improve the coordination of preventive services between plans and employers, BBGH formed the Health Services Advisory Committee (HSAC) (which involves both plans and employers) to produce a consensus on guidelines for preventive care. The HSAC includes health plan medical directors and representatives from BBGH, member companies, the California Department of Health Services, and the University of California-Berkeley, School of Public Health. These guidelines allow employers and other purchasers in California to measure and compare the use of preventive services across the health plans that they offer.

The group has decided to base its recommendations for preventive services guidelines on the United States Preventive Services Task Force because they are recent and review 169 preventive services for 60 target conditions (Table 2). The recommendations are also summarized in a guide for use by clinicians. All participating health plans and employers agreed to follow these guidelines.

Once the guidelines were adopted, HSAC developed a uniform data set for preventive services (Table 3). All plans agreed to measure care according to these guidelines.

Many employers wanted preventive services data on the plans sooner than was promised. A group of eight BBGH employers decided to collect information on the use of these services by using an employee survey. The 20-question survey, which was mailed to a sample of more than 10,000 employees, asks about the actual delivery of preventive services. Results of the survey will be used to audit data provided by the plans to confirm rates for mammograms and pap smear tests.

Coalition Purchasing Activities

What of the skeptics of value-based purchasing? They say that employers cannot purchase health care based on value because they do not know how to measure value, performance, and outcome. Others say that market forces have failed to control the cost of health care, and we therefore should allow the federal government to take control. In response to the first point, data that measure the cost and quality of health care and take into account such variables

TABLE 2

Preventative Care Guidelines Adopted by the Health Services Advisory Committee for Healthy Adults Between the Ages of 19 and 64*

Preventative Service Screening	Time Frame
Height/weight	Periodically
Blood pressure	Regularly
Nonfasting total blood cholesterol levels	Every five years
Pap smear test	Every 1–3 years
Clinical breast examination	Annually, beginning at 40
Mammogram	Every 1–2 years, beginning at 50
Tetanus/diphtheria vaccination	Every 10 years

* Based on the recommendations of the US Preventative Services Task Force, 1989. From Bay Area Business Group on Health, San Francisco, CA. Used by permission.

Counseling is recommended periodically in the following areas: smoking, nutrition, exercise, alcohol and drug use, sexually transmitted diseases, injury prevention, dental health, and unintended pregnancy.

Note: Individuals with symptoms or at high risk for disease may need additional services or more frequent interventions.

as severity, age, and comorbid conditions do exist. Information systems have been operating, testing, and refining data compilation, measurement, and analysis since the early 1980s. They may not be perfect, and there may be room for improvement, but we currently have no "gold standard." These approaches to accountability are an evolving and ongoing process. The notion that we must wait until data evaluation systems are perfect before purchasers begin to "buy-right" has been rejected by coalitions.

In the past, US market forces failed in health care because purchasers lacked or had inadequate information with which to make good purchasing decisions. Now that information is available and purchasers know the right questions to ask to track the performance of providers, market failure can be

TABLE 3

Uniform Data Set for Preventative Services*

Area	Data
Smoking	No. of smokers No. with recent "quit"attempts Length of time since quitting Factors contributing to "quit" attempt
Blood pressure	No. who have had their blood pressure measured in the last two years
Pap smear	No. of women who have had pap smear tests in the last three years
Mammogram	No. of women between 50 and 65 who have had a mammogram in the last two years
Blood cholesterol	No. of individuals who have had cholesterol levels measured in the last five years
Clinical breast exam	No. of women between 40 and 65 who have had a clinical breast examination in the last two years
Counseling	No. of individuals who have been counseled about smoking, nutrition, exercise, and other areas in the last three years

* From the Bay Area Business Group on Health, San Francisco, CA. Used by permission.

corrected; this is where coalitions have laid the groundwork. The coalition success stories involve innovative approaches to purchasing, suggesting that with a modicum of effort and persistence, employers and purchasers can change the health care delivery and financing environment. Changing the incentives for providers and promoting integrated or organized systems of care are coalition strategies for reform. Coalitions are working at the local level to affect these changes to the system while recognizing that there are aspects of health care that must be addressed through some form of legislation, such as reform of the small group insurance market.[3]

In May 1994 a report entitled *Community-Based Healthcare Reform Through Employer Group Purchasing—An Assessment of Select Initiatives*[4] was released by the Health Action Council of Northeast Ohio, the National Business Coalition on Health and the Ohio Manufacturers' Association. Prepared at the request of the employer coalition board of directors, the report defines models for purchasing and provides an analysis of different strategies and methods involved. The goal of the report is to provide an overview of general guidelines to consider and issues to address in designing a purchasing program. Table 4 lists the criteria most important to coalition success.

With regard to quality and performance information, almost every coalition included in this assessment was at a different stage of development, or took a different approach to the quality/data and performance component of group purchasing. Several coalitions used the RFP process to define and request specific types of clinical/quality information, which were later incorporated into the actual contractual agreement. Sometimes the plan or provider is unable to respond to the actual request at the time of the negotiation but will include in the contract a commitment to work with the employer group.[5]

The report also indicated that in some coalitions there were existing or developing initiatives toward communitywide collection and analysis of performance information. The quality assurance component may be delegated to the hospitals, with oversight by an employer/hospital medical staff committee to review utilization and any quality-of-care issues. Some coalitions take a slightly different approach where the employer group collects claims and analyzes and distributes the information.

The Memphis Business Group on Health (MBGH) has saved money for its member companies through its efforts to collect information from, and then selectively contract with, area hospitals. Coalition members have experienced an average increase of 6% per year in their health care costs for five years, compared to a national average increase of 15%. Given that other hospitals have also held their prices steady, the entire community has benefited. Today, in response to concerns that coalition purchasing tends to benefit only larger employers, MBGH has designed an insurance product for small employers based on present provider contractual relationships. In a joint venture with an

TABLE 4

Criteria for Measuring Coalition Success

- ◆ Significant expenditure savings for employers
- ◆ Documented improvements in quality of care
- ◆ Increased or increasing availability of quality/performance data
- ◆ Improved relationships with providers
- ◆ Market restructuring/increased provider integration

insurer, this product is being offered to small employers in Memphis and surrounding areas. For the first time in this market, small employers will have a customized, managed product alternative with a track record for cost-effective, quality healthcare.

Employer members of the Colorado Health Care Purchasing Alliance have averaged single-digit health care inflation trends, below Colorado averages for health care costs. During the first three quarters of 1993, Alliance members realized a savings of over $19 million as compared to previous health care expenditures, representing a 15 to 1 return on their Alliance investment.

In January of 1993, the board of the Houston Area Healthcare Coalition authorized the formation of a metropolitanwide healthcare purchasing organization (HPO). In the fall of that same year, the coalition completed the first phase of their project, which involved collecting inpatient data in a diagnosis-related group (DRG) format from 34 area hospitals for their insured population. The database reflected 161,000 cases or $1.7 billion in paid services. Over 30 employers representing more than 250,000 covered individuals have signed letters of intent to participate, while 35 hospitals have submitted charge and length-of-stay information as a demonstration of their good faith to cooperate in the process. The purchasing group finalized the allowable rates for participating hospitals structured on a DRG basis for inpatient and on ancillary service categories (ASCs), developed by the Health Care Financing Administration (HCFA), with other specific case rates based on procedure.

A quality-of-care data vendor has been retained to address issues using severity-adjustment software. Specifically, the vendor will determine if differences in quality, length of stay, and costs are due to differences in the severity of illness within patient categories. The HPO will use this system to ensure that contracted hospitals continue to meet quality standards that are jointly established by the HPO, hospitals, and physicians. The coalition and the individual hospitals will share in the cost of the quality initiative. Outpatient hospital and physician office services will be monitored from a quality perspective as well, through the HPO's data manager. Streamlining administrative paperwork is also a major goal of the HPO. In addition to the electronic claims submission and payment to providers, the purchasing group will set up interactive voice-response technology for obtaining claim payment status, administering provider, employer and patient satisfaction surveys, enrolling participants, and for conducting patient outcome surveys. The final objective of the Houston coalition purchasing group is to seek a strategic alliance with insurance/underwriting partners to facilitate small employer participation in the group.

The two main business coalitions in Wisconsin sponsor group purchasing activities. The Employer Health Care Alliance Cooperative in Madison, Wisconsin, spun off from the local health care coalition in 1990 in order to identify and contract with quality, cost efficient providers. The Alliance now offers a full menu of group-purchased services, including contracts with clinics, hospitals, physicians, mental health providers, and chiropractors. The Alliance also maintains a claims database and generates comprehensive financial and utilization information for members. Employers in the Milwaukee area and beyond are also involved in group purchasing through the Health Care Network of Greater Wisconsin.

Other coalitions are moving in the direction of more specialized group purchasing by diagnosis or procedure. For example, the Detroit Area Health Council is involved in a coronary artery disease project which has several components, including the establishment of a consortium of regional heart care centers, physicians, purchasers, payers, government, and consumers. A major objective of the consortium is the development of information systems and the dissemination of data. In March 1993, the Council released a report that included information on the demographics of the region, health status indicators, heart care services capacity, utilization, outcomes, and financial impact. Included in the report were hospital-specific mortality data for Medicare recipients undergoing CABG and angioplasty from the US Department of Health and Human Services Medicare Hospital Information Report.

The consortium has also established a Purchaser Advisory Working Group that, among other things, is charged with identifying, designing, and recommending strategies so that purchasers can use comparative performance information to reward provider performance and to buy and use health care on the basis of quality and value. An additional mandate of the project is to raise the standards of care for treatment of people with heart disease across the entire community, an effort that will be monitored by the collection of standardized data from all heart care sites. A future area of project focus will be to evaluate which centers and which techniques are most effective in preventing the need for cardiac care.

The Health Policy Corporation of Iowa in Des Moines, Iowa, has formed a not-for-profit subsidiary called Community Health Purchasing Corporation to collectively purchase health care in central Iowa. The Corporation began the effort with a cardiovascular health demonstration purchasing project. The project has now expanded over time to include a comprehensive purchasing strategy.

Founded in 1988, Nashville's business coalition, the Employers Healthcare Cooperative, now shares its health care purchasing program with eight other cities and more than 1,060 employers in six states. Three other health care coalitions are involved (Richmond and Roanoke, Virginia and Reading, Pennsylvania), a manufacturing executives association (Fort Smith, Arkansas), and four employer-only group purchasing organizations (Fort Wayne and Indianapolis, Indiana, Knoxville, Tennessee, and Dallas and Ft. Worth, Texas). All are sharing their buying power, overhead cost, claims data, and savings. More than 247,000 employees are covered under the program, with a total of 618,000 covered individuals.

Because they represent over 50% of employer health benefit costs, hospitals were chosen as the initial focus for direct contracting. Since the program was launched the member groups have saved more than $20 million, documented on a claim-by-claim basis in hospital costs, and savings at urban hospitals have averaged over 15%. Almost 40 coalitions are involved in group purchasing, including large cities such as Chicago, Denver, and Orlando, as well as smaller and medium sized cities such as Birmingham, Alabama, Lake Charles, Louisiana, and Ann Arbor, Michigan.

The overall influence of business coalition efforts is difficult to measure; however, some programs have been clearly viewed as a success by their constituents. When the Ozarks Area Business Group on Health (OABGH) was first formed in Springfield, Missouri, in 1990, no managed care program was available in the area. In 1991, Springfield was dominated by two large hospitals (with over 600 beds each) and two smaller community hospitals, and although several HMOs and PPOs had sought a market presence in the community, there was significant reluctance on the part of the health care community to even talk to them. Neither of the two major hospitals saw the need to be Blue Cross-participating, nor in any way alter the manner in which they did business. By forming a coalition, contracting with a 200-bed community hospital in a market share-driven, per-diem-based contract, and using available data to determine the value of a discount-based program, OABGH successfully developed a "first generation," coalition-developed PPO, OptionHealth. OptionHealth is available not only to self-insured members of OABGH but also to small employers with as few as one employee. OptionHealth is not mandatory for coalition membership and not all members use the product. During 1993, 28 members of the 67 member organization saved more than $729,000 from OptionHealth alone.

While the experience of OptionHealth is notable, the success of OABGH is much broader than the savings generated. While the absolute amount of the dollars being redirected as a result of OptionHealth is not inconsequential, its real impact has been to act as a wedge with which to open the fee-for-service door.

Partially in response to OptionHealth, both major hospitals in Springfield have now developed Physician Hospital Organizations (PHOs). One has contracted with a series of PPOs outside the immediate Springfield area and the other has become a participating hospital with Blue Cross. Two worker's compensation managed care organizations have been formed and are soliciting business, while a joint venture between providers and purchasers is in its early development. One of the large hospitals has begun selling its cardiology services on a bundled charge basis, and the community hospital with which the coalition contracts has become a local leader in managed care by initiating other contracts with non-OABGH members and other PPOs across the country.

To suggest that OptionHealth has been the only impetus to change is unrealistic. Nevertheless, in a small area such as Springfield, a group of employers coming together in a way that stimulates competition and redirects large sums of health care dollars is startling enough to cause the entire system to take note of impending change.

As another example, the Savannah Business Group in Georgia represents 22 employers. The coalition contracts with 160 physicians and a hospital network for its PPO. After a three-year hospital contract, it is estimated that the savings in hospital costs to members has been 36–42%. Quality standards are incorporated into hospital contracts to promote efficiency. One coalition member, Savannah Foods and Industries, is paying $2600–$2800 per employee per year, as compared to other areas where indemnity coverage is $4200–$4600 per employee per year.

A 14-county rural coalition of 96 employers, the Southeast Missouri Business Group on Health in Cape Girardeau, recently began offering its own insurance product, Value Management Health Plan, to be administered by Blue Cross and Blue Shield of Missouri. The plan includes three alternatives for insured employers, as well as the option of self-insurance.

Consumer Education Projects

Some coalitions are directly involved in educating consumers about quality-of-care comparative hospitals and other providers. The emphasis on consumer health information must be accompanied by an emphasis on the credibility of the data disseminated. The St. Louis Area Health Care Coalition, a consortium of the area's largest employers, including McDonnell Douglas, Union Pacific, and Edison Electric, helped to bring consumer information to the St. Louis Area by prepurchasing and distributing over 60,000 copies of a magazine called *Health Pages*. The magazine provides both general health care information about such topics as breast cancer, prostate cancer, and Medigap insurance. It also includes community-specific comparative information about managed care plans in the St. Louis area, including quality of care information on such indicators as pediatric immunization, mammography, and pap smear rates. The Pittsburgh and Atlanta coalitions are helping to bring the magazine to their cities, as are groups in other states, including Florida and Iowa. Michigan, Minnesota, and Ohio coalitions are interested as well.

The business coalition in Washington state, the Health Care Purchasers Association (HCPA) located in Seattle, has also been involved in a consumer education project. In 1991, the coalition published a 32-page health care consumer guide to educate employees to become more prudent buyers of care. Included in the guide are chapters on doctors, hospitals, HMOs/PPOs, medical quality, surgery, emergency care, maternity care, and diagnostic tests. Over 40,000 copies of the guide have been distributed, and other coalitions in Vermont and Springfield, Missouri, have reprinted the guide for use in their areas.

In June of 1993, Health Policy Corporation of Iowa, working with researchers at New England Medical Center in Boston, developed assessment tools to enable consumers, employers, and the public sector to evaluate health plans. The John A. Hartford Foundation funded the study as part of an effort to establish a Community Health Management Information System across Iowa. Using a number of measures, the survey described consumer health, as well as consumer's evaluation of their health plans and providers.

Future Directions of Coalition Involvement in Quality Initiatives

Given the level of interest and potential activity around health care system reform, it is difficult to project the future direction of health care coalitions. One aspect of reform that seems fairly consistent across most proposals is the move toward more managed systems of care. Coalitions' traditional emphasis on individual hospitals, physicians, and other health care providers has just begun to shift its focus on integrated, managed, or organized systems of care. As discussed earlier, many large employers and some states are involved in efforts to evaluate managed care systems using HEDIS 2.0. Indeed, the Joint Commission on Accreditation of Healthcare Organizations, which has traditionally evaluated individual hospitals and other providers, is now moving into the accreditation of networks of providers. While purchasers, coalitions, and consumers will have a continued interest in individual physician and hospital performance, this will be done increasingly in the context of managed care.

A second issue in reform which may become manifest in health care coalition activities is the tension between efforts to support the public availability of provider information and provider efforts to implement internal continuous quality improvement (CQI) methods. Some argue that publishing comparative information, particularly about individual physicians or hospitals, may counter internal efforts to improve performance in a nonthreatening way, and may also interfere with the notion of "partnering," both of which are central ideas to CQI. These concerns can be addressed by insuring that data are accurate, credible, and presented in a responsible fashion. The focus on "customers" in CQI also ensures the continued need to make good information available to the end-users of health care—purchasers and consumers.

Coalitions will continue to be involved in projects that balance these issues and may provide insight for health care policymakers. For example, the

Berkshire Business Group on Health, a business coalition in western Massachusetts, is involved in a project that is collecting data on physician and plan-specific patient satisfaction and health status, which are available publicly only on an aggregate basis. Next year, however, the information may publicly identify the performance of individual physicians and managed care plans.

A more fundamental question is how health care coalitions will develop in response to state health care reform. It is possible that group purchasing activities conducted by health care coalitions could effectively end as large employers are required to buy care either on their own or through state-established health purchasing alliances, which group all other purchasers into a very large purchasing pool. Under other scenarios, coalition purchasing activities could be strengthened if viable alternatives to publicly established purchasing alliances are offered. Key factors affecting the future of the coalition movement include national and state efforts to reform the delivery and financing of health care, antimanaged care legislation, and attempts to obtain waivers from the federal government.

One health care reform scenario might involve coalitions acting as the organizer of a competing health care delivery system in a community, particularly for those coalitions that have developed group purchasing activities, and who might not find it difficult to offer their contracted networks to newly constituted health care alliances.

A final scenario could involve the ascendancy of a policy function for health care coalitions as health care reform is implemented on a state and local basis. Indeed, one of the goals of NBCH is to foster health reform at the local level where services are actually provided, received, and paid for. The policy function of health care coalitions could take on a number of roles. In some communities, the coalition could serve as the convener of all parties to implement health care reform; in others, they may simply represent the purchaser interest in larger policy forums.

An example of such a broad-based commitment to a comprehensive approach to "Improving the Health of the Community" is the Greater Detroit Area Health Council, the oldest business group on health in the nation, as well as one of the largest. The group has a strong track record of public stewardship and long-term planning efforts, such as a campaign to encourage vaginal deliveries among women who had previously delivered by cesarean section; development of the Hospice of Southeast Michigan; the AIDS Consortium of Southeast Michigan; the Outpatient Surgery Organization and Financing Project, and the previously mentioned coronary artery disease project. The Health Council was the driving force behind the Coordinated Community AIDS Program, which raised over $2 million to organize a regional response to the AIDS crisis.

Health care coalitions have long been involved in issues related to the public accountability of hospitals, other health care providers, and health plans. As early supporters of publicly sponsored databases, they were in the forefront of collecting comparative information on hospital performance. Many are committed to coalition-sponsored data projects, many of which have evolved into group purchasing activities or consumer education projects. While their future fate is uncertain, coalitions have effectively served as agents of change in their communities and as laboratories for many of the activities currently being promoted on a national basis.

Ultimately, whether broad-based or focused, the coalition movement has played a critical role in the paradigm shift from treating sickness to promoting health, wellness, and prevention. A related activity in many cities is the move from evaluation of individual health to a comprehensive assessment of the health of the entire community. After such an assessment, goals are established with timelines against which improvement can be measured. This is just another strategy to quantify and document the ultimate success of community health reform, the goal of which is to improve the overall quality of life and health of every individual in every community.

References

1. National Business Coalition on Health: *Health Care Information Systems and Data Initiatives*. Washington, DC, Feb 1994.

2. National Business Coalition on Health: *1993 Membership Survey.* Washington, DC, Jul, 1993.

3. Sullivan S, Kunkle C: *ValueBased Purchasing: The Road to a Healthy Market,* Washington, DC: Medical Interface, 1993.

4. O'Brien A, Shaller D, Casey P: *Community-Based Healthcare Reform Through Employer Group Purchasing: An Assessment of Select Initiatives.* Cleveland, OH, May, 1994.

5. Casey J: Employer coalitions spearhead value-based purchasing. *Health Benefits Newsletter*. Alexandria, VA, Oct 1993.

Chapter Five

PURCHASER QUALITY MEASURES
Progressing from Wants to Needs

Robert W. Hungate, MBA

The old saying, "Wants are insatiable," applies to purchasers' wants for measures of hospital quality. Each release of information has led to requests for more data, not the hoped-for satisfaction, creating a tension over the value of the health care services the hospital provides. When costs were lower and the value of medical care was intrinsically trusted, payers simply paid for services rendered. However, as costs have risen and public information about possible benefits has increased patients' expectations, payers no longer simply pay medical bills, but purchase health care on a more prospective basis.

Purchaser attempts to verify or establish the value of what they pay for has created an increased "hassle factor" for hospitals and other providers, contributing to even higher administrative costs. Yet as long as providers merely respond to purchaser wants, data on quality of care may provide an important educational service, but will never satisfy the information needs that drive those wants. Those needs will remain unmet until common measurements for patient expectations, purchaser commitment to quality, and physician and hospital performance can be established. Wants, by their very nature, may obscure the true needs—the requirements. Only by identifying these underlying requirements can hospitals meet purchaser needs.

Background

Purchasers and Hospital Quality

Whether the purchaser is a future health alliance, today's union trust fund, an employer, or Congress, all have a basic need to reconcile the value of the health care delivered for the money spent. When purchasers' "wants" for quality measures are closely studied, it is clear that they are seeking a justification for paying as low a cost as possible, as was the case in both Pennsylvania's legislation[1] and Cleveland Quality Choice.[2] Unfortunately, measures that simply document differences in resource use between locations may be used to justify selective contracting to reduce spending, when the true need is to maximize health benefits for the money spent. From a macroperspective, the question is, if the care you deliver costs more, how much better do your patients do? How much of the difference is a *risk-managed* difference and how much a real result?

Purchasers include patients, payers/sponsors, and fiscal intermediaries, whether the latter are a traditional indemnity insurer or managed care organization. Patients are often ignored as purchasers because benefit designs are typically determined by employers or other payers. Payers/sponsors ultimately must include the costs of sponsorship in the value of their goods or services. For the insured population, fiscal intermediaries have historically functioned as the primary payers. The evolution of fiscal intermediaries as a cost-plus, service-utilizing activity is traceable to their formation.[3] As a result, fiscal intermediaries typically respond to three sets of consumers, i.e., the patient, the sponsor, and the physician/hospital (provider). Payers/sponsors, especially large self-insured employers, were the first to react strongly to rapidly rising health costs by shifting from a payer to a purchaser role.

These purchasers now use three broad plan types to provide health benefits. Standard indemnity coverage is the classic model which leaves choice at the provider level and to the complete discretion of the patient. The health maintenance organization (HMO) is again a classic model that represents the continued separation of the patient from the costs at the point of utilization but transfers the responsibility for choice to the plan's management. The last major category and the most rapidly growing is a hybrid of the other two. It includes plans such as preferred provider organizations (PPOs) or Point of Service options for HMOs that leave a measure of choice with patients but with attached differential costs. These differentials usually take the form of no cost for the use of "in-plan" providers but higher cost for the use of "nonplan" sources of care. Purchasing decisions relate to both the type of health plan (e.g., indemnity, PPO, HMO) and controls over selection of health care providers, as well as controls over decisions to use selected medical procedures (Table 1). At each level of decision making, information needs exist. Imperfections in information at each level limit the ability to achieve efficiency through market driven forces.

How does hospital quality fit with purchaser needs? Historically, hospital choice was the province of the physician, who was not a purchaser. In recent years, patients have become more active in health care decision making and want to participate in the selection of hospitals; however, their choice may be limited by their sponsors, or the managed care organizations, to a single hospital. When choice is restricted it is not clear that quality-of-care needs can be met by statistical reporting of satisfaction or patient outcomes within a given institution. A recent appeals decision (McClelland vs. Health Maintenance Organization of Pennsylvania) regarding an HMO's responsibility for gate keeping decisions,[4] while specifically applying to a physician, would be equally applicable to a hospital if it assumes the responsibility to deliver all needed care for a fixed price. In the cited case, biopsy or histological examination of a surgically removed mole was not done. The patient later died from undiagnosed, untreated melanoma. Hospital quality may be only one component of the

TABLE 1

Quality of Care Issues by Purchasing Level

Purchasing Level	Quality of Care Issues
Insurance plan	Enrollee satisfaction with insurance plan Health status of insured population Treatment effectiveness threshold accepted by plan for coverage Cost effectiveness threshold accepted by plan for coverage
Health care provider	Satisfaction with care from specific providers Comparative outcomes by providers
Medical procedures	Possible outcome given patient risk factors Possible adverse events

larger need—the expectation that the patient is receiving the best, most efficient, total process of care for the outcome sought.

Hospitals have a key role in the control of health care processes. Increasingly, hospitals are being asked to contract for total episodes of care. In this form of contracting, lack of control of health care processes can lead to increased cost on the institutions' part and hence poorer financial performance or higher prices. These "quality-of-care" problems when reported publicly create several significant problems. Public reporting is punitive by its very nature, and as a result, providers will tend to underreport problems. Underreporting may mistakenly suggest that the problem is not significant, hence it goes uncorrected, with the continuing higher cost.

The continuing improvement model applied across institutions is a possible correction of this problem, as it creates a system of nonpunitive sharing of process information. A number of hospitals have joined others to share data to compare or benchmark their own performance on many quality indicators in a nonpunitive, quality improving way. However, continuing quality improvement programs across institutions can be data intensive and expensive and will only be sustained if they add value to patients and purchasers as well as institutions.

Purchasers, whether benefit managers, managed care organizations, or patients, need to know if the expected benefit of a health care intervention is worth the proposed cost. The patient directly judges health care benefit when incurring cost for services. Intermediaries and final sponsors must adopt proxies for patient judgments. It is in that context that the need to measure hospital quality becomes evident. It should also be clear that hospital quality alone is an inadequate definition to meet patients needs. The result of an intervention really becomes the basis for patient judgment. While the necessity, appropriateness, efficacy, and efficiency with which an outcome is achieved are clear contributors to an outcome, it is predominantly the outcome itself that relates to expectations, and whether they are met or exceeded. Both intermediaries and final sponsors will in the long run need to measure performance on the same terms that patients judge it. The variation in purchaser role and physician/patient medical decision-making processes are shown in Table 2. Current system performance tends to be focused on first-dollar coverage and the structural aspects of benefit design. As both patients and payers become more informed consumers of health care, however, performance is increasingly being motivated by patient choice.

Changing Health Care Market

While federal political processes have not ratified the decision, it appears that the United States will adopt market mechanisms to ensure an appropriate cost of health care for both individuals and society. If this is true, the health care market must move the use of resources and achievement of health results to the point of optimal marginal-gain for the individual. This balancing of the marginal value of health care with the marginal value of other expenditure options—government, housing, food, clothing, or entertainment—is based on perception. Markets seem to work best when value is determined by the purchaser.

While it is changing rapidly, the health care market for the last 40 years has largely not been market-driven. The health insurance mechanism of paying for care removes the assessment of value at the time of receipt of health care services. Purchasers, acting in the benefit management mode, have taken the early steps of conversion. Value assessment is typically considered when the benefit manager makes insurance purchasing decisions. For value to be part of the purchasing decision, the benefit-management role carried out by purchasers is critical to the operation of an effective market regulation of the health care system.

TABLE 2

Medical Decision-Making and the Purchaser Role

Physician/Patient Relationship	Purchaser Role
◆ Physician as decision maker	Traditional
◆ Informed choice	↓
◆ Physician/patient consent	↓
◆ Patient as decision maker	↓
◆ Choice limited by insurance plan	Nontraditional

Purchasers' Wants Versus Needs

What Do Purchasers "Need"?

Health care reform generally means one of two things, i.e., guaranteeing universal access of health care to all individuals, and guaranteeing value by holding providers accountable for health care quality. Since the information system to quantify these needs does not yet exist, persuasion, influence, and politics in general, become the controlling forces determining "wants." For purchasers to base their decision on need, rather than wants, information that is purchaser-friendly must be further developed. The chapter by Cronin and Kunkle describes coalitions' current efforts, which reflect the importance of measurement in all their initiatives. Despite significant cost in data collection for quality measures, less than the expected shifting of patients to high-quality, low-cost institutions has occurred. It would appear that no measurement system has yet met purchaser needs. The state of the art of measurement systems continue to be part of the problem, since these systems are not yet adequate for use by purchasers. Iezzoni has described differences between various first generation measurement systems and approaches to risk-adjusted outcomes that tend to limit their utility.[5]

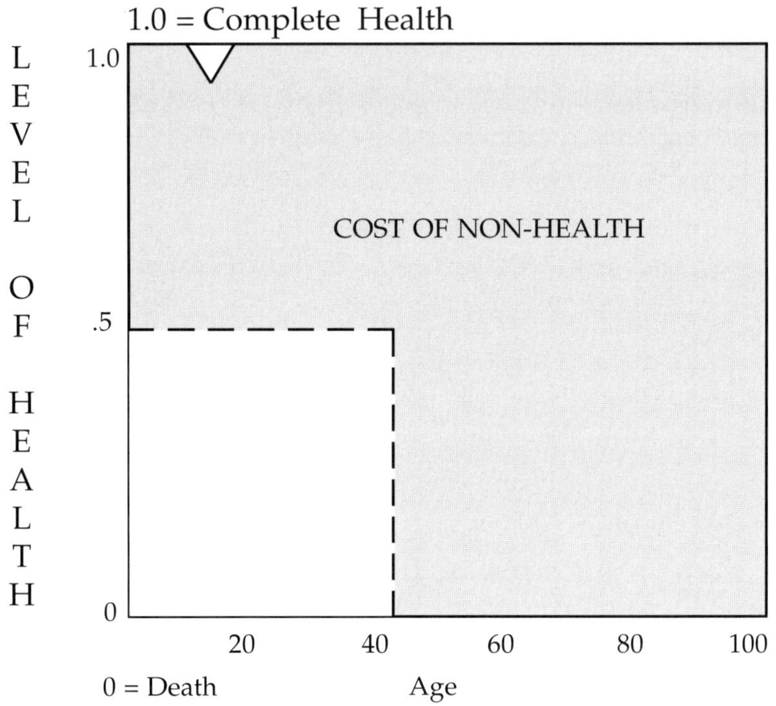

Figure 1. *A simple representation of state of health. Full health, as 100%, is expressed as 1.0; absence of life, death, is expressed as 0. Graphically portrayed in the upper horizontal solid line is an individual who has experienced a healthy life, but suffered an attack of appendicitis at an early age, recovered quickly with no loss of function, lived an active life until age 100, and died suddenly. This is among the best scenarios of health that can be anticipated.*

The opportunity costs of a significantly less healthy life are portrayed by the dashed line. This life represents a neonate, probably a low birth-weight one, who was severely compromised, perhaps from prebirth conditions or by a failure of process control during birth. The patient lived to age 40 in this depiction. The shaded zone represents the cost of non-health.

When assessing value, health is the high quality product, and nonhealth—for example, unexpected death or loss of function—is a cost. These nonhealth events become the macrofocus of *Healthy People 2000*, a national articulation of objectives for improving health.[6] If purchasing functions are to work to patients' benefit, then some recognition of the costs of nonhealth must be part of the language. Viewing the system this way offers hope for making public health methodologies more visible, perhaps even congruent. A sample of such a model is provided in Figure 1.*

It is the translation of these macro-objectives to the episodic individual patient conditions, encounters, and results that become the language of quality for a value purchasing system. Quality of health care per se becomes a judgment of *process*.

As a result, medical appropriateness, necessity, effectiveness, and efficiency have both cost and quality implications. Using the diagrammatic representation of this cost/quality interrelationship (Figure 2), it is clear that the highest quality of health might cost the least. Purchasers want to maximize the portion of their total health care bill spent on quality, while minimizing that spent on nonquality.

For purchasers, a significant control problem exists. One's state of health is more than just the result of health care received; heredity, life-syle, living conditions, etc., all have significant impact. Purchasers' realization of these other, sometimes less expensive, ways to impact health enhances their desire to know exactly what has been gained for the health expenditure. This demand for answers has been an unaccustomed and uncomfortable one for health care. For the customer, quality is measured by doing the right thing and doing it well—appropriateness and necessity, and effectiveness and efficiency.

Public Availability of Information

Patients' understanding of the medical options available to them has grown more sophisticated in recent years. In our grandparents' time, medical knowledge was the exclusive property of the physician. The covenant of trust between patient and physician was based on this knowledge. Today, patients are often privy to medical findings—once the exclusive domain of the health care profession—before their physicians. Newspapers regularly feature stories on the latest contributions to medical technology, serving to raise expectations for achieving maximum health and prolonging life. Mortality of the patients treated by hospitals and physicians are released for public scrutiny. Increasingly, purchasers of health care are organizing to enhance their knowledge and purchasing power, both in the form of business coalitions as well as private lobbying efforts.[7] In short, this chain of events has tended to undermine our confidence in

* For a discussion of the distinctions between quality of care and quality, see *Quality Review Bulletin*, 1993, for an exchange of letters between the author and Avedis Donabedian, MD.

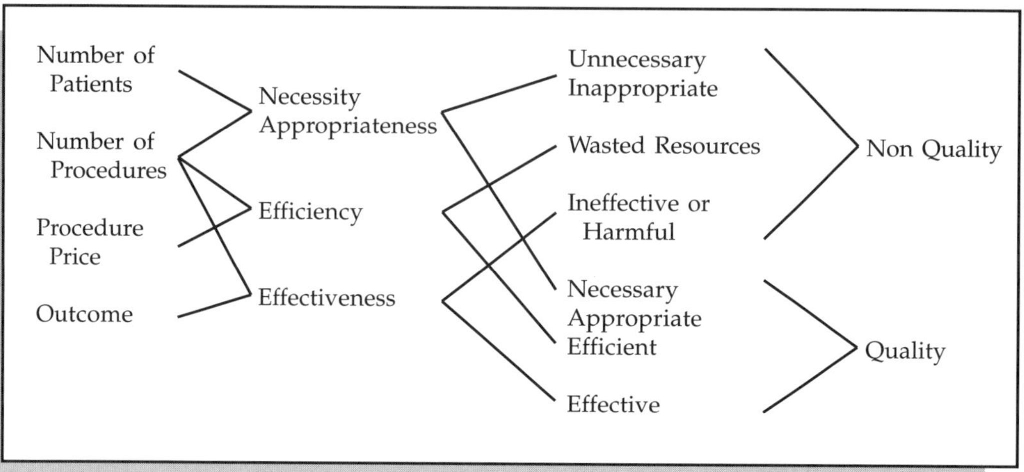

Figure 2. *Quality/cost equation.*

the physician-patient relationship and in our health care system. In the midst of this uncertainty is the making of a new, rapidly evolving health care market.

Impact of the Information Revolution

Concurrent with the public availability of information has been rapid evolution of information technology. The rate of change in the technology of information has never been faster. A national priority is the development of electronic data interchange (EDI) for the purpose of moving health care claims processing to more efficient levels. The health insurance industry has responded with the Workgroup for Electronic Data Interchange (WEDI), whose objective is to implement EDI for routine use in the industry by 1996.[8] On a broader level, the "electronic data highway" is now expected to become reality. Such a system would permit very rapid access to individual and collective data about patients' medical records. The founder of the Lotus Corporation, Mitch Kapor, has created a not-for-profit foundation, The Electronic Frontier Foundation, to stimulate broad adoption of this technology.

Creation of the data highway is a key element in creating a cost-effective computerized patient record. The feasibility and benefit of such a record is now recognized,[9] and electronic medical records are now under rapid development in many settings. Proposed federal legislation would fund the development of such a record. Both vendors and users have created and joined the Computerized Patient Record Institute (CPRI) to promote orderly adoption of the standards essential to ready transfer of information between plans and providers, including careful attention to protection of patient rights to privacy. Both of these steps are made possible by the rapid decrease in cost of the memory to contain ever more detailed data, and the software to convert that data to useful information. Referred to in the industry as "Moore's Law" (named after Gordon Moore, Intel cofounder), memory chips available on the market double in both density and speed every 18 months. This technology trend lowers cost and enhances individuals' power to tap into it.

An added benefit of this technology comes in the form of expert systems. These systems have been in varying stages of development for more than a decade now. An organization, The Society for Medical Decision Making, exists to foster the development of such systems. The Agency for Health Care Policy and Research (AHCPR) has recognized the potential of this capability in making guidelines available to professionals.

The Office of Technology Assessment (OTA) recently released Benefit Design—Clinical Preventive Services to inform the debate on setting a minimum benefit in health system reform. It found that many common preventive services were offered not on statistical support documenting benefit to patients, but on the belief that these services would result in health benefits.[10] An even touchier issue that is clearly of purchaser interest is the cost-benefit of preventive services. When data collection becomes less expensive as a result of the electronic medical record in its two primary forms, encompassing the patient's life and each episode and encounter, observations about variations in patient experiences can be used to significantly augment clinical trials with true clinical results.

In summary, trends include:

- emergence of electronic data interchange as a national priority;
- electronic patient records;
- the declining cost, coupled with increased power of computers to provide information;
- demonstration of expert systems that effectively augment professional control of medical processes; and
- realization that effectiveness may be more critical than efficacy, as proven in clinical trials.

Combined, these trends let us envision a future quality-of-care information system quite different from what we have previously tolerated. The information "map" of the future will involve the integration of claims data with clinical process control, medical record, and patient-supplied health status data; all are needed to fully describe patient outcomes. Although we have been forced historically to choose between claims data (with its inadequacies) and medical record data (with attendant high costs), information systems should let us focus on what is really needed to allow purchasers to assess value and providers to conduct self-measurement to improve care.

Benefit Management

Benefit managers must balance the countervailing pressures of satisfying employee wants and management of costs. While "wants" for benefits may be insatiable, the funds to pay for them are limited. Moreover, benefit managers pay for things they do not personally receive and must justify these expenditures to their employers. "Win-win" conditions are met when the beneficiary, employee, dependent, or retiree achieves a health status commensurate with the motivation, loyalty, and productivity their employer receives from that expenditure. Controversy exists over the establishment of a uniform (and predictably expensive) benefit design. To date, attempts to create universal coverage of some minimum benefit have created larger price tags than today's politics have been willing to fund.

Health care costs have been a major concern of industry for almost 20 years; many different cost-containment tools have been tried, refined, or discarded. These tools have evolved from first-dollar coverage, through changing benefits and selective contracting, to quality improvement. A large and thriving consulting industry has grown around managing health care cost, part of the administrative expense of our country's "nonsystem" of delivery. These tools have largely been inspections and external interventions of previously undisclosed aspects of the care management process, whether it be hospital or outpatient based. Figure 3 reflects the results of a poll taken in 1993 of employers' ratings of the effectiveness of various programs to contain health care costs. Listed as least effective of those reported are second opinion programs. At the onset of employer interest in cost containment, second opinions were judged as very effective. Similarly, both utilization review and precertification also are eroding. Delegation of these judgments to an HMO or other intermediary managed care organization has meant that the organization becomes the pur-

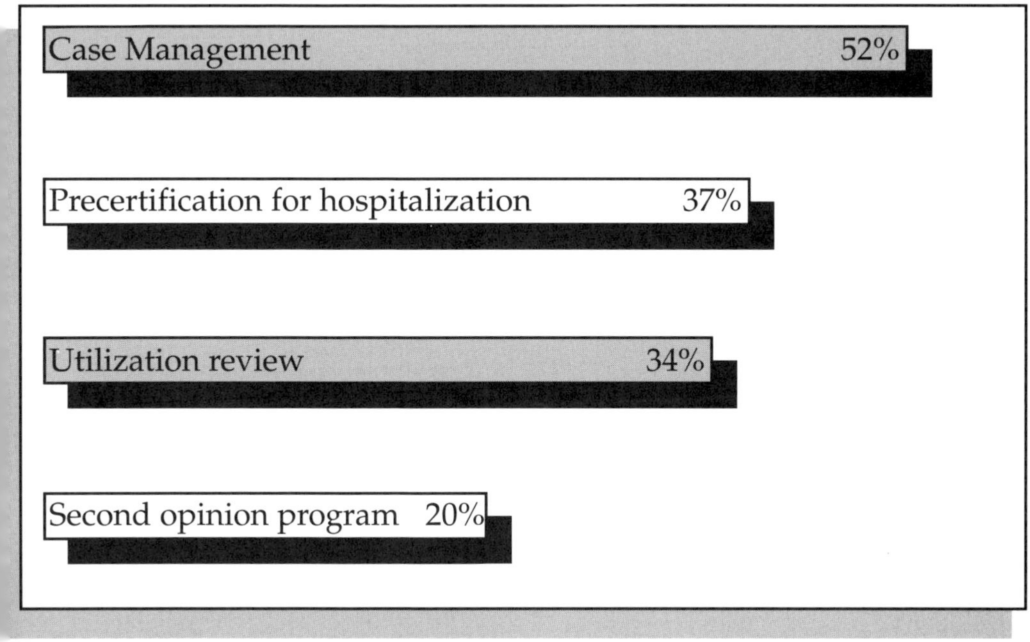

Figure 3. *Effectiveness of cost-containment programs. Percentage of employers who rate the following programs effective in containing health care costs. (From* Business & Health *1993 Executive Poll, May 1993, Survey of 410* Business & Health *readers. Montvale, New Jersey: Medical Economics. Used by permission.)*

chaser. General Motors, Hewlett-Packard, and now the Health Care Financing Administration (HCFA) because of risk differences in the population managed have questioned the price paid for HMO services, i.e., its value.

The Massachusetts Group Insurance Commission, in evaluating the cost of plans that serve its members, found that 75% of its high-cost cases occurred among the 25% of enrollees that were part of the indemnity plan.[11] HCFA's evaluation of Medicare risk contracts, conducted over four years by Mathematica Policy Research, concluded that contracted HMOs had been paid 5.7% more than was warranted, even after a 5% lower cost than the average per capita cost per enrollee. Healthier, lower-cost individuals had selected the HMO option.[12]

Another approach to the risk management aspect of benefit management is in Minneapolis, where nine employers agreed to a common benefit design in order to get effective price competition between plans.[13] In a significant response to this initiative a consortium was formed, consisting of two

TABLE 3

Benefit Management Structure

Population Managed	Management
Employed—Self-Insured	
◆ Large, mature, union organized	Human resource, union
◆ Large, non-union industry	Human resource
Private Sector employed—Insured ◆ Smaller, union and non-union	State legislatures, state insurance commissioners, brokers, owners, unions
Private Sector Employed—Uninsured	
◆ Still smaller and newer	Same as above
Unemployed	State legislatures
Poor	Congress, state legislatures
Federal Employed	Congress, FEHB
◆ NonDOD	Defense Department, CHAMPUS
◆ DOD	
Retired	
◆ Medicare	Congress, HCFA
◆ Medigap	Congress, human resource
◆ Military	VA, DOD, CHAMPUS

HMOs, Group Health and Med Centers, and Park Nicollet Medical Center and the Mayo Clinic. These employers expect that 100,000 members will enroll in Choice Plus, the name given the new plan in 1994.

Displayed in Table 3 is the current benefit-management structure of the US health benefits industry. This organizational structure represents the primary purchaser, and hence market manager, of the US health care system. It is clear on inspection that managerial lines of responsibility are clearest in three segments of the system: large self-insured employers, Medicare, and the US Department of Defense. It is also clear that for some segments of the system, either funding has not been forthcoming, or benefit management has been inadequate in achieving an effective benefit-management system for those segments. Small employers have clearly suffered under the system as it now functions. It is also evident that there is no information system in place to support decisions about the care offered. Small employers would benefit most by a system that provides information on costs and benefits of health.

While political reform may alter or entirely replace the existing management structure, what will remain constant is purchasers' need to balance cost with health care benefit for their employees. Since information needs are the same for employees and benefit managers, it seems advisable to concentrate on defining information needs for both groups. Good information may help significantly in revealing the existing imbalances in the health achieved for funds expended across different population groups. If health reform can correct the "job lock" nature of our current system and guarantee that people never lose coverage when they change employers, then this benefit-management structure will iteratively define a minimum benefit structure, as costs are balanced with a the need to attract and motivate employees. But for this to work, every individual must be covered by a health care program and not be free to purchase insurance only when illness occurs. It is not yet clear if the political will to recognize this individual responsibility exists. Employees are less and less likely to have a single employer during their employed years. In large organizations, the productivity loss of disgruntled employees because of a denied benefit is a more critical priority for corporate success than achievement of absolute minimum health care costs. It is the presence of these tensions that assures a ready use of valid data.

Behavior Range of Patient/Health Seeker

Patients want to be healthy, stay healthy, or recover full health. If health is 70% determined by life-style,[14] then measuring hospital quality accounts for less than all of the health system's real value. But with the high expense and acute nature of hospital care, the emphasis has been almost exclusively on hospital quality. If quality is defined as meeting or exceeding expectations, how those expectations are established will have a pivotal impact on judgments of quality. Two major factors—information sources and patient behavior—affect these expectations. Media attention to technology breakthroughs as well as HMO advertisements for "all the health care you need" are factors in the information realm. Patient behavior in reacting to physician advice is another important, information-based factor.

Patients can be grouped into four general behavior styles: (1) traditional; (2) informed consent; (3) collaborative; and (4) patient choice,[15] based on the form of interaction they expect to have with their health care providers.

Traditional patients want the physician to take full responsibility for deciding and doing. The patient or the provider may fear that information will erode their trust.

Informed consent encourages patient passivity in the interaction and willingness to unquestioningly accept information as to risks and potentials.

Collaborative patients are more likely to set realistic expectations by interacting with the care system and relevant physicians.

Patient choice extends the collaborative model fully so that the patient, rather than the physician, makes the final decision. This behavior style is likely to have the highest probability of matching expectation. On the other hand, the quality of result may be conditioned by misinformation the patient uses in making that choice, especially when that choice is concealed from the physician. When a patient believes "Once a cesarean section, always a cesarean section," professional judgment may be severely constrained. If true needs are best expressed by realistic expectations for outcomes, and if patient behavior is not accounted for in the process of care, then the manner in which the patient will determine quality is uncertain.

If the shift to a quality improvement mode of management is to be successful, development of a common set of measurements to satisfy both the employee (patient) and the boss (purchaser) is essential. This challenging assignment frustrates both employees and benefits managers. It is clear that we are woefully unprepared to describe the real benefit of effective management.

Purchasing Levels

Purchasing occurs under the three primary health system reform approaches. The purchasing arrangement, whether single payer, managed competition or employer-based, serves the function of transferring money from those who may need care to those who deliver care. "What" is managed is similar if not the same in all approaches; it is "who" manages that is different. In any of these approaches to purchasing care, some amount of money is available for the provision of health care services. The responsible purchasing entity will have to decide on the relative investment that should be made in various diseases, conditions and interventions. These funding decisions will affect both quality and availability of services. Regardless of the purchasing approach, decisions will be made regarding which patients receive what treatments for what conditions. Equity in those decisions will require attention to value (health) expected for health care (cost) expended.

In aggregate, health care costs are the totality of the number of patients multiplied by the number of services provided to those patients, multiplied by the cost of those services. Purchasers can reduce costs by acting on any one or all of these variables. They have been willing to do so. These efforts can be initiated at three levels in the system: the *plan* level, the *provider* level, and the *procedure* (or *service*) level. To adequately meet purchaser needs under these options, value measures—which may be implemented through an intermediary—at all three levels are needed (Table 1).

The desire and willingness of purchasers to manage to this level of detail is visible in several rapidly growing fields of activity, especially utilization review and precertification. The field of precertification was initiated as a result of the small area variation studies of Wennberg,[16] Chassin,[17] and others. The growing sophistication of this activity is reflected in the use of guidelines, such as Rand's,[18] in the structured determinations of necessity and appropriateness. Medstat's rapid growth as a supplier to employers of comparative claims data illustrates the demand for valid rate and cost data at the procedure level. Finally, the Community Health Management Information System (CHMIS) initiative being funded by the Hartford Foundation seeks to make comparative procedure information broadly available on a geographic basis, reflecting the largely local nature of health care. This initiative initially focuses on claims data and will as a result provide good information on utilization and prices. It will not yield absolute values, i.e. measures useful for evaluating alternative procedures and outcomes until usable outcome information becomes a part of the system. Employers, concurrently with their own proactive evolution as purchasers, have been broadening the base of purchasing activity by increasing cost sharing with employees.[19]

Plan-Level Purchasing

At the plan level, employers and employees are the purchasers. Employers select plans to offer to their employees during open enrollment. Employer choices are based on a combination of price, past performance, and image. Of these three, only the first—price—has quantifiable comparative utility. Not surprisingly, it is the primary focus of purchasers. Unfortunately, risk-adjustment methodologies do not yet exist to correct for existing market imperfection (i.e., the selection of indemnity plans by patients with greater health care needs). If an employer always contracted with a single plan vendor, then risk selection would not be an issue, as competing plans would always bid for the same population. Nevertheless, employee choice at the plan level would be eliminated. Kaiser Permanente, a large HMO, has consistently refused to be the single plan chosen, feeling that choice on the individuals' part is important. In general employers have found that presenting employees with options under open enrollment is more effective in the balancing of satisfaction and cost. Recently some leading employers, most notably Allied Signal and Xerox, have acted to subcontract the management of risk to a single overriding plan, which in turn manages the enrollment with options made available to employees. Cigna, in committing to hold Allied's health care cost constant over the three years of its initial contract, assumed all selection risk. In turn Cigna contracted with other managers for the population enrolled there. The process to be managed has not changed, only who is managing that process.

In managing open enrollment, employers must decide between contribution policies. It has been demonstrated that employees tend to select plans based on the lowest premium cost to them.[20] Through contribution policy, employers affect which plan employees choose. If plans adopt the Enthoven/Kronic advocated contribution policy[21] a fixed dollar amount is established as sponsor contribution, preferably based on the low-cost plan, and the increased costs of other plans are collected as part of employee premiums. In this approach, adverse risk selection to a plan, as often happens when indemnity coverage is offered in addition to an HMO, results in higher premiums being charged to higher cost individuals. If this greater cost is a result of greater utilization (but with the same underlying health conditions), then it is equitable. If the costs are a result of conditions requiring greater costs,* then the true purpose of health insurance—protection against the higher costs associated with nonhealth—has not been served. It seems to be the antithesis of the desired end. Because resolution of this question has not been possible some employers have assumed a policy of a constant percentage contribution. This has the effect of absorbing most of the cost of variation between plans by the sponsor with only attenuated price incentives to employees. Finally, some employers vary their policy from enrollment to enrollment based on whatever seems to minimize

* The Clinton Health Care Security Act recognized this system deficiency and assigned its resolution to the National Health Standards Board. Some method of collective judgment will be essential to making the system work for the benefit of, not disadvantage of, those patients whose conditions, when appropriately treated, would lead to higher costs.

employer cost and maximize employee acceptance of the options offered. These two joint imperfections of risk selection and the employer contribution to benefit costs create a far from perfect market at the plan level. If good measures existed at the plan level to assess health relative to risks managed, then employers/purchasers could risk-adjust premiums and establish a market-driven policy for the employer contribution toward health care benefits.

Provider-Level Purchasing

Until such a system of risk selection across health care plan options evolves, employer demand for provider level data will continue. Even after that need is met, plans will still need provider level data to carry out their delegated responsibility. It is provider level information that has received the major focus in employer coalition efforts. Depending on benefit design, choice of physicians is a mix of plan and employee choice. Choice of hospital then involves the physician as well as the plan and/or employee. Historically, physicians made most of these choices based on their affiliation and local knowledge, placing great reliance on the Joint Commission as their guarantee of quality, but with little or no regard for cost. Cost decisions for employees tend to be driven by employer and the employee selected plan option with copayment considerations. They tend not to be prospective unless a preferred provider option with differential costs exists. Since cost to an employee usually consists of a mix of a deductible and copayment, no true alternative cost between institutions' decisions can be made. Rather, if a quality differential is perceived, and if the patient decides the magnitude of the difference will be affordable for the "better" alternative, then the better alternative will be the choice.

Perception of quality may be an important force in selection of health care services. For instance, teaching hospitals have generally not had the occupancy problems that community hospitals have encountered, as inpatient stays have decreased. Patients perceive teaching hospitals to be better, perhaps in part because they tend to be more expensive. Whatever the case, employers with large suburban employee populations, where community hospitals exist, have seen patients use more distant teaching hospitals. Both employee and employer may have paid more for care based on perceptions of quality rather than information on quality.

For the provider level market to become a true market, and hence deliver to plans the efficiency their purchasers seek, provider level measures of risk adjusted outcomes will have to evolve. Accompanied by prospective pricing of packages of services that are complete and meaningful, like the

Coronary Artery Bypass Graft (CABG) initiative at HCFA,[22] these products will become essential to meeting purchaser needs.

Procedure Level

At the procedure level, today's market is extremely imperfect. For patients without plan copayments, no cost is incurred for medical services or procedures. Insurance plans operate with physician agreements that limit plan obligations to a reasonable and customary charge. Evidence of the inefficiency of this market exists in the range of what is reasonable as allowed by HCFA intermediaries in their payment of Medicare claims. The US Department of Health and Human Services (HHS) in studying the impact of technology[23] collected information on different procedures for which they felt they might be "overpaying." The resulting data displayed a 3 or 4 to 1 ratio between the highest and lowest allowable charge. Figure 4 shows their findings for lithotripsy, a now common procedure. HHS' Inspector General's office surveyed 20 Medicare carriers to compare the maximum amount they allowed physicians to charge for kidney lithotripsy in 1987 and 1988. Of the 20 carriers, 13 had maximum limits averaging $1,525, and seven had maximum limits averaging $748. The higher limits are unreasonable, says the Inspector General, because they are linked to payments for the surgical removal of kidney stones, which is more time-consuming than lithotripsy. In related work at the Physician Payment Review Commission it was found that these variations were not the result of variations in practice cost. Given that these reasonable and customary prices evolved from an indemnity insurance system, where the physician was one of the key customers, especially in the case of Blue Shield, it is not surprising to see this result. As noted earlier, employers increasingly ask their employees to share in the cost of utilization through copayments. Nevertheless, it is the rare patient that will question their physician's charge. Even more rare is the patient who will question before the procedure. In addition, the reasonable and customary charge, which may result in the patient paying much more than the expected 20% of the bill, is not known before the visit or procedure resulting in the cost.

Even with this magnitude of cost uncertainty, the uncertainty of health gain from certain services is even greater. While immunizations have relatively defined certainties of outcome, imaging and many diagnostic tests have significantly less direct linkage between intervention and health gain. Since these tests are the ones most subject to public expectation, significant induced demand is possible. Even in an HMO, where one might expect more tightly controlled procedure utilization, rates of use are not far different from those under indemnity coverage. Patient expectations can determine the use of services. Markets

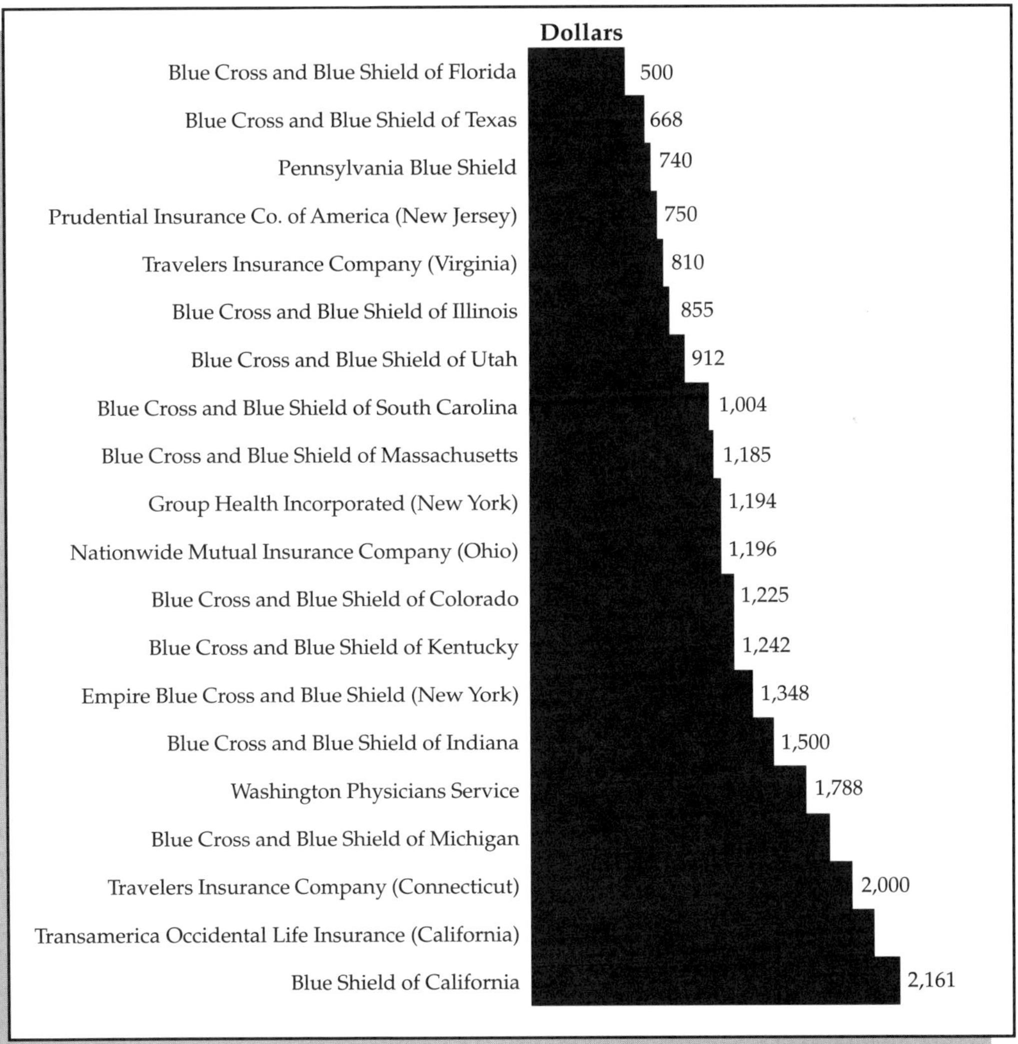

Figure 4. *Variations in physicians' charges for lithotripsy. (From Department of Health & Human Services:* Health Technology Trends. *December, 1990. Used by permission.)*

will develop at the procedure level only when a measure of financial participation is placed on patients, and the uncertainty of health care outcomes associated with specific services are understood by the patient. Without some discipline at this level, the components that go into provider package prices and then plan costs will still not deliver the desired efficiency. To compound matters, a bit more risk adjusting for presenting patient characteristics will be necessary to make copayments an effective purchasing tool. Ideally, an imaging procedure for an asymptomatic but highly vocal patient should carry a higher copayment than one that meets all the appropriateness criteria. Unfortunately, benefit design is limited to determining which procedures are part of a benefit; precertification is used to try to separate these inappropriate tests. It might make much more sense to give patients better probabilities accompanied by an affordable copayment, and leave the judgment to be made by the patients. Unless patients are made aware, they will have little way to judge. On the other hand, if the physician does not have the means to make this same probability assessment, how will utilization be controlled? Clearly, if it is not based on knowledge it will be done in some arbitrary way, perhaps consistently by health care plans, perhaps not. While physicians may not wish to have their judgment of test appropriateness questioned or kept track of, they may prefer the patient who questions over an insurance precertifier.

The patient is largely in control of the processes that are likely to be impacted. The educational value of giving patients enough information to make judgments to perform, or not perform, a test should not be underestimated. Information on the reason to take a test and expected probability of results, becomes the kind of control data that has proven useful in industrial processes.

Impact of Technology on Procedure-Level Purchasing

The Foundation for Informed Decision Making, with its landmark work with interactive video,[24] provides an example of how patients' needs can be met based on knowledge of the implication of procedures. The Foundation offers an interactive video intended for patients with benign prostatic hypertrophy who are candidates for transurethral prostatectomy, as well as videos for other conditions. In the video, patients who have chosen to undergo the procedure, as well as those who have not, are interviewed. Some who had elected "watchful waiting" describe why they chose that option and how their life-style has been affected. Patient characteristics are assessed by the physician and used to estimate the probability of specific outcomes based on information from past surgical outcomes. Patients in the video describe their treatment outcomes, accompanied by the probability of that particular outcome. The probability of mortality from the procedure is also reported. Group Health of Puget Sound and Kaiser have both reported significant reductions in surgery rates in populations exposed to the interactive video.[25]

While the author welcomes this contribution and feels that the video should be a precondition for surgery, additional issues remain. Questions arise, such as: Are those who now elect watchful waiting merely postponing what will become a riskier and more expensive operation later? What about alternative therapies, Proscar for example, which is now prevalent in ads on the sports page as an alternative to surgery? How can we assure that the video provides the most current medical information? Suppose that the particular surgeon and hospital involved have underlying performance statistics that differ significantly from the probabilities built into the video system? How can the patient be assured that the probabilities reported in the video reflect the current state of the art in clinical practice? The probability of death due to the insult of anesthesia declined significantly over time. How is that mortality factored with the surgical mortality? These questions all illustrate the need for continued data collection of actual practice, change of technology, etc. In the small-area work variation studies that preceded this video, Wennberg found that physician expectations for favorable outcomes were higher than the actual outcomes observed in study populations.[16] At least in part, the interactive video also corrects physician expectations about outcomes. Left somewhat unsettled is just how this new technology, which has cost attached to its development, maintenance and use, will be adopted by the health care system. Will urologists embrace it as an augmentation of the professionality of their practice? Or will they resent its intrusion on their professional responsibility and training? Will traditional patients appreciate the information? Should patients be required to view it? Purchasers acting individually can impact this, in fact need to, but what added tensions and cost might that bring to health care? Similar questions can be raised about the professional acceptance of other efforts to formalize medical care processes. Other approaches include the establishment of practice parameters at the American Medical Association and credentialing at the American College of Physicians.[26–28]

If all these questions are resolved, the systemwide adoption of this and other approaches to informing patients and managing expectations can yield the information needed to achieve congruence among patients, purchasers, and physicians. This congruence can span the issues of necessity and appropriateness, and over time effectiveness, so that price can be set by comparative efficiency of providers—the value purchasers have long sought. This ideal condition would meet purchaser needs, both patient and sponsor.

Information Map for the Future

In the future, outcomes will be described by some combination of claims information and medical record and health status information, a merger of purchaser, patient and provider interests in a common system. Such a merger appears to be essential to converting today's inspection-based system of management to a measurement-based improvement system of management. Process information will evolve most completely from the evolution of practice management systems and hospital information systems as they move from being predominantly administrative to becoming medical information. Evolution of this information map is essential to establish the commonality of effective communication for the various constituencies of health care. Patients, physicians, nurses, and purchasers must be able to reconcile their views by talking about the same things, not talking past each other in the belief that they are exercising their sole responsibility. The information map enables the more precise exchange of ever more specialized information, as the absolute amount of information continues to increase.

Driven by the waste and damaged trust and confidence caused by bad information, all parties to the system have a vested interest in improving health care information. When we knew less about health and disease, when options were fewer, when only physicians had information, and payers paid all the bills, we did not need this information. Now it is painful to live with its absence.

Who assumes responsibility for the information map? Since patients are at the end-link of the value chain, their needs will most likely define it. It seems likely that their interest will be a combination of quality of life as adversely modified by loss of bodily function and or disease. Patient interest in specific measures is driven by specific needs, whether it be pregnancy, back or chest pain, or malignancy. Health issues are general and not very compelling when we are healthy, which is most of the time. Most of that time not much detail is needed. In fact, we generally accept word of mouth information about the validity of data available on physicians, hospitals, and health plans. Nevertheless, the patient's employer or purchaser of insurance can decide that a plan is too expensive. When choice is restricted, the patient with a medical condition needs to know that the new providers are as good or better than the ones that were given up. Patients may be very reluctant to accept the benefit management view that the new option is better. Does the benefit manager making the decision have the same medical problem? Does he or she use the same plan and provider? We are more likely to trust established physician relationships. It is

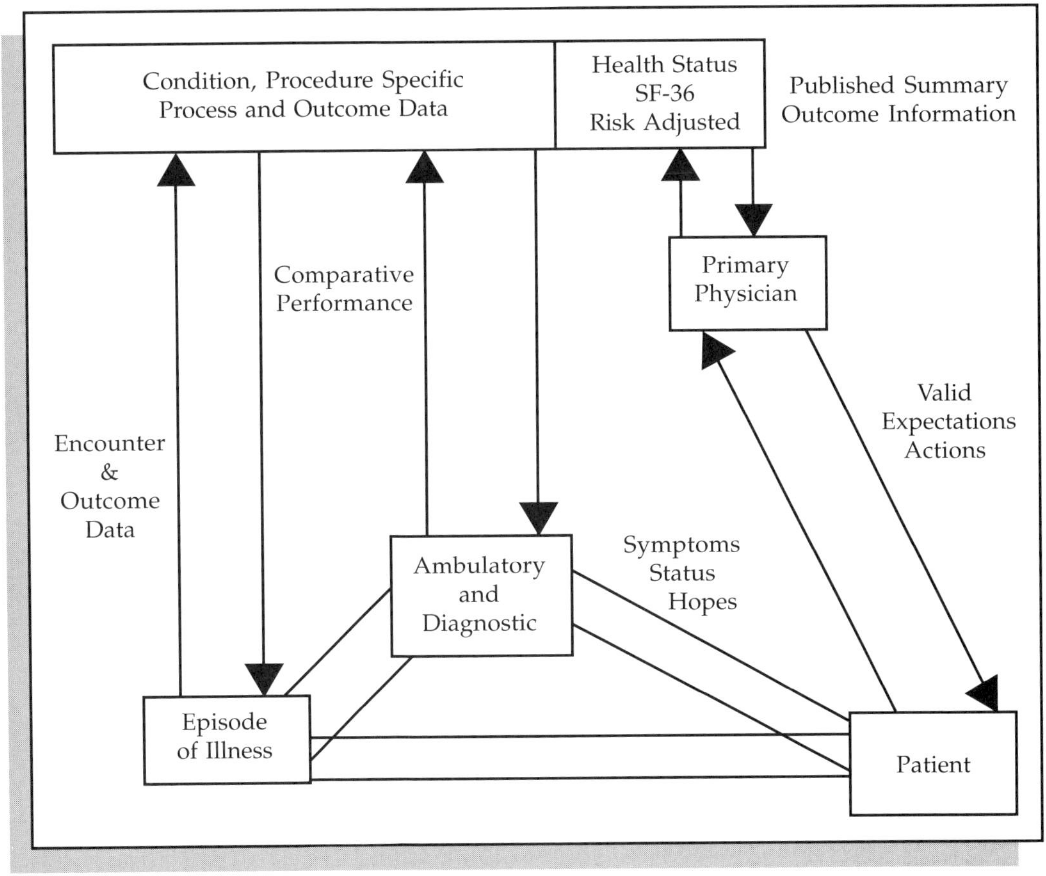

Figure 5. Structure of a measurement-managed system.

unlikely that the current provider will say that the new choice is at least as good, maybe better than the services that they can provide. Without disease-specific measurement that justifies restricted choice in location of care, the providers who are losing patients are likely to derail the process by making patients uncomfortable with the need to change their site of care. With the current information system, it is difficult for purchasers to make change decisions that will balance employee satisfaction and perceived value when choice is restricted.

It is intriguing to reflect on how these judgments are made today in instances of malpractice suit. Obviously, judgments are made after the fact. Those judgments are heavily based on two factors, the extent of injury and whether the process of care was up to the standard of care. Whether that standard is a local one or a broader national set is immaterial to the award. The standard that is used for awards is left to the collective wisdom of competing attorneys, expert witnesses, and a jury whose greatest commonality is the prospect of being a patient. This classic "bad-apple" approach is hardly part of a quality improvement program. The bumper sticker which stated, "If you think education is expensive, try ignorance," could be paraphrased for today's outcome-information system. Leaving health care information systems unaddressed could be viewed as systemic malpractice among an increasingly worried patient population.

A possible structure for a measurement-managed system using an outcome information flow for continuously improving health care as its driving force is described in Figure 5. This representation recognizes the need to reemphasize primary care, to reorganize the payment system in order to move from micromanaging the system with inspection tools to create measurable, accountable subsets to the system; and to build a risk-adjusting methodology that will make capitation-payment systems operate to the benefit of the patient, not the risk avoider, as all current systems do. While this structure has some logical appeal, it has not yet seen implementation; in fact, it probably cannot be implemented until the confidence in measurements themselves is a little more developed. I think it was Peter Drucker who said, "If you can't measure it, you can't manage it." It seems to be bearing the test of time. With today's emphasis on managing care or competition, or both, surely its time has come in health care.

Measuring the Measures

In the future quality-of-care system, it should be possible to concentrate purchaser information needs on the statistical outcomes of care processes. Today's lack of outcome measures directs purchaser attention to intermediate process indicators as a proxy for quality. Intermediate process measures can work well in areas of certainty, where judgments are black and white, but the measures become less informative as the underlying certainty decreases.

There are five requirements for outcome measures: validity, feasibility, believability, sensitivity, and importance.

Validity—Is the measure valid for ascertaining the presence of quality? Customer satisfaction—the meeting or exceeding of expectations—is the gold standard for validity in continuous improvement models. For hypertensive patients, for example, is the maintenance of blood pressure within prescribed bounds a valid measure? For some perhaps it is; for many others, however, inadequately controlled blood pressure may not cause discomfort. In fact, the side effects may cause more discomfort and inconvenience (and they may have been unexpected). The clinical measure of blood pressure, then, is not necessarily valid as a measure of the patient's health status. A direct assessment of health will probably be necessary to augment the clinical measurement to have a valid measure for the outcome of hypertension management.

If patients and purchasers are to judge on statistical measures of outcome with enough detail to allow for disease condition, then those responsible for the processes to achieve those outcomes must agree with the validity of those measures. It is this observation that has provided the cross-system basis for the Valid Risk-Adjusted Outcomes (VRAOM) project at MassPRO. Still in its infancy, this project proposes to collect risk-adjusting information, probably accompanied by process information for three heart diagnoses/procedures, acute myocardial infarction, coronary bypass grafts, and percutaneous transluminal coronary angiography. The project hopes to take advantage of the pioneering work done by HCFA in its Cooperative Cardiovascular Project and the New York state's release of CABG data. Repeated study of quality indicates that process control lies at the center of its continued presence and improvement. Guidelines, whether personally established by training and ethics, by societies supporting a professional specialty, or by an institution or hospital, become one of the tools for defining expected outcomes.

As Dr Masselli, Medical Director at MassPRO, stated in describing their VRAOM project's customers:

> *"...the physicians...for education and behavior (practice) improvement...the hospitals...for basic quality improvement (CQI and QA) and (both for) confidence in data for reporting score card data, and for contract negotiation. Purchasers...for making value decisions in the purchasing of health care services...Score card reports are here to stay... to gain the confidence and support of the medical community, a long term, well promulgated/participative medical team approach will gain the long term support, credibility and confidence of physicians."*[29]

Process information sharing between entities, as occurs with the Joint Commission indicator program and with the Maryland Hospital Project, fosters the attention to process comparison and improvement, and benchmarking to best performance. If organizations are in fact expecting different outcomes when they are using the same process, how will the patient or purchaser compare them? Do patients and purchasers need to review the entire set of process controls? Perhaps it would be better to limit process management by patients and purchasers to those parts of the process they can control, i.e., life-style, adherence to medication orders, appropriate payment systems. Specialty societies, in recognizing the importance of justifying their groups' contribution for compensation, will probably find it cost effective to lead the development of the data systems that demonstrate their outcomes, and enable them to detect and quickly communicate to others, improvements that are identified and proven.

Feasibility—Can the information be reliably and cost-effectively collected? Feasibility was carefully addressed in the Health and Employer Data Information Set (HEDIS) work.[30] Our ability to measure health care processes and outcomes depends on the state of automation of the information-collection process in the particular health care system. In a way, we have a chicken and the egg phenomenon. Unless there is a demand for measures there is no demand for the data collection, hence no demand for the tools to make it feasible. The whole process-outcome debate slows data development. The wish for certainty has created a reluctance to provide outcome measures, perhaps in recognition that the outcomes process is not able to control those factors most responsible for outcomes. This issue of feasibility in that case is selfdefeating from the start.

Believability—Can the measure achieve patient ownership? Since many clinical processes are more in the patient's control than in the clinician's control, it is essential to have measures that make sense to patients. The aforementioned interactive video work of the Foundation for Informed Decision Making[24] grapples directly with this need. The video on benign prostatic hyperplasia, for example, translates clinical measures such as impotence, incontinence, and mortality into meaningful, believable terms when described by other patients.

Sensitivity—Does the measure of quality vary between locations of care? Does it vary *enough* to provide guidance about differences? David Edsall[31] points out that for anesthesia deaths to be a statistically valid quality indicator of the hospital's performance, 10 years' worth of data will need to be collected for high-risk patients; for healthy patients, 30 years would be needed. Other anesthesia outcome measures, such as discomfort (e.g., vomiting) and myocardial infarction rates, may be more sensitive than mortality. Anesthesia has evolved from the bottle of bourbon for removal of the arrow, through ether, electroanesthesia, and acupuncture, to today's very sophisticated processes. At one time, the anesthesia-associated death rate was probably the best indicator, then lack of pain; now perhaps it should be measures of discomfort or secondary complications.

Related to this anesthesia example is the illustration of the importance of economics and the demonstration of the link of process control with outcome improvement. In the early seventies, malpractice insurance cost for anesthesiologists were rapidly rising as awards under "anesthesia accidents" increased. A process control intervention was adopted by anesthesiologists as a standard of care which, though requiring added capital investment, both reduced malpractice costs and improved patient outcomes. Knowledgeable purchasers, perhaps erroneously, have been led to the conclusion that similar opportunities exist throughout the health care system. These expectations are fueled by the observable differences among intervention rates for conditions such as cesarean section and CABG in different geographical areas. Surgery, being most definable, is most visible. In the absence of data, purchasers are likely to conclude that lower rates, hence lower costs, are always good. Sensitivity to factors other than simple rates will be essential to shifting this expectation.

Importance—Does the outcome measure make any difference to the patient? In the case of anesthesia, the traditional measures (death and pain) certainly still have significance. On the other hand, the volume of anesthesia gases used may be an outcome of importance to environmentalists, but is probably not of real consequence to patients. Vomiting or myocardial infarction are important outcomes to patients, although in the absence of measures they may not know there are differences between the likelihood of these events across different providers. As long as knowledge of these measures is lacking, they would seem to lack importance. Once information systems permit their measurement, their importance may increase.

Three Sample Measures Considered

Information on quality of care, not only for purchasers but also patients and providers, should meet certain expectations. Three frequently used "quality" measures are cesarean section, mammography screening, and CABG mortality. Their sensitivity, feasibility, validity, believability, and importance are plotted in Figure 6.

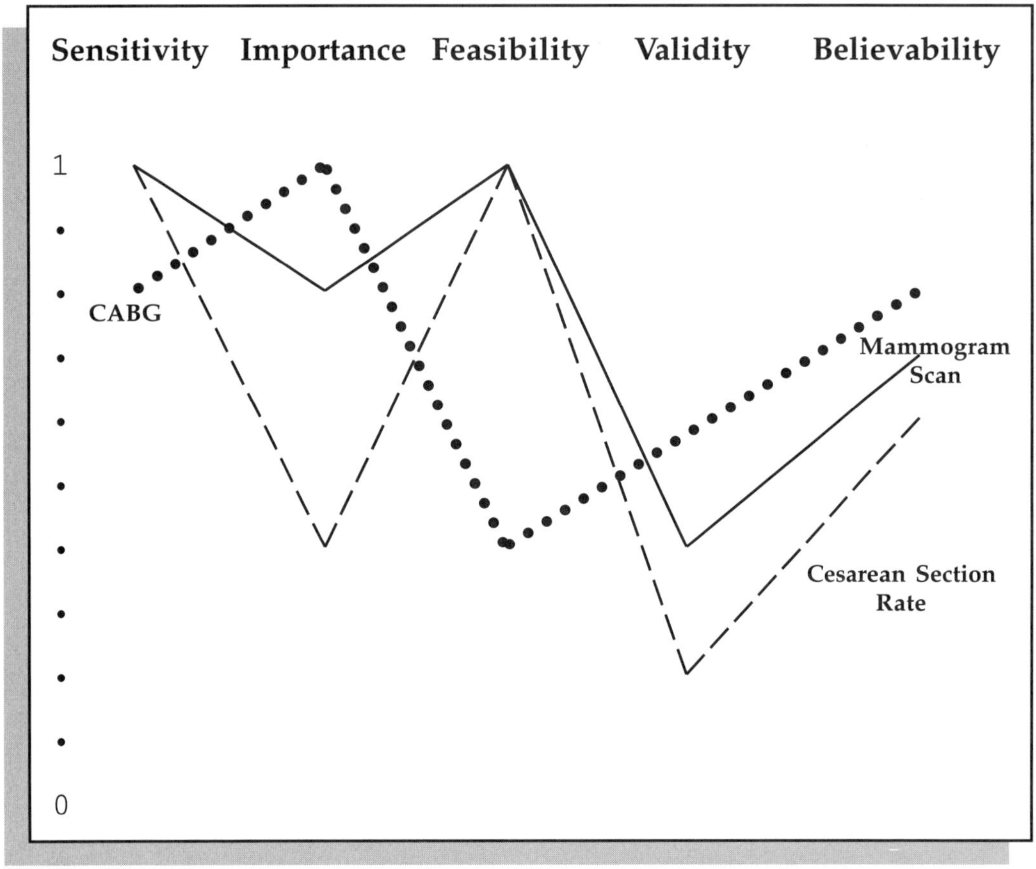

Figure 6. *Assessment of commonly used measures. Assessments close to 1 represent high levels of sensitivity, importance, feasibility, validity, and believability. The scaling was estimated from 0 to 1, in accordance with the common form of presentation of health status measures.*

Cesarean Section Rate

This population-based measure is often singled out because cesarean sections cost more than vaginal deliveries under current payment systems. Some payers, including Blue Cross of California, have addressed this by changing their terms. They now pay a single price for delivery, whether cesarean section or vaginal.[32] Will purchasers care about this measure if the cost risk is borne only by the provider? Although the measurement varies between hospitals (sensitivity) and is easy to collect (feasibility), it has questionable significance in result (validity), is not an end in itself (importance), and has a low believability score. The decision to perform a cesarean section is a process issue.

Healthy People 2000 expresses two outcome goals to reflect improvement in maternal and infant health.[6] The nation should reduce infant mortality to no more than 7:1000 births. Low birth rate should be reduced to no more than 5% of live births. A process goal is also stated, i.e., to increase first trimester prenatal care to at least 90% of live births. Perhaps that single process intervention is all that is needed to achieve the goal, which seems unlikely but possible. It is questionable whether the process goal is necessary if valid measures of birth outcomes were provided to purchasers and benefit managers specifically for the employees or populations for whom they purchase care. Risk adjusting of those outcomes is clearly needed. Many different types of risk adjusters will need to be considered. For instance, infant mortality may need to be adjusted for the socioeconomic status of the parents. Measurement processes will improve especially if initial outcome measures indicate potential problems. In the search to verify the data, there will be opportunities to improve both the measurement process and the system for delivering patient care.

Mammography Screening Rate

Mammography screening rate sounds like an important measure and the measure is sensitive to variation. Moreover, measuring the screening rate is feasible, but it is not a valid measure of result because it provides no assurance the proper treatment is provided in a timely fashion. Controversy exists about the cost-effectiveness of mammography screening, specifically, when to start screening and how often to repeat the test. Certainly OTA did not set the issue to rest in its review of preventive measures for benefit design.[10] The Canadian National Breast Cancer Screening Study was specifically done to examine efficacy of screening. For both rating cohorts, 40–49 and 50–59 years of age, screening was shown to detect more node-negative small tumors, but at seven years screening had no impact on mortality. When I read the report I begin to wonder if we are really even on the right path. If the operable cancers are the slow growing ones, they could probably be detected adequately by self examination if individuals were well trained and if periodic audits were available. The fast growing cancers are less frequent in the population than total cancers, leading both to fewer events to detect and more frequent need for screening to permit detection in time for effective treatment. It is very hard to argue that mammography screening rate is a quality measure, given the controversy surrounding the effectiveness of the technology. The case for screening for prostatic cancer is equally unclear as a quality measure. At the same time, I distinctly recall a billboard in the Midwest where an HMO promised 100% Prostate Specific Antigen Screening. Population death rates for the two conditions have similar orders of magnitude: in 1993 there were an estimated 46,300 deaths from breast cancer and 35,000 deaths from prostatic cancer.

Kaiser-Permanente, which has recently released its internal quality measures in the 1993 Report Card for the Northern California Region, has begun to show how early detection is occurring and is developing survival information by cohort,[33] a much more believable quality measure. These are the kind of data, for example, that can be used to chart progress toward the goals of *Healthy People 2000.*

Mammography screening rates alone provide a valid indication of how well a process for detecting cancer is managed by a plan. Such measures provide information that helps set patient expectations. When combined with other measures, as Kaiser has begun and published, purchasers and their sponsored population can then see how well a frightening part of "nonhealth" is managed, and then decide where to entrust their dollars and lives.

CABG Mortality

When risk adjusted, the rate associated with coronary artery bypass graft surgery is probably the best outcome measure available. Continued work in data collection systems and risk-adjusting methods should solve the current feasibility and validity limitations. This measure was virtually the first used, and because of the high cost and serious impact of the procedure, it has found a ready market among purchasers. Why else would President Clinton single out this particular treatment in his speech to Congress introducing the administration's Health Care Security Act?

For outcome measures to be fully effective, they must be condition-specific, not merely procedure-specific. This process is probably most advanced with coronary bypass grafts. HCFA, using its internally developed quality measures, has begun to purchase CABG surgery from selected centers. HCFA's Cooperative Cardiovascular Project will no doubt advance the public accountability agenda. We hope this will broaden the quality measures so that as mortality diminishes new measures with adequate sensitivity will continue to drive the improvement process.

Conclusion

The multilevel complexity of the components that make up health care are what must be purchased cost effectively, which will require meshing benefit with cost to improve the efficiency of the our health care system. Most of the political debate focus is on the who will do this, a single payer, an alliance, a plan, or an extension of those who do it today. This debate has simply assumed that once the assignments are clear the job will get done. The "grunt work" to make information-based decisions a reality lies in the detail of relating procedure to outcome, compiling those to episodes to encompass all providers contributions, and then relating this information to costs. Risk adjusting at the patient level, provider level, and at the plan level are variations on a theme. No amount of statistical manipulation will substitute for the development of valid judgments at the detail level. This fundamental truth is at the foundation of all systems of quality control. It is at this foundation that the information for a value-driven health care system will get established. This information gets articulated as a purchasing language, because today that's where the benefit and cost get resolved. Any shift in the locus of that decision will have no impact on real results unless these purchasing information needs are met.

The ultimate measure of quality will be a mix of population-based measures that are determined to be sensitive to detect differences, feasible to collect, valid with regard to the outcome of interest, important to patients, and believable. These measures will depend on evolving health status measures for their full utility.

Risk adjusting is becoming generally recognized as an essential ingredient to a purchaser driven system. Without it, the care that must be managed is too variable to make value comparisons valid without large populations. Individuals are not large populations, yet they need valid expectations for outcome, based on their own risks, not those of uncomplicated people that might have been the subject of clinical trials. Most readers are by this point in this chapter extremely disappointed that explicit purchaser needs for hospital quality-of-care information have not been spelled out. In fact, none of the examples used in this chapter singles out the hospital for specific measurement of its quality of care. It is the author's firm conclusion that purchaser demands for hospital-specific quality-of-care information are simply wants based on the inability to get other meaningful data, coupled with the demand for value of health care services purchased. Hospital care is only part of the process that yields outcomes, so measurement systems need to address not only hospital care but ambulatory and other care settings.

To meet needs for appropriate decisions the information will be conveyed at Plan, Episode/Provider, and Procedure levels. Table 4 presents in a generic form the content needed at each of these levels for sound decision making. We will know we have achieved an information system worthy of the twenty-first century when we have information for patients that is disease-specific, statistically valid, based on functional outcome, and available in a suitable form to achieve patient understanding of expectations for results appropriate to their presenting conditions and process-management preferences.

Plan-level measures will encompass and summarize valid patient-level expectations and performance to those measures. Internal plan and provider information is also needed about comparative processes and risk-adjusted outcomes data that ensures the ability to meet, and continuously improve, appropriate patient expectations. This information will focus on the case or the episode of care, and provide the information feedback to care providing personnel that lets them achieve the excellence of result that providers and their patients seek.

Appropriate Expectations

As with most pioneering efforts, the initial attempts to measure quality have had many faults. As health care delivery continues to lose its shroud of secrecy, it is likely that information services will evolve to provide benchmarking capability to providers on increasingly specific episodes of care; many first generation products are already present. If health care measurement systems are thought of in the same way as were the first automobiles after the horse and buggy, then they are properly regarded.

Meeting patient and purchaser needs in the manner described will not be an overnight occurrence. But it will not take as long as might be expected. The factors driving the information revolution occurring outside the health care field have significant momentum and are beginning to make their impact on health care. The science-based discipline of the medical education system evolved from the information tools of its age to a highly effective profession. That profession, acting for the benefit of its collective patients, created the Joint Commission in recognition that individual doctors could not undertake the oversight necessary to ensure quality of care for hospitalized patients. The

TABLE 4

Levels of Quality-of-Care Information

Level	Type
Plan	Satisfaction Health status measurement Treatment-effectiveness threshold Cost-effectiveness threshold
Disease/treatment/outcome	Probable outcome Possible adverse events
Hospital, physician, nurse	Satisfaction Control

health care profession, hospitals, and the Joint Commission now have a new control problem, the management of information. The Joint Commission has catalyzed the move to a future that, as Yogi Berra put it, "Ain't what it used to be!" Purchasers have become dissatisfied enough to clearly state that the old ways are no longer acceptable. Purchasers cannot tell providers what will be acceptable information. The questions that must be asked often require the type of training received by physicians and other health care providers. Because the profession has a control problem and those who pay their bills are unhappy, physicians now face a whole new world. Change from near certainty to almost total uncertainty is never fun. Yet self-directed change is a lot more invigorating than that demanded by external forces, regardless of source, government or private. Over time, physicians will increasingly realize the professional enhancement, even preservation and protection, that can accrue to them individually and collectively from the active pursuit of data.

The early beginnings of the information revolution will become a steamroller of change. Quality-of-care information offers the potential to restore professional autonomy, based on specific measures of accomplishment, instead of today's continued questioning, inspection and distrust. Hospitals that understand the information revolution will be able to implement information systems that bring this power to physicians. Patients and payers will welcome the hospital information leadership that can promote the sharing of process and outcome information at ever more detailed levels. Some of this change is currently visible in the benefit management of certain components of health care. First it was only mental health and substance abuse benefit-management programs, then rehabilitation; now we see cardiovascular possibilities. This change is synergistic with the information needs of patients and providers. As costs pressures continue to intensify, demand for health will not stop, nor will the generation of ideas and tools to measure outcomes—hence the need for valid measures. Trust simply does not work when information is available.

Commonality is not the only critical factor in this information system. Continuous improvement as a methodology depends fundamentally on operator collected information, and on operator ability to alter process. Reform efforts must empower physicians while correcting the system information deficiencies. Building an information-managed rather than a structure-driven system, which empowers a continuously and measurably improving system, remains the critical challenge that purchasing must help to effect.

Audit

Patients will not be healed by a treatment whose clinical results were falsified. Purchasers also will not trust self-reported data, even if it is that self-reporting that enables the best result for today's patients and even better results for future patients. In addition, patients do not really wish to be told after the fact that the quality of care they received was not the best. They need to know that there is a verification process, by some party independent of the result, in order to be comfortable that the information is not self serving. Although flawed in important ways, the HCFA release of mortality data was an independent judgment. Some of our administrative overhead may need to be spent in verifying that detailed data are collected accurately and in appropriate ways to avoid a punitive inspection. An investor in publicly held securities has the benefit of an extensive auditing system to assure validity of largely self-managed and reported financial data. Penalties for falsification are severe. Surely, health is as important as money and worthy of audit.

Hospital Role

A hospital is a critical part of the process for restoring health to the best possible level. The hospital's measure of quality is its ability to manage health care processes to best achieve expected outcomes including patient satisfaction. The Joint Commission's Agenda for Change recognizes the Commission's critical role in providing the assurance, no longer just to physicians but to patients and purchasers as well, that process control in hospitals is sufficient to achieve the outcomes that are expected by both physicians and patients. The magnitude of the details necessary to demonstrate management of process is so great that it will probably never reach the "best seller lists" for purchasers, whether fortunately or unfortunately. It defies meaningful summary. Yet the presence of this process control is pivotal to physicians' and patients' joint achievement of the best possible outcomes for patients, given the presenting conditions and the state of the art. It is this reconciling of results that facilitates analyses that can finally meet the true needs of the benefit management function as articulated in purchasing behavior. If health system reform translates to an integrated delivery system—the managing of process through shared resources—then surely hospitals' information management resources must be a key part of this agenda. Hospitals' leadership will determine their success in meeting purchaser needs. Getting these measures will take time and dedication, because purchasers have the need, but not the knowledge, to develop them. With a focus on many different pieces of the elephant, purchasers ask question after question about their wants, seldom achieving their needs in the process. Only if those who provide the care, and hospitals are where the focus usually starts, understand the true nature of the problem, and begin to address it, will we make headway on meeting true purchaser needs.

References

1. State of Pennsylvania Mandate: Health Care Cost Containment Council Act of 1986 (P. L. 408, No. 89).

2. Woods P: Shopping for quality: The Greater Cleveland Quality Choice Project. *Nurs Econ* 8:319–21, 1990.

3. Starr P: *The Socialization of American Medicine*. New York: Basic Books, 1982.

4. Anonymous: Gatekeeper is agent of IPA-model HMO. *American Medical News* Aug 9, 1993, p 9.

5. Iezzoni LI: Severity standardization and hospital quality assessment. In Couch JB (ed): *Health Quality for the Twenty-First Century*. Tampa, FL: American College of Physician Executives, 1991, Ch 8.

6. US Department of Health and Human Services: *Healthy People 2000: National Health Promotion and Disease Prevention Objectives*. Bethesda, MD, 1991.

7. LaChapelle JV: Cancer: Taking charge. *AARP Bulletin*, March 1994.

8. Workgroup for Electronic Data Interchange, Report, pp i–iv. Hartford, CT, October 1993.

9. US General Accounting Office: *Automated Medical Record: Leadership Needed to Expedite Standards Development*. Washington, DC: U.S. Government Printing Office, April 1993.

10. U.S. Congress, Office of Technology Assessment: *Benefit Design in Health Care Reform*, Report #1-Clinical Preventive Services, OTA–H–580.

11. Mercer-Meidinger presentation to Massachusetts Group Insurance Commission.

12. Medicare to stop pushing patients to enter HMOs. *New York Times* December 27, 1993.

13. Torchia, M: How Twin Cities employers are reshaping health care. *Business and Health* February 1994, pp 30–35.

14. Fries JR, et al: Reducing health care costs by reducing the need and demand for medical services. The Health Project Consortium. *N Engl J Med* 329:352–54, 1993.

15. Green JA: Minimizing malpractice risks by role clarification: The confusing transition from tort to contract. *Ann Intern Med* 109:234–41, 1988.

16. Wennberg JE, et al: An assessment of prostatectomy for benign urinary tract obstruction: Geographic variations and the evaluations of medical care outcomes. *JAMA* 259:3027–30, 1988.

17. Chassin MR, et al: Variations in the use of medical and surgical services by the Medicare population. *N Engl J Med* 314:285–90, 1986.

18. Woolf SH: Practice guidelines: A new reality in medicine. I. Recent developments. *Archives of Internal Medicine* 150(9):1811–18, 1990.

19. Enlisting employees in the battle to cut health care costs. *Business and Health* June 1993, p 24.

20. Marquis S, et al: *Participation in Alternative Health Plans: The Role of Financial Incentives in Medicare Beneficiaries' Decisions*. Santa Monica, CA: Rand Corp, 1991.

21. Enthoven A, Kronick R: A consumer-choice health plan for the 1990s: Universal health insurance in a system designed to promote quality and economy. *N Engl J Med* 320:29–37, 94–101, 1989.

22. Wilensky GR: From the Health Care Financing Administration. *JAMA* 266(2):191, 1991.

23. US Department of Health and Human Services: *1990 Health Technology Trends*. Bethesda, MD, December 1990.

24. Kasper J, Mulley A, Wennberg J: Developing shared decision-making programs to improve the quality of health care. *Quality Review Bulletin* 18(6):183–90, 1992.

25. Gapen P: The beginning of a beautiful friendship: Videos geared toward building 'robust' patient-doctor partnership. *Managed Health Care.* October 1993: 65–66.

26. Roberts JS, Radany MH, Nash DB: Privilege delineation in a demanding new environment. *Ann Int Med* 108:880–86, 1988.

27. Nash DB, et al: Evaluating the competence of physicians in practice: From peer review to performance assessment. In Gonnella JS, Hojat M, Erdmann JB, Veloski JJ (eds): *Assessment Measures in Medical School, Residency, and Practice: The Connections*. New York: Springer Publishing Company, 1993, Ch 3.

28. Use of practice parameters as standards of care and in health care reform: A view from the American Medical Association. *Joint Commission Journal on Quality Improvement* 19(8):322–29, 1993.

29. Minutes of first VRAOM Technical Committee Meeting, Waltham, MA, January 18, 1994.

30. Corrigan JM, Nielsen DM: Toward the development of uniform reporting standards for managed care organizations: The Health Plan Employer Data and Information Set (Version 2.0). *The Joint Commission on Quality Improvement* 19:566–76, 1993.

31. Written communication. David W. Edsall, MD, Chairman, Department of Anesthesiology, Burbank Hospital, Fitchburg, MA, February 22, 1994.

32. Department of Health Services, State of California: *Report for the Maternal and Child Health Branch.* Sacramento, CA, June 1989.

33. Kaiser-Permanente Northern California Region: *Quality Report Card.* Oakland, CA, 1993.

Chapter Six

HOSPITAL ADMINISTRATORS IN AN ERA OF CHANGE AND INCREASING RESPONSIBILITY

Susan Koskoff Glazer, MBA

J. Richard Gaintner, MD

Public accountability in health care is an idea whose time has come, although hospital leaders will need to set the vision for how accountability fits into the mission of their institutions. The driving force behind the need for clear accountability is the public belief that the rate of increase in the cost of health care is simply unacceptable. The question raised in the minds of many people is what benefits (and for whom) does the public receive for all that expenditure. Many Americans are without health coverage altogether, and those with coverage find it increasingly difficult to keep up with the rising costs of premiums.

In the absence of specific individual or organizational criteria for measuring clinical outcomes, standard public health criteria have been used to measure the dollar value of what we spend. Measured by these standards, the US results are mediocre at best. Infant mortality in the United States places us 21st among 24 industrialized nations, and 12th in life expectancy at birth for both men and women.[1] Although these indicators are important, they are difficult to improve upon through our current health care delivery system, which is primarily a system for treating disease. To produce significant gains in health status indicators, two things must happen: individual behavior must change (e.g., diet, exercise, smoking cessation) and public policy must focus on broad issues like education, job training, violence prevention, and reduction in poverty. The current national health care debate is not primarily about these concerns, but rather about improving access and lowering costs in the current health care delivery system.

As few indicators other than health status are in place to determine how we are doing, developing new, more specific, access and accountability measures are at the forefront of the current national debate. Central to many health reform initiatives is the idea of educated consumers making informed health care purchases based on information that will allow comparison among care providers. How to accomplish this is the key question. To be effective, performance measures must offer clarity and consistency, and reflect a consensus on what is important. Clinical outcome measures will be crucial components for the scoreboard, but access, patient satisfaction, and cost will also play important roles in identifying successes.

Public concerns about access, cost, and documented quality, along with the relentless movement to managed care and capitation, are the primary external forces acting on the chief executive officer (CEO) in the current environment. Within that context, the focus of this chapter will be on how a tertiary, urban academic medical center might respond to these concerns; what leadership the CEO can provide, how demand for accountability is currently expressed by the CEO's constituencies, and what strategies seem appropriate to best serve patients and ensure a place in the market.

Hospital Constituents

The tertiary hospital has many constituents who demand accountability. Outcome measures have not been high on most constituent agendas, although clearly that time is coming. In an urban teaching hospital the constituents include the surrounding neighborhood; the broader community throughout the region; community hospitals and health centers with their associated physicians; the business community and employers in particular; federal, state and local government; insurers, including managed care organizations; accrediting agencies; and the media.

In addition to these external constituents, internal ones include patients, families and friends, physicians, employees, volunteers, and donors. Although not focused on outcome measures, each of these internal and external groups have demands for accountability to which the CEO must respond. For example, local neighborhood community groups, many of whom represent poor urban communities, view accountability from the perspective of increasing access to care, and increasing the funding available for needed community projects. Quality is frequently assumed. We have responded by developing an active community- benefit program dedicated to building ties with community health centers in Boston, providing medical coverage, managerial support, and direct financial aid.

In addition to individual hospital efforts, the Boston teaching hospitals have been working together on how best to cooperate with community health centers, the mayor, and the city health department to improve the health status of our surrounding neighborhood. One project we have collectively undertaken this year is to develop a mechanism to guarantee a $10 million loan fund for Boston's community health centers, to improve their access to capital so that antiquated plant and equipment can be replaced.

Government agencies have historically equated accountability with regulatory concerns (e.g., fiduciary responsibility, organizational structure, fraud and abuse) or, increasingly, with tax exempt status. A quick survey of our hospital (Deaconess, Boston, Massachusetts) indicates that considering only regulatory agencies, we have had contact with over 80 organizations during the past year. In anticipation of federal questions regarding tax exempt status of hospitals, we undertook a detailed review of hospital and physician practices vis a vis available governmental guidelines for determining tax exempt status. The utilization review and quality assurance activities of insurers, although usually couched in terms of quality, almost always represent concerns about cost containment. Significant staff time is spent answering questions from insurers about the status of patients admitted to the hospital. In a typical month, our utilization review staff receives over 500 phone calls from insurers asking about the specific progress of individual patients. This is clearly aimed only at expeditious discharge and has very little to do with quality. Such activities make one even look forward to capitation.

These constituents' concerns vary greatly, and in some instances, are mutually exclusive. For example, providing community benefits may increase quality of care for neighborhood people and is consistent with the hospital's overall mission, and may even help to document its tax exempt status. Nevertheless, managed care providers are not interested in these activities, and do not want these efforts to be funded from premium dollars. As the growth of managed care causes revenues to shrink, money to support these initiatives will be increasingly difficult. The challenge is to find ways to balance these legitimate demands and, at the same time, steer a course that ensures institutional survival. Often institutional efforts are judged in the press, which can be more critical of teaching hospital efforts than community groups themselves.

Internally, accountability also involves balancing competing interests. Meeting the demands of patients for high quality, comprehensive care, the physicians' desire not to have clinical choices limited by external factors, the need to maintain a stable and satisfied work force, and the requirement to successfully compete on the basis of cost all vie for the CEO's attention.

Although it is difficult to steer a path among these frequently competing interests, keeping *values* clearly in view helps: that is, focusing on service to patients and communities, maintaining institutional values, and providing value (i.e., balancing cost and quality). The Board of Trustees must share this commitment, and the ability of the CEO to involve the Board in solutions to current problems is crucial to the continued success of the institution.

The Changing Hospital Delivery System

Managed Care

In addition to meeting the needs of constituents, hospitals are faced with the challenges of a rapidly changing health care delivery system. In fact, it is inconceivable that any health care reform package Congress is likely to pass will bring more changes that affect the deliverers of care than those changes already underway. Chief of these changes is the relentless growth of managed care.

Currently, 35% of Massachusetts residents are enrolled in managed care plans, placing Massachusetts first in the country in terms of managed care penetration. Nevertheless, patient care in Massachusetts, when compared to places such as California, has just begun to be "managed." Physicians and other caregivers are faced with how to maintain quality and value as pressure mounts to keep down inpatient admissions, and continue to reduce lengths of stay.

Initially the growth of managed care in the tertiary hospital environment was felt primarily by its intrusion on the traditional practice of medicine and by its downward effect on revenues. Once contracts were obtained, requirements for precertification, monitoring of lengths of stay, and retrospective review of claims for payment added a significant "hassle" factor, as well as significant costs in added staff time. Managed care payors made little effort to describe these requirements in language other than what they were, i.e., exercises in cost cutting.

Physicians and administrators alike decried the interference and inconvenience of these requirements, especially as they consumed time which could better be spent in activities directly benefiting patient care. Revenues were also adversely affected, as most patients covered under these plans were not "new business," but rather patients who had switched from better paying traditional Blue Cross indemnity plans. Initially, however, the growth of managed care did not bring decreases in tertiary volume.

As managed care in our area continues to be more "managed," however, the traditional "referral and return" business that is the mainstay of most tertiary academic medical centers has begun to be significantly eroded. Pressure grows to keep hospitalizations in local facilities where costs are likely to be lower, or, to avoid hospitalizations altogether. Full capitation of patient lives threatens to radically realign financial incentives. The academic medical center is forced by these circumstances to consider new products.

"Subcapitation" of tertiary care for a fixed per member per month fee offers one possibility of sharing in the risks and rewards of the capitated system as it emerges. Under such an arrangement the tertiary center would agree to accept a fixed portion of the capitated fee from either insurer or primary care group to cover all the tertiary care needs of the capitated patient panel. Problems in developing this product include ensuring that there is no adverse selection in the original patient panel, setting a capitated fee, negotiating stop loss provisions, and developing the internal systems to distribute the risks and rewards equitably between tertiary hospital and its physicians. One of the most difficult tasks, however, will be to come to agreement with the primary care provider on what constitutes tertiary care, since the financial incentives from the primary care group will favor "turfing" difficult cases to the tertiary partner. The solution to this problem will probably entail some mix of initial guidelines and a dispute resolution system to resolve difficult cases.

Another product that may be attractive is tertiary "case management" of difficult medical or surgical conditions, such as diabetes or AIDS. In this case, a fixed annual fee would be charged by the tertiary provider to the primary care group for which the appropriate tertiary specialists would assume the total management for the designated patient that is usually reserved for the primary care physician in the community.

The development of these and other products will require complex information systems that combine both clinical and financial information, as well as information that can demonstrate the value of these products in achieving savings without sacrificing patient care. As these products evolve, significant change for physicians will be required. Requests for outcome measures will grow, and physicians will be increasingly called upon to publicly share results. Bidding for "Center of Excellence" contracts often involving complex surgical procedures such as transplants routinely involve comparing outcomes among competiting institutions and physicians. Although most physicians are comfortable with the informal peer review that forms the basis of referral networks, even those with excellent records find it difficult to accept the idea of public scrutiny with all of its possibilities and pitfalls. It is clear however, that this is exactly the kind of information that is becoming more readily available as outcome measures grow.

The changing environment will also affect how physicians groups are organized. In most academic medical centers, physicians are organized by individual specialty groups. Integrated multispecialty groups will provide a much more suitable vehicle for sharing the financial risks and rewards of capitation. We are in the process of changing our faculty practices into a true multispecialty group and it is a difficult, but crucial process. Physician leadership, administrative support, and the appropriate financial incentives are all issues which must be resolved. The CEO is required to play a key role in facilitating the process.

Much positive benefit is available to physicians under capitation. Although there may be a reduction in revenue, especially for specialists, the trade-off expected will be a reduction in the "hassle factor" insurers impose. Most physicians might gladly accept this trade-off.

Physicians will also have to reorient to some degree their concept of accountability. Physicians have been trained to be accountable to individual patients. They have not, generally, had to think much about the common good of populations. As resources become scarcer, question of common good versus individual need will arise more often, and physicians, like it or not, will be called on to play a role in the resolution of these dilemmas. Success for most hospitals will depend on maintaining relationships between senior management and physician groups. It is perhaps the CEO's single most important task.

Building a Network

Building a network and having partners is another way in which tertiary centers can mount a defense against the current changes. No tertiary hospital in this day and age, regardless of how large or sophisticated, can go it alone without partners. A network provides a base of primary care physicians that can provide some of the traditional referral and return business to the tertiary partner. Some tertiary hospitals have adopted the strategy of buying primary care physician groups that are therefore employed by the tertiary center to ensure this necessary referral base. Much of our effort however, has gone into networking with community hospitals and their doctors throughout the region, assuming that as we have hospital affiliates, both the physicians and the geographic neighborhoods associated with those hospitals become likely sources of referrals.

Existing networking arrangements range from traditional physician-to-physician relationships to actual purchase of small community hospitals. We have made a major commitment of manpower and funds to developing an integrated health network that includes a number of community hospitals along with our tertiary center. We acquired our first community hospital more than a year ago. Three other hospitals are expected to become part of the system by the time this book is published. These organizational ties bring to the network physicians and neighborhoods associated with them, which will increase our referral base, and provide a lower cost platform to support new product lines.

The goal of the Network is to provide optimal, cost-effective care for patients while positioning Network members to take advantage of the growth and changes in the managed care market and the changes that might result from national health reform efforts. The Network will link primary, secondary, and tertiary providers in a continuum of patient-centered care which ensures patients access to community hospitals and physicians, as well as to highly trained specialists at an academic medical center.

To be successful, the Network will have to offer insurers and other purchasers of care a reasonably broad geographic base, a consistently high quality of patient care, and a competitive cost structure. To accomplish these goals, it is envisioned that the Network will have a number of independent community-based physicians and hospitals who will remain the primary source of health care treatment for patients in their service area. The Deaconess will serve as the tertiary provider for the system, although other Network hospitals may have specific expertise that will encourage referrals from other Network members. To ensure quality, continuity of care, and cost-effective delivery, Network members will have to be linked by strategic plans, information systems, and management structures that facilitate Network integration.

As community partners are added, maintaining the quality of the system as a whole will increasingly become a challenge. There is the necessity for objective quality and outcome measures in such a system that can form a basis of consensus between tertiary physicians and physicians practicing in the community setting.

Providing Quality of Care

Current Hospital Activities

Offering high-quality patient care is at the core of any hospital's mission. Outcome studies provide a means for hospitals to assess their own performance and judge it against internal standards, as well as providing a means to judge their own institution against others, both locally and nationally. Benchmarking can stimulate reexamination of clinical operations with the goal of improving patient care and/or increasing efficiency.

The Deaconess participates in a number of studies where clinical outcomes are judged against national and regional norms. One example involves comparing outcomes of percutaneous transluminal coronary angioplastys (PTCAs), sponsored by the Northern New England Cardiovascular Disease Study Group, a physician-organized group that develops and exchanges information regarding the treatment of cardiovascular disease. The goal is to continuously improve the quality, safety, effectiveness, and cost of medical interventions in cardiovascular disease. Participating physicians and hospitals regularly compare outcomes using in-hospital mortality data and nonfatal adverse outcomes as primary indicators of quality. In addition, the hospital is participating in the development of the Joint Commission's Indicator Measurement System (IMS) as a "beta 2" test site for oncology indicators, and a "beta 3" test site for infection control indicators. This effort by the Joint Commission is a continuation of the shift marked in recent years from the former Joint Commission standards, which focused almost entirely on physical plant and record keeping, to one which is more patient centered. Although there will be difficulties in achieving consensus on what will be appropriate in an outcome-oriented Joint Commission review, given the historical importance of Joint Commission accreditation, it will be well worth the effort to achieve consensus.

In addition to outcome studies, the standard tools of quality assurance, utilization review, review of credentials, risk management, and other quality review activities provide other means of looking at institutional quality. Continuous quality improvement (CQI) programs offer an important approach to improving efficiency and effectiveness. So much has been written about CQI that it has become almost "motherhood and apple pie." CQI is an extremely powerful concept when woven into the corporate culture of any institution. It encourages and empowers employees to take responsibility for improving the environment in which they work, no matter at what level they are operating. To be successful it must become part of the culture. It says that no matter where you are you can improve!

During the past two years at the Deaconess, we have identified over 75 discrete projects from work redesign to interdepartmental cooperative planning, where problems have been solved through CQI initiatives. Two examples taken at random from different ends of the spectrum involve evaluating the procedure for "do not resuscitate" (DNR) orders in the critical care unit (CCU), and a project aimed at bringing together facilities staff with clinical staff to develop better means of preparing renovated space for business after major construction requirements had been completed.

Both projects have been implemented by bringing together diverse groups of staff that did not ordinarily work together. The problems were defined, data collected and reviewed, changes recommended, and solutions monitored. All involved in both projects felt the time spent resulted in an improvement in care to our patients.

Having a faculty group practice, as opposed to a large number of independent physicians, is an additional aid to ensuring quality, as well as being more efficient for the purposes of managed care contracting. As physicians practice together and have the opportunity to exchange clinical information on a regular basis, peer review, and evaluation become more prevalent and meaningful.-

Developing Outcome Measures

As outcome measures play an increasingly important role in the public concept of accountability, more and more effort is going into development of regional, national, and local guidelines and standards. Although very valuable, standards that are both acceptable and useful will be difficult to develop. Some recurrent problems that have arisen with outcomes measurement are indicated in Table 1.[2]

There are, of course, very good reasons to encourage the development of outcome measures, no matter how difficult. Even with the crude measures now available, it is clear that quality varies widely among institutions and across the nation, and that much patient care could be improved. Two graphs reporting results from recent studies of these variations (Figures 1 and 2) depict, respectively, an estimated percentage of inappropriate care provided to the elderly, and a significant variation in overall hospital mortality rates from the expected norm.[3,4]

The case is clear for developing outcome data. Even as acceptable outcome measures are developed, however, the question arises as to how much difference such data will make to a large teaching hospital in terms of obtaining managed care contracts or increasing market share. Our guess is that it will not make a significant difference, at least in the next few years. Although market share is not, of course, the primary reason to offer high-quality care, those of us "toiling in the fields" should anticipate little direct market benefit from providing such care. Meeting standards of care as they develop will be a necessary component for success, but it will not be sufficient by itself.

TABLE 1

Recurring Problems with Outcomes Measurement*

- ◆ Measures are not statistically meaningful or accurate
- ◆ Results are not comparable across institutions
- ◆ Measures are not severity-adjusted (for patient acuity)
- ◆ Measures are not risk-adjusted (for patient demographics)
- ◆ Indicator has no direct link to provider action
- ◆ Data cannot be collected (due to technological constraints)
- ◆ Data are prohibitively expensive to collect
- ◆ Results are "gamed" or manipulated

* *From Health Care Advisory Board:* Line of Fire: The Coming Public Scrutiny of Hospital and Health System Quality. *Washington DC: Health Care Advisory Board, p 17, 1993. Used by permission.*

The first reason for this apparent paradox is that to date, the "quality" argument has not overcome payors' bias in favor of the standard of lower cost. In large part, this is due to the fact that as an objective body of "quality" data does not exist, insurers remain free to ignore largely anecdotal information and focus on cost. Even academic medical centers, which previously could capture market share based on reputation, are finding that reputation is carrying less weight. Capitation exacerbates this trend, as those holding the financial risk are challenging the historical practice of referring complex cases to colleagues "downtown," where more of the capitation payment may be consumed.

This bias in favor of lower cost was discussed in a *Wall Street Journal* article headlined "In Health Care, Low Cost Beats High Quality."[1] Citing the findings of a recent survey by Foster Higgins, an employee-benefit consultant, the article states "the survey of 102 managed care organizations and 127 hospi-

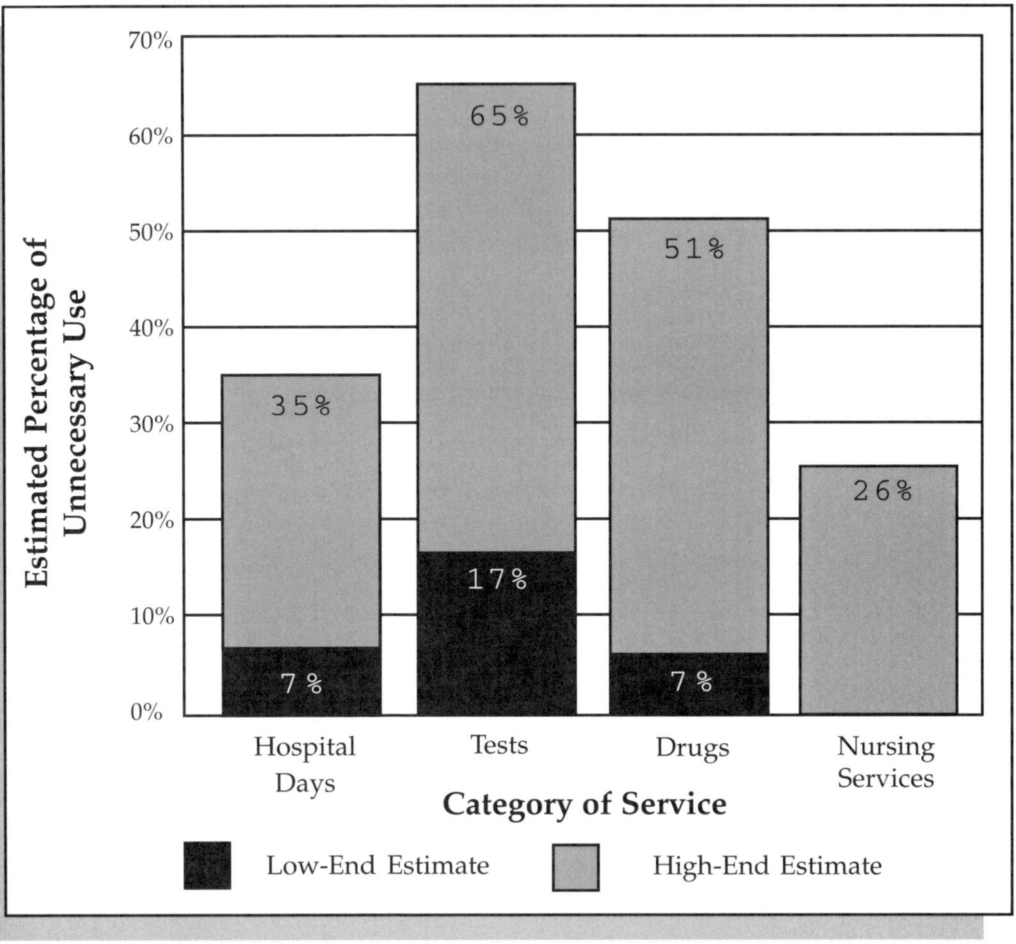

Figure 1. *Problem in inappropriate care, and in all aspects of hospital service as well. (From Brook RH, et al:* Appropriateness of Medical Care for the Elderly, An Analysis of the Literature. *Santa Monica, CA: The Rand Corp, 1989. Used by permission.)*

tals found that by a large measure, subjects rated price over quality as the major factor for success in their markets over the next three to five years." (See Figure 3.)

A second reason why outcome measures will not increase market share is because of the phenomena referred to by the Health Care Advisory Board as "the steepening curve of quality."[6] As Figure 4 shows, as outcome measures are produced and accepted, the quality curve will continuously steepen, and more,

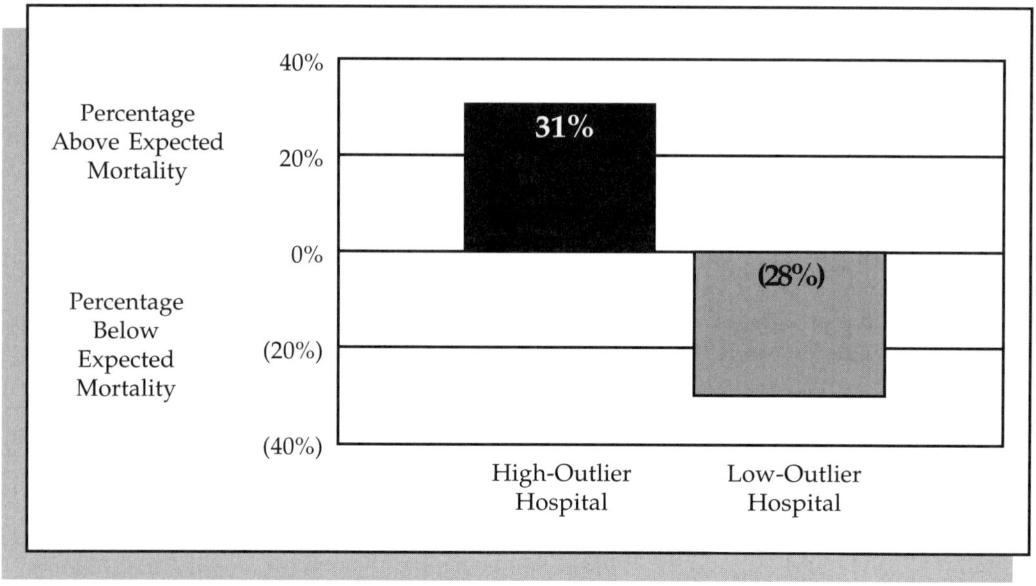

Figure 2. *Overall hospital mortality rates. (From Luft HS, Romano PS: Chance, continuity and change in hospital mortality rates.* JAMA *270:331–37, 1993. Used by permission.)*

not less, will be expected in terms of quality. Thus, a hospital will have a difficult time distinguishing itself on the basis of quality for any significant period of time, as most others will be able to "catch up" continually to those in front.

Finally, it will be difficult to gain market share on the basis of quality because there will simply be more institutions in the acceptable range than there is business to go around, even after closure of institutions that cannot meet minimum standards of care as they develop and change. What is acceptable will be clearly defined, and, as shown above, most institutions will be able to meet acceptable standards. With too much "high quality" capacity, price, and to a lesser degree, access and patient satisfaction will prevail. To use Boston as an example, there are more than a dozen teaching hospitals that would certainly pass any basic quality threshold test. Very sophisticated quality outcome measurements would have to be developed to detect significant differences in overall care among these institutions. Such differences however, even if discovered, are not likely to increase market share in the absence of price advantages.

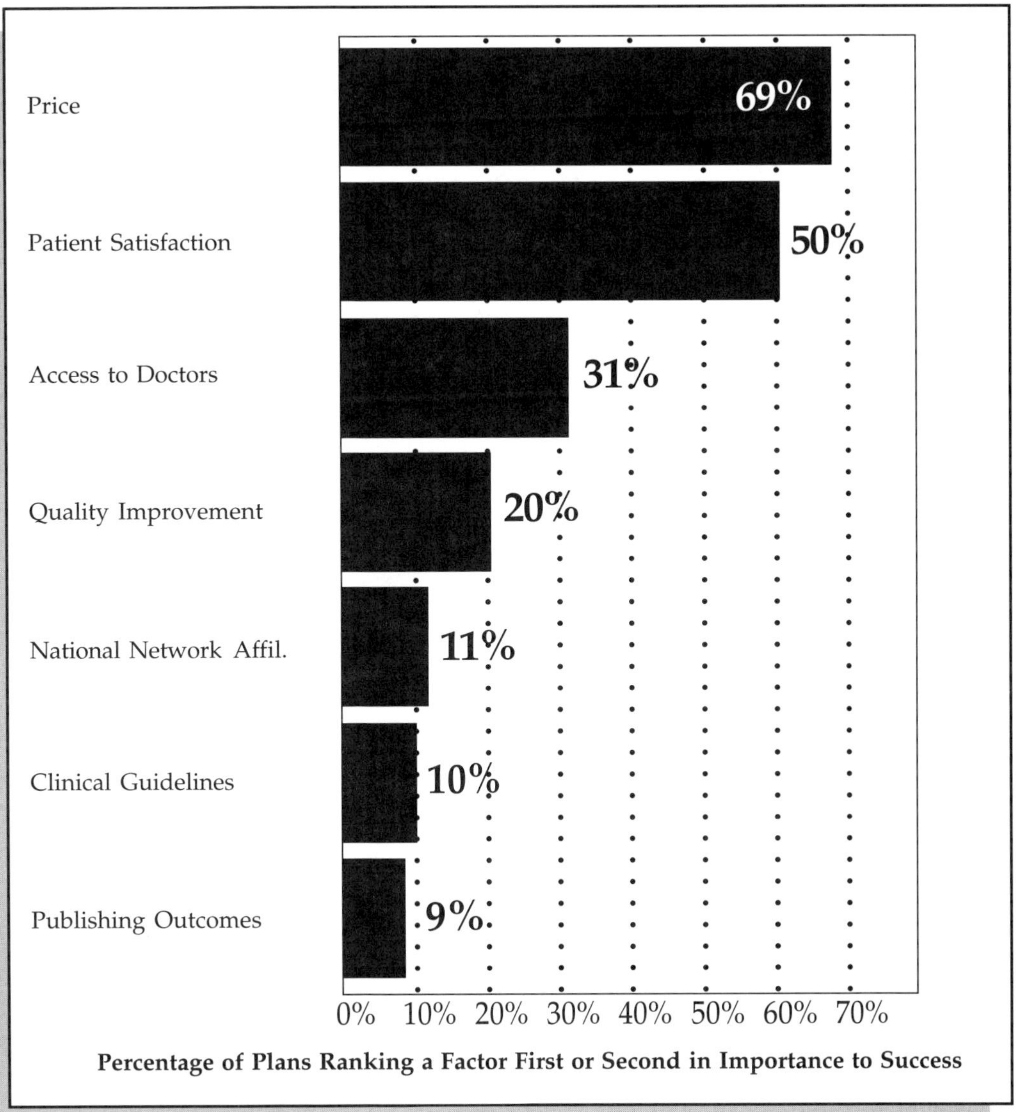

Figure 3. *Price versus quality: how 102 managed care organizations ranked factors important to success in the market place. Percentage of plans ranking a factor first or second. (From Higgins F: In health care, low cost beats high quality.* Wall Street Journal *January 8, 1994. Used by permission.*

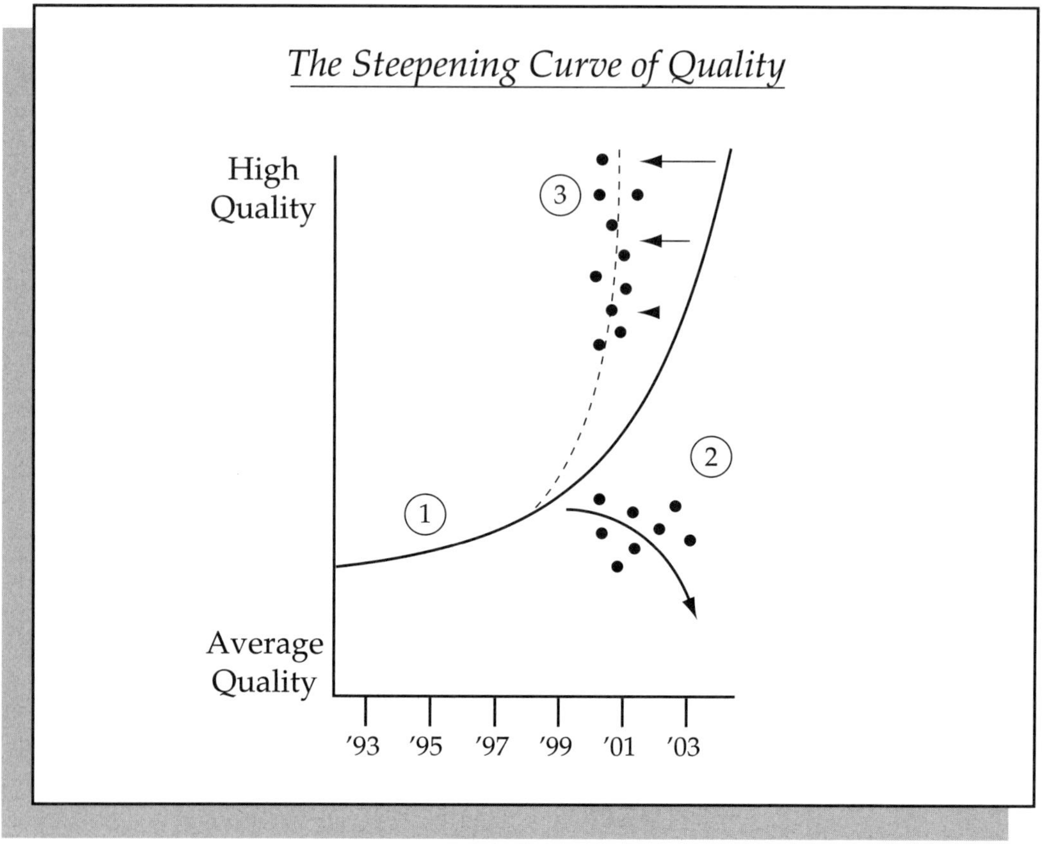

Figure 4. *Advisory board view on quality positioning. Three salient options: (1) the quality curve steepens over time; more, not less, will be expected; (2) outlier institutions that remain stubbornly below the curve over time will be marginalized and forced to close; and (3) outlier institutions above the curve may find their advantages increasingly short lived; curve could shift "to the best" faster and faster over time. (From Health Care Advisory Board:* Line of Fire: The Coming of Public Scrutiny of Hospital and Health System Quality. *Washington, DC: Health Care Advisory Board, p 62, 1993. Used by permission.)*

As price remains the primary decisive factor in market share, teaching hospitals face an interesting challenge. Most have maintained that there is added value in the higher price of receiving care at the teaching hospital, but it is unclear whether this assertion will stand up to scrutiny. One preliminary study from Pennsylvania questions this claim, and suggests that teaching hospitals offer no better outcomes at a significantly higher price (Figure 5).[7]

Other studies of specific tertiary procedures may suggest otherwise, and demonstrate the value of tertiary institutions for highly specialized care. Center of excellence contracts for very complex or new procedures such as organ transplants reflect this belief in the marketplace. For these complex problems, the learning curve may be steep enough so that for some period of time one or two hospitals in an area may have significantly better outcomes that will warrant specialized contracts from insurers that are not so price sensitive. If the volume of such procedures remains low (due to, for example, organ availability and/or certificate of need regulations) one or two institutions may retain their competitive edge for these procedures for a significant period of time. Such procedures however, represent a very small portion of even the most sophisticated academic medical center's business.

As the cost debate escalates, an important task for the CEO of a teaching hospital will be to ensure that reimbursement for education and research are part of the value and quality debate, and are not lost in the race to become the lowest cost provider. Appropriate financing for these activities needs to be recognized as crucial to our continuing success in improving the treatment of disease and training of future providers.

Moving from the individual hospital to the "systems" point of view, we are seeing the first indications in the Boston area that health care systems will be rated on quality. A coalition of large public and private employers that together purchase insurance for more than one million people have formed the Massachusetts Healthcare Purchaser Group and issued its first, very preliminary "report card." The *Boston Globe* of February 17, 1994 covered the report in an article headlined "A mixed bag for Mass. health insurers...purchaser group says firms kept rate hikes down, but quality of care varies."[8] The article noted that although the group measured outcomes along only a few parameters, they found significant differences among the health plans surveyed. As a further step, the group will be using the National Committee for Quality Assurance (NCQA) Health Plan Employer Data and Information Set (HEDIS) performance measures to begin a more complete evaluation of local health plans. The goal of the project is to help employers make a market-based and collective approach to purchasing health care.

In a different, but related direct patient marketing effort, the Harvard Community Health Plan (HCHP), the area's biggest health maintenance organization (HMO), recently published advertisements attesting to their accreditation by the NCQA. HCHP characterized this accreditation with the headline "To a health plan, this is an Oscar."[9] The ad went on to say that the NCQA is the foremost judge of a health plan's performance, thereby awarding itself a kind of "Good Housekeeping seal of approval." Having qualitative data accessible to patients would be a good substitute for this kind of advertising.

Whatever the limitations of clinical outcome studies are in terms of increasing market share, they will clearly benefit patients. As standards are developed and hospitals gear up to meet them, more patients will receive the kind of care that is now available from only the "best" providers. As outcome studies lead to the development of standards of care however, an important concern is to be sure that such standards leave room for innovations that mark important contributions of academic medicine to improved diagnosis and treatment. Our hospital, for example, was a pioneer in developing a technique for limb revascularization in patients with diabetes. Formerly, limb amputation was the prevailing standard of care. If standards of care become more formalized, and amputation is the standard of care and a cheaper procedure, what is the mechanism for funding a promising new procedure until it can be determined whether the standard of care should be altered?

Finally, the growth of capitation, as discussed above, will bring new challenges that can be positively affected by the increased acceptance of outcome measures. As the financial incentive under capitation supports providing less, rather than more care, the concern is that so little care may be provided that health status will be compromised. Although most care remains clinically beneficial, clearly gains can be made by reducing unnecessary care. There is real danger however that such reductions in care might go too far, cutting into services that are beneficial to patients. As the Health Care Advisory Board noted in its publication "In the Line of Fire" outcomes tracking can provide the safety net, preventing the elimination of too much care by setting the standard for what is acceptable (Figure 6).[10]

Assessing Value

It is of course impossible to survive in today's market without focusing on cost, as well as quality. The impact of managed care which results in both reduced volumes and increased sensitivity to price have required hospitals to look at substantial reductions in cost in order to successfully compete. In this era of

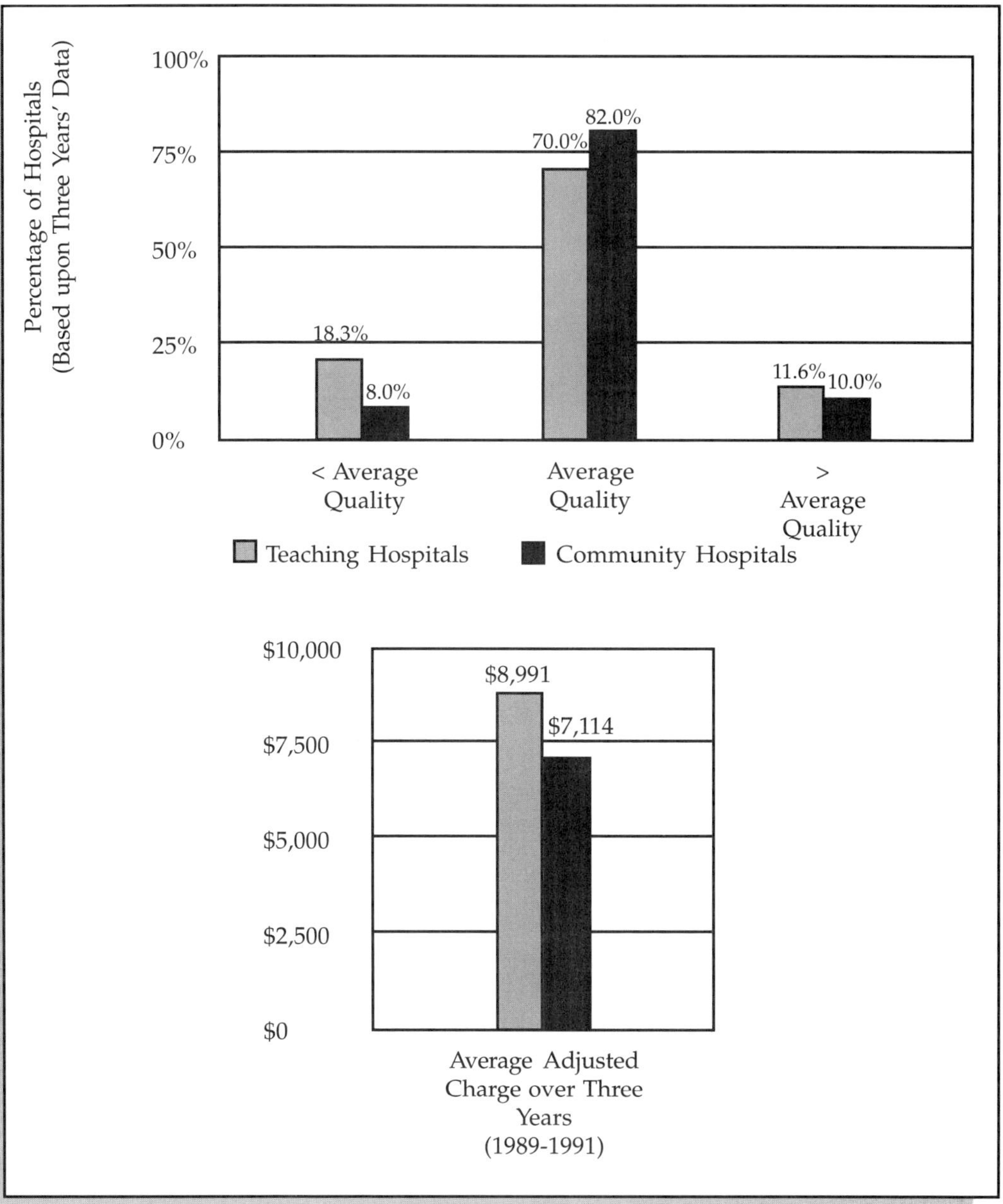

Figure 5. *Are the "best" truly best? Data suggest that teaching hospitals offer no better outcomes, but at a higher price. (From PA Health Care Cost Containment Council:* Summary Reports of Pittsburgh-Area Hospitals, 1989–1991. *Pennsylvania Department of Health; Advisory Board Analysis. Washington DC: Health Care Advisory Board, 1991. Used by permission.)*

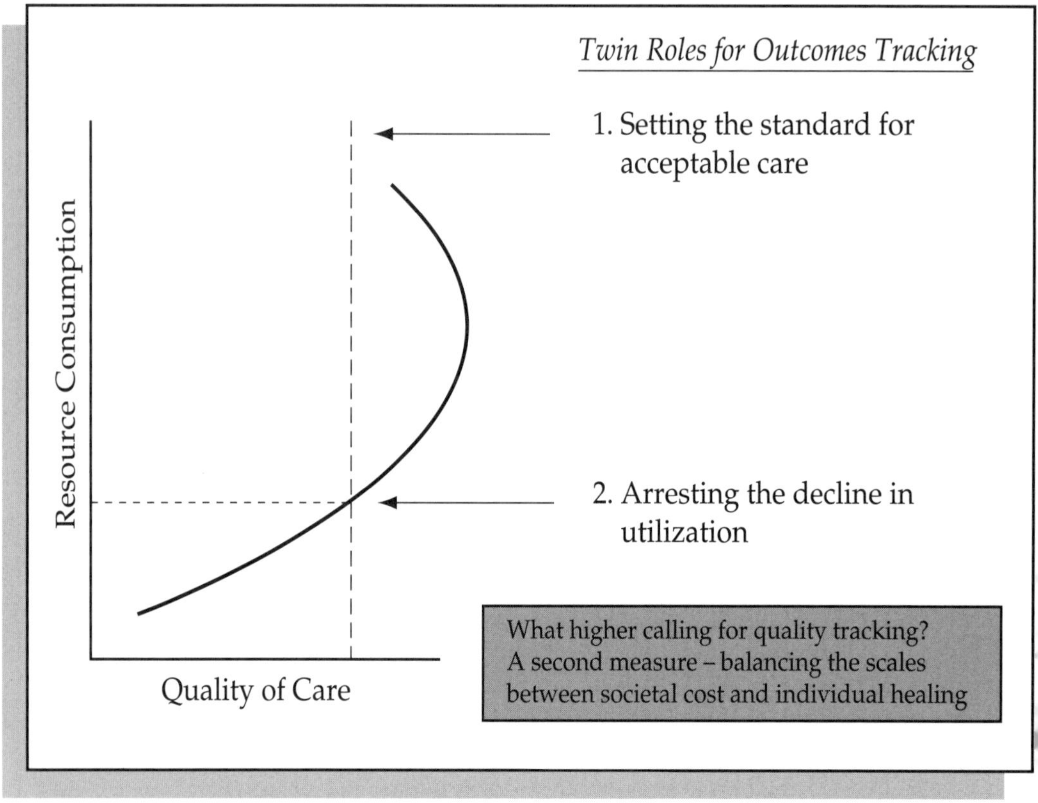

Figure 6. *The golden era for outcomes tracking; safety net undergirding capitation. (From Health Care Advisory Board:* Line of Fire: The Coming of Public Scrutiny of Hospital and Health System Quality. *Washington, DC: Health Care Advisory Board, p 71, 1993. Used by permission.)*

affiliation and consolidation, physician groups and potential hospital partners, as well as managed care organizations are looking for institutions with lower cost platforms with which to associate. As physician groups are increasingly capitated, business will go to those hospitals that use the fewest capitation dollars, assuming that quality is sound. The challenge is to make these necessary cost reductions without going below the threshold of what is acceptable quality to both physician staff and senior management.

One concept that is useful in making these decisions is to consider these challenges in the context of providing *value*. Cost, quality, and efficacy can be thought of as the determinants of whether a hospital is providing value to all of its constituents, as the formula below suggests.[11]

$$\text{Value} = \frac{\text{Quality}}{\text{Cost}} \times \text{Efficacy}$$

Quality is measured in terms of the scientific and technical aspects of what is being done, along with the degree of satisfaction on the part of the patients. Cost is self explanatory. Efficacy refers to the appropriateness or effectiveness of what is done. If efficacy is zero (i.e., the procedure did not benefit the patient, no matter how well or at what cost it might have been performed), then the value will always be zero! Obviously the highest value is produced if quality and efficacy are high and cost is low. Appropriate balance is the key.

In the internal hospital environment, different groups are interested in different parts of the value formula. Physicians, for example, historically have been most interested in scientific quality, and possibly to a lesser degree in efficacy, but have not generally been concerned about cost. Although there is growing pressure on physicians to consider cost, this concern frequently places the physician in a conflict of interest with his or her role as patient advocate. One way to partially resolve this dilemma is to help physicians focus more on efficacy.

Efficacy is not, of course, always easy to determine. Tertiary medicine is full of examples of very high-cost interventions that may be life saving to a few, but may have a relatively low success rate when applied to a population as a whole. Bone marrow transplants for women with advanced breast cancer is one such intervention, much discussed publicly. Despite these difficult cases however, many common interventions and treatments can benefit from considerations of efficacy or what works. Algorithms of care, such as those underway in the Deaconess Department of Surgery, are good examples of these initiatives. Concern paid to efficacy, coupled with the already existing physician concern with quality, will inevitably result in cost savings.

Patients have most often focused on their satisfaction, which for them has served as a surrogate for quality. Patients have not often thought about efficacy, rather they have wanted something "done" without often knowing its real usefulness. They have been interested in cost only when paying directly. Physicians and other care givers must draw the attention of patients to the efficacy portion of the formula, discourage requests for unnecessary care, and continue to raise awareness that no matter how good one's insurance, health care is paid for by all. The CEO can provide leadership to encourage this effort.

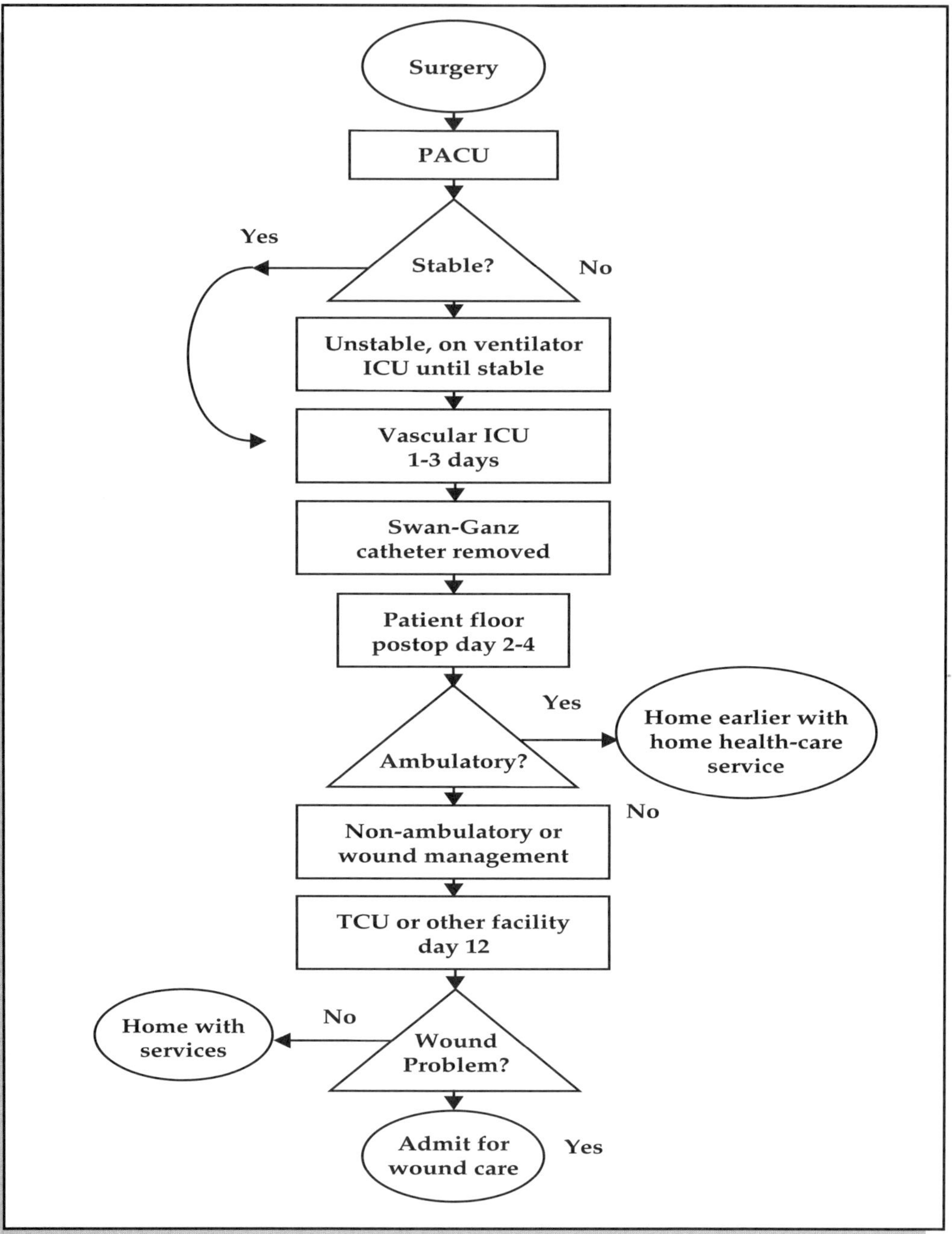

Figure 7. *Prototype of algorithm for vascular surgery: in-hospital component. Key: PACU = postanesthesia care unit; ICU = intensive care unit; TCI = transitional care unit.*

Dealing with all aspects of value for patients will help to resolve substantially a significant part of the current national health care dilemma. The public wants to contain overall health care costs, but without sparing any expense with regard to individual health demands or the care of loved ones.

Finally, insurers are major constituents for any hospital CEO. Although they talk a great deal about quality, as we have already discussed, their focus has been almost entirely on the cost portion of the value equation. Here the job of senior management is to direct the attention of insurers to quality measures as they emerge, and to the balance between cost and quality. To date, national "centers of excellence" contracting for complex tertiary care procedures such as cardiac surgery and transplants represents the major foray of insurers into serious consideration of quality outcome comparisons among institutions. With the exception of these highly specialized services it has been difficult to make a quality argument that overcomes price sensitivity. Whether this changes may depend in part on the quality of the outcome information itself as it emerges.

The Deaconess is involved in a number of specific activities that examine the question of providing value, as illustrated in the following examples.

- Department of Surgery physicians are involved in the development of algorithms of care or critical paths for common surgical procedures done at the Deaconess. The goal is to enhance clinical decision making, and reduce variation in treatment and therefore reduce unnecessary utilization. An additional goal is to improve communication and collaboration among all care providers involved in a particular surgical intervention. Each algorithm identifies necessary laboratory tests, x-rays, and consultations, and includes outcome results that expand the traditional morbidity and mortality parameters to look at quality of life indicators. The physicians involved have seen the necessity of undertaking such exercises, and believe that it will better enable them to meet the clinical needs of their patients as well as prepare their department for the coming changes in the delivery of care. A working model of a portion of an algorithm of care involving vascular surgery is shown in Figure 7. It demonstrates the kinds of decisions that have to be made, such as the definition of "unstable," as the algorithm is developed.

- Patient satisfaction is another indicator of providing value. Our hospital has been sending out a survey to each patient discharged since 1983. The current return rate is 34%. This year, surveys will be sent to a random selection of outpatients as well. Although it is difficult for patients to judge the true scientific quality of the care they receive, their

TABLE 2

Employee Opinion Survey*

Rank	Category	Mean Year I	Mean Year II	Year II - Year I	IND
1	Hospitality—Employees	4.09	4.19	0.10	S
2	Community Image	4.13	4.17	0.04	I
3	Performance Orientation	4.15	4.02	-0.13	S
4	Leadership Effectiveness	3.88	3.94	0.06	S
5	Job Satisfaction	3.86	3.92	0.06	S
6	Downward Communication	3.77	3.83	0.06	S
7	Hospitality—Management	3.74	3.79	0.05	I
8	Cooperation	3.64	3.70	0.06	S
9	Hospitality—Administration	3.53	3.58	0.05	B
10	Overall Management	3.50	3.55	0.05	B
11	Positive Recognition	3.46	3.54	0.08	S
12	Hospitality—Physicians	3.08	3.15	0.07	B

* This report shows total hospital means by assessment category. Date is ranked in order of highest to lowest means. The mean values range from 5.00 (highest) to 1.00 (lowest). Key: S=significant; I=insignificant; B=borderline. (From Corporate Systems, Inc. Report: EOSY2R2. 1993. Used by permission.)

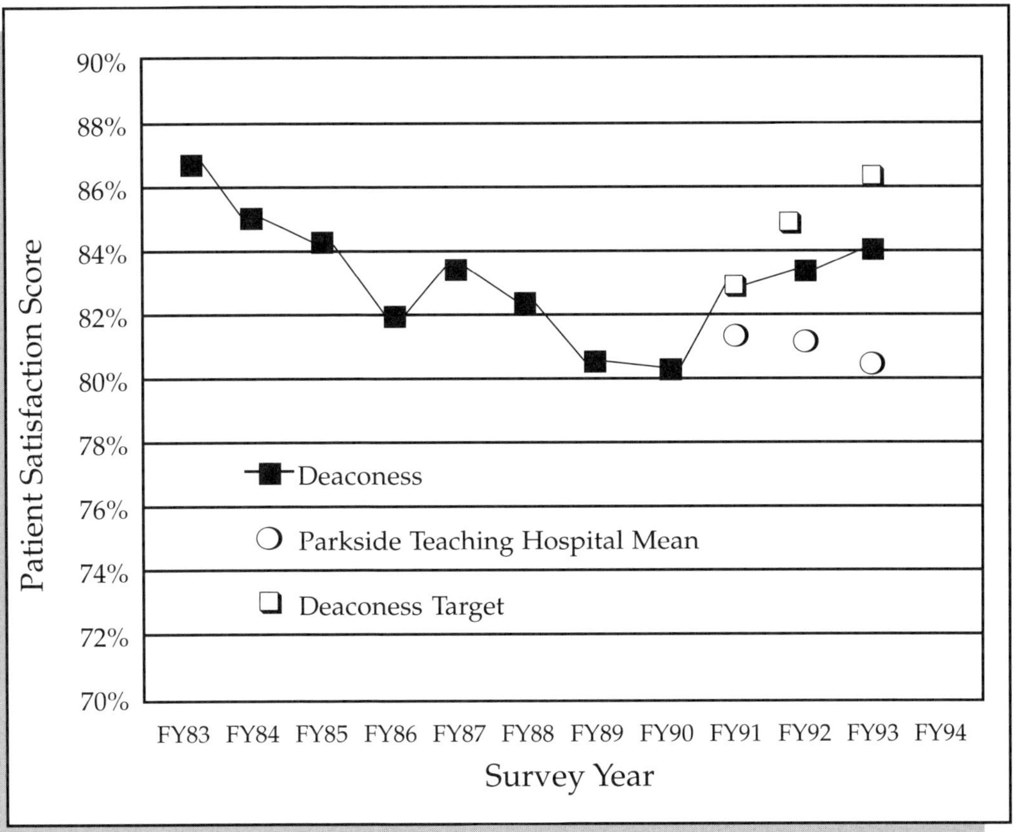

Figure 8. *Deaconess and Parkside inpatient satisfaction results. (Courtesy New England Deaconess Hospital, Boston, MA.)*

comments on service, their experience with housekeeping or dietary departments, and their answer to the question, "Would you recommend the Deaconess to a friend or family member?" tells us whether patients perceive that we are providing value. We use the surveys internally to continue to identify target areas of improvement and we chart the responses to these questionnaires on a regular basis, as shown in Figure 8. It is likely that such data will be useful externally as well, as patient satisfaction becomes part of the acceptable group of outcome measures that become part of the hospital's "report card."

In addition to our internal review, we review our progress against national parameters on a regular basis. Our data are compared to the national

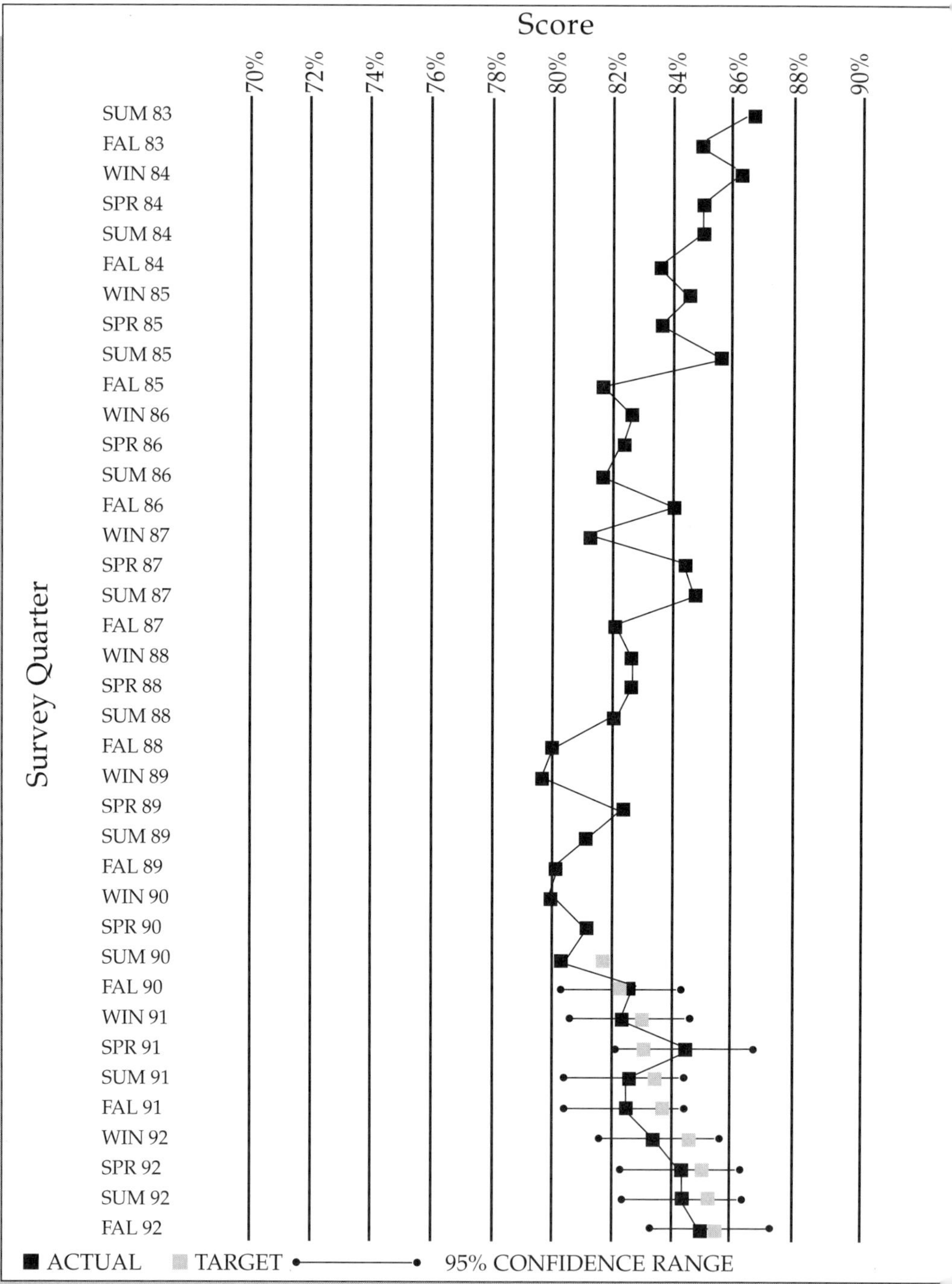

Figure 9. *Combined department aggregate of patient satisfaction survey results. (Courtesy New England Deaconess Hospital, Boston, MA.)*

Parkside data and charted against those of other teaching hospitals participating in the Parkside database (comprising 106 teaching hospitals and 166 nonteaching hospitals). This begins to give us some idea how we will do when such data become public (Figure 9).

Although not related to value per se, an employee opinion survey is also administered as part of our CQI process, making management more accountable to employees. From these surveys, we identify specific targets for improvement that will make the Deaconess a better place to work. Table 2 groups the results of individual survey questions into 12 overall categories and asks employees to rate how the hospital is doing in these major areas on a scale of 1–5.

Meeting the Future

As the environment rapidly changes, it is important that the academic medical center teaching hospital remain focused on its traditional missions of patient care, teaching, research, and community service. The strategies required to maintain these goals, however, will be radically different. Most tertiary hospitals and their associated physician groups will have to learn how to be part of larger networks, where they may be one among a number of colleague groups, and therefore not able to function as they did historically—as a stand-alone institution. Furthermore, both hospital and physician groups will have to do the cost cutting and restructuring that will be necessary to take advantage of the managed care products that will be developed in the market. Thinking of the term "market" in relationship to traditional roles will be a significant adjustment in and of itself.

The CEO must provide leadership that compels the institution to meet its obligations to its patients and its communities in this environment. Maintaining institutional *values* and focusing on *value* will offer guideposts. Public accountability offers a challenge and an opportunity to demonstrate commitment to the high standards that have traditionally marked academic medical institutions.

References

1. U.S. Department of Health and Human Services: *Health Care Financing Review* 13(4):53, 55, 65, Summer 1992.

2. Health Care Advisory Board: *Line of Fire: The Coming Public Scrutiny of Hospital and Health System Quality*. Washington, DC, 1993, p 17.

3. The Rand Corporation: *Appropriateness of Acute Medical Care for the Elderly. An Analysis of the Literature*. Santa Monica, CA, September 1989.

4. Luft HS, Romano PS: Chance, continuity and change in hospital mortality rates. *JAMA* pp 331–37, July 21, 1993.

5. Winslow R: In health care, low cost beats high quality. *Wall Street Journal*, January 8, 1994.

6. Health Care Advisory Board: *Line of Fire: The Coming Public Scrutiny of Hospital and Health System Quality*. Washington, DC, 1993, p 62.

7. Pennsylvania Department of Health: *Summary Reports of Pittsburgh Area Hospitals, 1989 –1991*, PA Health Care Cost Containment Council; Advisory Board analysis. Washington, DC, 1991.

8. Stein C: A Mixed Bag for Mass. Health Insurers. *Boston Globe* Feb 17, 1994.

9. Advertisement, Harvard Community Health Plan, *Boston Globe* Nov 26, 1993, p 33.

10. Health Care Advisory Board: *Line of Fire: The Coming Public Scrutiny of Hospital and Health System Quality*. Washington, DC, 1993, p 71.

11. Gaintner JR: Commentary on economic indicators of health care problems. *Health Care Delivery: Current Issues and the Public Policy Debate.* Association of Academic Health Centers, 1991, pp 47–48.

Chapter Seven

ARE HEALTH CARE QUALITY IMPROVEMENT AND PUBLIC ACCOUNTABILITY COMPATIBLE?

Robert J. Panzer, MD

Are health care quality improvement and public accountability compatible? The most appropriate answer is "maybe." While health care quality improvement and public accountability are highly compatible in theory, as currently implemented, they do not usually fit together well. This occurs because of organizational conflicts, time limitations, and measurement techniques that are in their infancy; even effective organizations have difficulty achieving both internal quality improvement and external public accountability. Nevertheless, there are several potential ways to overcome this incompatibility.

There is much rhetoric as to how quality improvement and public accountability can best be achieved. Superficial approaches to both quality improvement and public accountability are easy to combine in theory. Few would argue about the necessity of public accountability. After all, quality improvement is centered around the "customer," and the "public" in public accountability is the customer of health care. Furthermore, statements of solutions from different groups often begin with phrases that we can all agree with, for example, "Given that we are committed to the highest quality care..." and "So that patients can choose the best possible care...." It is the following parts of those sentences that tend to reflect a diversity of approaches to this dilemma, incorporating heavily the perspectives and attitudes of those presenting the ideas. Many existing efforts are based on strong opinions but lack scientific support.

There are three fundamental questions about any quality improvement effort that can also be applied to public accountability and raise important issues:[1] (1) What are we trying to accomplish? (2) How will we know that a change is an improvement? (3) What changes can we make that will lead to improvement?

Too often, our efforts in creating or improving a system fail to carefully address the first two questions. Public accountability and quality improvement are both means rather than ends; a thoughtful understanding of what each is trying to accomplish as suggested by the first question is a prerequisite to maximally achieving their goals. The second of these questions is also critical; it is easier to make the case for change than to measure and show that any particular change advocated is better than the current state or other alternatives. Frequently, those with good intentions do what seems best without having a systematic way to determine in advance, or after the fact through monitoring, that improvement actually occurred.

In this chapter, the compatibility of health care quality improvement and public accountability will be viewed from the perspective that both concepts are important, but that several key issues are impeding their successful realization. Many may (correctly) perceive a bias towards the "total quality management" perspective and a view that community level cooperation is key to success. In this chapter, the view of health care quality improvement will be dominated by hospital experiences, where many of the earliest health care quality improvement efforts have occurred, though much of the success in achieving quality improvement and public accountability has occurred at health maintenance organizations (HMOs) or at the community level.

The goal of this chapter is to first lay the foundation for a system that works to achieve both continuous quality improvement and public accountability by exploring key issues and obstacles. Differences in vision and paradigms will be presented. Some experiences from the Rochester, New York health care system will illustrate key issues. Issues that are usually "undiscussable" obstacles in the debate will also be described. I will then recommend an approach to how the best purposes of quality improvement and public accountability can be met in a community-based fashion that exceeds current independent efforts.

Health Care Quality Improvement Issues

Vision of Health Care Quality Improvement

The ideal vision for a hospital or other health care organization implementing quality improvement in its largest sense ("total" quality management) involves a long-term transformation of how the organization defines its direction and deploys its energies. Leadership sets direction based on the organization's mission and vision, selects key strategic quality goals for breakthrough, and deploys resources to meet those goals. Clinical, support, and administrative groups work cross-functionally to solve problems and make their contribution to the organization's progress. Individuals and teams apply quality improvement approaches to their daily work, keeping their focus on both external customers (especially patients) and internal customers (e.g., fellow employees) that need their support to perform their contribution to patient care. Information systems guide efforts with valid information about patient outcomes, hospital processes, and feedback from those inside and outside the organization. All of these efforts are focused on meeting customer needs and expectations, both those expressed by patients and those that reflect the purposes of health care.

This description may sound unrealistic to some, given the demands on the time of those who work in busy health care organizations. Are resources abundant or scarce? Some look at the busy hospital or HMO and see little time and money available for new efforts. However, the resources available through the people who work in such organizations are immense. For example, in a large hospital with several thousand employees, shifting a small percentage of total effort to quality transformation represents 100,000 hours or more, and millions of dollars.

Quality Improvement Principles

There are many ways to describe the core principles at the heart of continuous quality improvement. One useful set of principles[2] is listed in Table 1.

The first principle clearly relates to the external customer and thus in part to the concept of public accountability. On the other hand, the other principles are largely internally focused, still with the ultimate goal of meeting the needs of the customer (especially patients) at the highest level possible.

Different Models of Quality Improvement

The reality of quality improvement in health care organizations is usually much less than the vision implied by the phrase "total quality management" and all six of the principles listed in Table 1. This occurs, in part, because there are several patterns for the implementation of quality improvement in health care, each emphasizing different principles and priorities. While some health care organizations excel in a number of areas, as in business, there are few that come close to putting together all of the key components.

Implementation of health care quality improvement typically follows three patterns: a "business-oriented" approach emphasizing customer satisfaction, a "team-oriented" approach emphasizing problem solving, and a "total quality" approach emphasizing organizational transformation. While none of these types is pure, and all organizations implementing quality improvement have some of their features, their differences are important to the issue of public accountability.

In all three patterns, customer-mindedness, teams to achieve improvement, and organizational transformation are important. The importance of these three concepts varies. The rate of change and the degree to which the organization works at the cutting edge varies as well.[3]

TABLE 1

Quality Improvement Principles

1. Customer-mindedness	The customers and their needs shape our organization and its work, not vice versa.
2. Systems and process orientation	Quality products and services result from quality systems, processes, and methods.
3. Quality obsession	Quality is the all-consuming focus of the organization.
4. Improvement through formal methods	An organization achieves quality by mastering the methods of improvement.
5. Prioritization to focus efforts	An organization pursuing quality directs and focuses its energies.
6. New meaning of leadership	There is a new paradigm of leadership. Managers must reformulate what it means to lead.

Business-Oriented Quality Improvement Model

For those organizations with an emphasis on the business side, the customer is the dominating focus. The first principle in Table 1, customer mindedness, is the driving force. Teamwork, cultural change, and the patient's health status are secondary in importance. With a business strategy, the key is the satisfaction of those who pay. In most health care situations, those who determine payments are a combination of the patient and the patient's agents, such as insurers, HMOs, or others. The patient brings volume and the agents bring the payment per service and, in some environments, whole groups of patients. For-profit hospitals and managed care organizations of various types may emphasize this aspect more, but even not-for-profit hospitals need income to support their organization and its growth. This model is prevalent in managed care organizations in highly competitive markets where they are highly dependent on customer satisfaction for their organizational health.

For organizations of this type, major themes for quality improvement include determining customer requirements, deploying quality-improvement resources to meet those requirements, and measurement of customer satisfaction to determine success.

Being accountable to the public is natural for such an organization, regardless of what effort it takes. If the sharing of outcomes information is one of the key customer requirements, obstacles (e.g., concerns about confidentiality) will usually not be allowed to get in the way. The necessary extent of public accountability is defined by the public (the customers). There is often also another layer of accountability as direct providers (e.g., physicians, hospitals) are accountable to the managed care organization as an agent of the public.

Team-Oriented Quality Improvement Model

Other organizations direct much of their effort in quality improvement toward training and creating teams to solve problems and achieve targeted improvements. For such organizations, the second (systems and process orientation) and fourth (improvement through formal methods) principles dominate, concerning the central roles of process improvement and the methods of achieving improvement. Meeting customer requirements and needs often drives the nature of the improvements. Consequently, being accountable to the public is one of the targeted efforts that such an organization *could* achieve, though internal improvement tends to be the focus in hospitals in this category.

"Total" Quality Management Model

While "continuous quality improvement" and "total quality management" are frequently used interchangeably, the words themselves carry different meanings that help distinguish certain organizations and their quality efforts. In total quality management, the key words are "total" and "management." In terms of the principles described earlier, the emphasis in a true total quality management organization is on principles 3, 5, and 6 in Table 1: quality is all-consuming, the organization focuses its energies around its vision, and the roles of leaders change. This begins to approach the meaning of total quality management embodied in the Malcolm Baldrige National Quality Award, earned by organizations such as Xerox, Federal Express, and Ritz-Carlton (and potentially by health care organizations in two to three years).

A total quality management organization would go further in addressing the public's requirement for accountability than those whose quality implementation is typical for the other two models. Nevertheless, this organization would relate to the public somewhat differently. In defining its vision, it would likely emphasize meeting the true *needs* as well as the expectations of its customers, including accountability. It would find that parts of its vision relating to internal customers conflicted with the concept of public accountability, since part of its attention would be devoted to internal customers such as physicians and other health care providers.

In a total quality management organization, to obtain full physician participation in achieving improvement, the open sharing of the existence and nature of quality problems would be promoted and likely be confidential. This confidentiality would be an expectation of physicians and would be necessary if they were to routinely step forward with problems that might otherwise remain hidden to the organization's leaders.

In an organization's transformation to a total quality management institution, the full participation and involvement of all the members of the team would be paramount. To avoid fear and protective behaviors, those who identify and share problems would not be disclosed to the public, but rather involved in the organization's efforts to improve. Poor performance would not be ignored. Yet such an organization would understand the role of fear of retribution in hiding the problems that it wants to find and resolve.

Public Accountability: The Vision Versus the Reality

The vision of public accountability for health care is compelling. Given the discussions in other chapters, this vision will not be pursued here in detail. However, key elements usually include the collection of meaningful measures of quality, providers taking responsibility for the quality of their care and patient outcomes as described by those measures, and the sharing of enough useful information with the public to guide their choice of the best health care providers. The "customer" is central to this vision, but here primarily as an educated purchaser.

The reality of public accountability in health care, like quality improvement, typically falls short of the vision. Evidence is lacking to show that there are quality measures that are valid, reliable, sensitive, and specific for distinguishing various gradations of health care quality. Quality measures often show hospitals, physicians, or other providers as having different outcomes. However, the state of the art does not provide confidence that most apparent differences in quality are real. Common stumbling blocks include reliable collection of information for the quality measures, the handling of differences in patient mix (including severity), and the linkage of outcome differences to specific processes, a linkage that would validate the conclusion that the organization's performance leads to the outcomes measured.

Cooperative national efforts, like those to develop the Health Plan Employer Data and Information Set (HEDIS) Version 2.0 set of quality measures, have advanced measurement in managed care environments, although some of the concerns about the validity and utility of various measures remain.

A continuing challenge for public accountability efforts is how to present information to the public in a useful, understandable way that is not confusing and full of statistics and annotations. From the scientific perspective, some such reports are problematic and undermine the trust of those whose information is presented, illustrating the gap between vision and reality. Commonly the precision to which numbers, such as mortality data, are calculated (for example, "3.9%") overstates the actual statistical confidence in that rate (for example, the 95% confidence limit for mortality for even high volume conditions by institution is often plus or minus several percentiles).

Similarly, past releases of statewide cost and quality data by the Pennsylvania Health Care Cost Containment Council included statistics that flagged deviations at the $p < .25$ and $p < .10$ level and did not account for the multiple hospital and condition analyses conducted. As a result, the initial reports did not clearly distinguish between organizations that had extreme variations in outcomes and those whose data were consistent with the variations expected by chance alone.

As another example, the New York State Department of Health released cardiac surgery outcomes by hospital and physician (in response to newspaper petitions) with detailed statistics. Most of the differences in outcomes were correctly flagged in the state's reports as being statistically insignificant. Yet the newspapers printed the raw mortality numbers, with accompanying stories raising concerns about any apparent local differences in outcome regardless of the size or significance of the differences.

Paradigms for Quality Improvement and Public Accountability

The way we think about and implement both quality improvement and public accountability are strongly affected by the framework or "paradigm" we use when thinking about health care in general. Some of these concepts are directly related to the quality improvement principles outlined earlier; others relate to how quality improvement works at the level of people in the organization. Some of the differences between the paradigms for quality improvement and public accountability are listed in Table 2.

Quality Improvement Paradigms

From the quality improvement perspective, one of the fundamental concepts is that most problems are the result of systems, not individuals. Neither approach ignores either category of problem, but quality improvement tends to focus first on the performance of the system, while public accountability tends to focus first on the performance of the provider.

A second key for quality improvement is its model of teamwork with well thought out ground rules and behaviors. The work of the team is confidential while it is in progress, promoting openness of discussion and "dialog."

Two of Deming's 14 points are highly relevant to this discussion, i.e., driving out fear and the harm caused by ranking individuals.[4] In his teachings, rankings are considered to be undesirable. He pointed out that the results one sees in any individual's apparent performance are a combination of the individual's efforts, performance of other parts of the team, performance of the system, resources, random variation, etc. Isolating the individual's performance in this complex equation is problematic. Deming also described the counterproductive effects of ranking individuals in the organization and over time.

Public Accountability Paradigms

The current health care environment tends to place those promoting public accountability in conflict with providers of care. This is consistent with the paradigm shift (both in reality and perception) toward health care as a business. In such an environment "caveat emptor" is an appropriate concept. Terminology directly reflects this in the "Buy Right" movement promoted by Ellwood and

TABLE 2

Differences in the Paradigms for Quality Improvement and Public Accountability

Quality Improvement	Public Accountability
Physician-patient relationship is special	Health care as a business
Systems/process thinking	Focus on performance
Teamwork	Measure individual and organizational performance
Confidentiality	Public's right to know
Drive out fear	Good providers have nothing to fear
Ranking is bad	Publish report cards, reward best providers, avoid worst
Finding problems praised	Problems are "bad" and should not occur

others.[5] The concept of "Buy Right" is that purchasers of care would make their choices based on value, incorporating both the cost of care and its quality. *Consumer Reports* becomes the model for informing the public, and is being made explicit through efforts in development by researchers at the University of Pennsylvania.[6]

From the perspective of many, the paradigm of health care as a business is useful since it explains behaviors and provides us with responses drawn from the experiences all of us have as consumers. However, the fundamental distrust we have for those marketing products to us (based on our strong personal experiences with advertising versus performance) does not necessarily create a positive environment for constructive change in health care.

Another "paradigm" issue relates to where the responsibility lies for quality problems. Most often with public accountability, the focus is on finding the individuals or hospitals that are at fault for poor outcomes (the "bad apples"). The public, through purchasers or as individuals, could then steer their health care to other providers. This is the usual way public accountability efforts are operationalized, even though it may not be the intent of its leaders who may intend to focus more on excellence.

Lessons from Decision-Making Models

To draw a potentially useful analogy, the relationship between providers (usually physicians) and patients can be described in terms of several alternative relationships in situations with difficult choices. Using words that may differ somewhat from how experts in ethics might describe the alternatives, these relationships might be called "paternalistic," "autonomous," and "contractual." In advanced total quality management organizations, the concept of "partnership" takes the contractual relationship further.

The older relationship between doctors and patients was one with substantial trust; the physician often was asked by the patient or the system to decide what was best and proceed. This "paternalistic" relationship assumed that the physician would always act in the patient's best interest and that the patient would usually not be sufficiently informed to make an adequate decision. Those opposing any form of public accountability often recall the times when this approach dominated the physician-patient relationship. Conversely, those supporting public accountability worry that private providers may decide what performance is adequate without involving the public.

A more modern "autonomous" model has the patient making key decisions personally, ideally informed by the best available information on the alternatives. The interactive videos for benign prostatic hypertrophy and other conditions developed by the Foundation for Informed Medical Decision Making are good examples of how patients can become knowledgeable about the choices. Public accountability efforts are usually most similar to this model. The availability of valid, easily understood information is key to the effective application of this model.

An intermediate model between the paternalistic and autonomous decision-making models has a relationship of a more "contractual" nature, where informed patients and physicians jointly discuss the options and come to an agreement on what each should do to optimize outcomes. This requires discussion and information, but the nuances of medical information can be shared by the physician—the information need not be fully interpretable by the patient alone. The interactive videos support this model particularly well. This may be closest to the quality improvement approach to decision making, where quality is in part defined as meeting the mutually agreed requirements of customers.

Further on this continuum is a relationship analogous to the business model in advanced quality improvement organizations, where the suppliers function as partners. They manage inventories, participate in management as indistinguishable team members, and take responsibility for controlling their own costs for the organization (against their narrow short-term interest but repaid through long-term relationships). This is an important model to keep in mind for how quality improvement organizations might work with those promoting public accountability. In the current health care environment, where the occurrence and management of significant health problems are related to patient, community, and provider actions, such a partnership makes sense and describes the best provider-consumer relationships. Similarly, the outcomes of health care for populations depend significantly on the behaviors of the purchasers of health care and the providers; with joint responsibility, a partnership seems more appropriate than a more distant buyer-seller relationship.

Experiences from the Rochester, New York, Health Care System

The Rochester health care system is often looked to as a model for how some of the best goals of health care reform can be achieved. It is a system built on a long history of cooperation dating back to the 1920s, driven by business leadership, and featuring high quality at lower cost.

In 1987 the Rochester Area Hospitals Corporation embarked on an innovative system designed to assess quality and hold hospitals financially accountable for their patients' outcomes. This experiment was linked to the payment system designed for the 1988–1990 phase of Rochester's Hospital Experimental Payment (HEP) program. It included the concept of a risk/award pool of money ($2 to $4 million) that would be allocated to the hospitals based on their risk adjusted performance in comparison to each other and national benchmarks.

The experiment to hold hospitals accountable for their outcomes and adjust financial rewards based on performance basically did not succeed. In part, this was due to time factors. For instance, an experiment that needed five years ended in three when financial issues arose independent of the quality component.

There were a number of specific issues that prevented successful implementation of quality assessment linked to financial accountability. One was that the state of the art of adjustment of outcomes for confounding factors that might differ among hospitals did not seem to be up to the task. Rochester used the MedisGroups severity-of-illness system during the experiment. Two major measures of outcome were chosen: adjusted mortality and adjusted "major morbidity." Major morbidity was the MedisGroups construct that looked at the severity of the patient several days into his or her hospital stay and drew conclusions about quality based on the rates of improvement or deterioration since the admission severity evaluation.[7]

When the Rochester hospitals carefully examined their data and the initially identified deviations at either the hospital or community level, they tended to find results that, in the view of both clinicians and researchers, were not convincingly linked to the quality of care. For example, high rates of "major morbidity" for certain surgical patients seemed to be driven by communitywide standards for routinely obtaining certain laboratory and radiologic tests after cardiac surgery, leading to a high rate of abnormal findings and "major morbidity" in patients having a quite unremarkable recovery. For medical patients, the persistence of preexisting laboratory abnormalities seemed to drive classifications of patients as having "major morbidity," rather than the occurrence of new adverse events that would lead to stronger concerns about quality. Of interest, based on feedback from its diverse customers, the MedisGroups system has evolved over the years, and has shifted its use of the term "major morbidity" to "nonresponders" in its most recent updates.

Mortality was ultimately used for interhospital comparisons after the utility of the "major morbidity" concept became questionable. However, the issues related to mortality were different. While the severity-adjustment system did a fairly good job of defining groups of patients with different likelihoods of death, the number of clinical categories with deviations from expected rates of mortality at the hospitals was barely different from what one would expect from chance alone. For example, after taking into account the number of comparisons being made at the level of "major diagnostic category," two significant mortality deviations (in either the better or worse direction) were expected by chance across the hospitals and only three were found in the Rochester data.

Thus, the quality "report card" as we implemented it based on severity-adjusted outcomes was felt to be lacking both credibility and sensitivity to any changes that might have existed. Largely because of these limitations, the decision of the hospital system, with the concurrence of the state, was that the reallocation of dollars based on outcome differences would not occur.

Interestingly, it was the semipublic nature of the report card (shared among the hospitals and the hospital corporation leadership with expectations of wider sharing in the hospital community) that raised concerns about accepting the deviations and reallocating the award pool without confidence in the validity of the individual findings. One might assume that errors in such a system would average out over time (like revenues with the diagnosis-related group [DRG] prospective payment system). However, accepting the validity of the deviations for allocation of monetary awards would be an implicit acceptance of their validity in concluding that certain clinicians provided better or worse care. Yet as noted, the hospitals' confidence in the measures was low and the concern about random variation was high.

The Rochester experience does not eliminate the possibility of valid measurement, but should promote caution. Some of Rochester's findings have helped to guide more recent quality assessment experiments, such as the one in Cleveland, where different types of measures have been selected. For example, rather than using a broad-based severity measure, Cleveland's system in part focuses on intensive care unit outcomes adjusted for severity with the respected "Apache III" system.[8]

In addition, the Rochester experiment did not include until its very late stages the kind of collaborative, multidisciplinary review of information at the community level that joint quality improvement would suggest. The perspective of this experiment initially leaned toward the public accountability model: hospitals would be guided by the findings of "report cards," responsible for responding with any internal quality improvement efforts that were needed, and provided a financial incentive to do so. Toward the end of the experiment the hospitals became truly knowledgeable about "continuous quality improvement" and "total quality management" as they became aware of the limitations of the information being generated. As the experiment was ending, they began conceptualizing their vision of community-level quality improvement, thinking of their joint outcomes as reflections of the "system," and investigating community issues such as access to emergency care.

In the Rochester experiment, the infrastructure and expertise for formal "continuous quality improvement" was not in place in the beginning; in 1987 only a handful of hospitals nationwide were involved in continuous quality improvement. As a result, the hospitals' efforts were not as process- and system-focused as they might have been, internal teamwork was not well developed, and fear was prevalent in the sense that many assumed that any adverse outcome deviations largely would reflect on individual physician's performance. The paradigm in place was not that of fully developed "total quality management." The results support the need for an environment supportive of quality improvement if full buy-in and participation of clinicians is to occur. Only several years later has a new continuous quality improvement effort guided by a partnership of business and hospitals begun to operate according to the new paradigms of joint quality improvement.

As noted, other efforts, such as the Greater Cleveland Health Quality Choice project,[8] have built on the Rochester experience and achieved some of the community level cooperation advocated in this chapter. Through learning from other communities and from active participation of clinicians from provider organizations, a more accepted, focused, and valid set of quality measures has been developed in Cleveland. Nevertheless, that effort emphasizes the buyer-seller themes and report card thinking from the public accountability paradigm.

"Undiscussables"

There are a number of issues that are usually avoided (often by both sides) in discussions of the different perspectives of quality improvement and public accountability addressed in this and other chapters.

An interesting concept about fear in organizations is that of "undiscussables"—topics about which many people have strong opinions which they share privately, yet will not discuss in groups or other public settings.[9] These issues are, in part, behind the reluctance of various parties to come together and are hard to overcome as long as they remain hidden.

Some of the undiscussables pertinent to the question of the compatibility of quality improvement and public accountability include:

- ***Lack of trust***—The lack of trust that the public and health professionals often have for each other.
- ***Physician performance variation***—The fact that physician performance does vary widely, with some physicians beyond the boundaries of what

the profession considers acceptable. Currently, licensing requirements focus on medical negligence rather than performance outliers and do not adequately address the issue of practice pattern variation.

- *Team performance*—The difficult concept that it is the performance of the team of physicians or other professionals that should be understood and managed, not just the specific outcomes of individuals. This is key to avoiding inappropriate incentives to individuals to personally avoid challenging patients.
- *Lack of resources and expertise to measure quality*—The task of judging quality and outcomes requires hard work and discipline that is often lacking. It is easier to obtain information and produce a report when it is not necessary to pay careful attention to having the right measures, the right sample size, and appropriate statistics.
- *The public's willingness to weed out providers imperfectly*—The public and their agents are likely willing to have some good physicians or hospitals harmed by accountability efforts, if overall, a larger number of poor providers is weeded out.
- *Broken commitments*—Commitments and promises are often broken in efforts like these despite the best of intentions.

These and other "undiscussables" impede open dialog about real issues, often making interactions between providers and agents of the public superficial at best.

Reconciling Quality Improvement and Public Accountability

The gap between the ideal goal and the reality of simultaneously meeting the goals of health care quality improvement and public accountability can be bridged in several ways.

Optimizing the Current State

When quality improvement and public accountability are separate, those managing each can still succeed in optimizing their part. Each effort done well can achieve a significant degree of success. As discussed in previous sections, the visions, paradigms, and decision-making models driving public accountability and quality improvement efforts are different, yet both sets are valid. The issues raised by those differences presented in this chapter, however, will be obstacles to cooperation and reduce the overall impact of the two efforts on the health care system and ultimately the health status of the population.

Effective public accountability efforts can guide the collection and publication of useful quality information. Effective quality improvement-oriented hospitals and other providers can meet the public's requirement for accountability.

Coordinated Efforts

Organizations advanced in quality improvement (for example, the Xerox Corporation) create special relationships with both their customers and suppliers. As a result, there can be mutual understanding, coordination, sharing of information, and a professional relationship. The quality and efficiency of each effort is enhanced when they work together.

Such a coordinated effort for quality improvement and public accountability can be negotiated between the providers and purchasers. This opens lines of communication, reduces conflict, and promotes linkages of the measurement work by those on the public accountability side to the process improvement work by those implementing continuous quality improvement.

By coordinating their efforts, public accountability systems and health care providers can each be more effective. Redundancy of data collection can be avoided. The focus of public data can be directed to areas where processes and individual performance can be affected. The providers can guide the public to high-yield areas rather than wait for the public reporting system to stumble on such opportunities.

Systems Integration

When considering the best approaches to quality improvement, the most effective combination of quality improvement and public accountability can occur when they are part of the *same* system. This kind of statement is easy to support in principle and some will say "so what" to this idea.

However, making a single system with both internal quality improvement and accountability to the public is not easy. A handful of communities have a good start in this direction, but it is likely that none are truly at this level of integration. Integrated delivery systems incorporating HMOs, hospitals, primary care practices, and home services (like a Henry Ford Health System) can also make major progress in this way since integration is part of the fundamental structure of the organization. The bridge to the public still needs to be built. The HMO/provider relationship, because it is internal, is a strength.

In its work on the concept of community-level integrated delivery systems, the GOAL/QPC Health Care Research Committee has developed a model for how quality improvement might occur at the community level. This committee is one of several created by GOAL/QPC, a Boston-area not-for-profit organization that specializes in defining and disseminating the worldwide cutting edge for total quality management. A Learning Collaborative has also been created together by the Institute for Healthcare Improvement and GOAL/QPC to advance community-level quality improvement.

In its work on community-level healthcare quality improvement, the GOAL/QPC Health Care Research Committee identified a number of key "thorny" issues to address:

- In integrating the system, key issues include how to establish innovative ways to collaborate, such as creating quality councils for clinical domains.
- In managing and improving the system, key issues include balancing individual and community expectations and values, developing a common information system, creating care maps or their equivalent at the integrated system level, and evaluating regional needs to guide resource deployment.
- In evaluating the system, key issues include linking outcomes to system processes and evaluating the integration efforts themselves.

If we had the public and the providers on the same "team," many of the issues of distrust, confidentiality, and honesty would be resolved over time. It is the making of the effort "internal" to a larger system that removes barriers and departs from the typical approach of discussing quality infrequently and cautiously. Only when individuals and teams work together over a long time can the continuous improvement be translated from individual organizations to the larger community or region. In addition, such a system of community-level quality improvement with public accountability itself requires continuous improvement, best guided by an ongoing management team.

Information Systems to Support Quality Improvement and Public Accountability

If health care providers implementing quality improvement and community forces promoting public accountability worked closely together, how would information flow?

Currently, reports to the public on health care providers are typically developed by a public agency, using data gathered from the providers through a cooperative but mandated effort. These reports are developed independently and then shared with the public and the providers. At times, as with the Medicare mortality reports from the Health Care Financing Administration (HCFA) and the MedisGroups reports from the Pennsylvania Health Care Cost Containment Council, the providers have a chance to submit comments that are added to the report before public release.

Information released to the public in most current systems suffers from many of the problems described earlier in this chapter. Despite the best efforts of their creators, the reports are often frustrating to both consumers and providers of health care. A series of reports coming from an integrated community-level system combining quality improvement and public accountability would be quite different.

If a community-level quality system were to report to the public, it might proceed as follows. The quality of care report is an "internal" report from one part of the system (the providers) to another part of the system (the community). The report would be structured and written like an internal report on any other sensitive issue. It would identify the key issues, show how the system deployed itself to improve, give the bottom line results on outcomes, and describe next steps to hold the gains and achieve further improvement. Individual's names would rarely be included and only if appropriate. Such a community-level system would recognize the need for confidentiality if important issues were to be rapidly shared and resolved. It would also be sophisticated in understanding the role of teams of providers and not punish those who made their own outcome results look worse by accepting the most difficult cases.

How would honesty be achieved in such a system? One way would be for the analyzing and writing groups to explicitly include advocates for the public. Such advocates could maintain confidentiality, yet assure the public that it is receiving an honest interpretation of how well provider groups achieve quality care. In communities with advanced quality improvement businesses, it is not difficult to find individuals with the right expertise to represent the public in analysis and honest reporting concerning health care performance.

The content of such reports would broadly address the state of health care in the community and how well providers do their part to optimize health. The perspective would be that of a complex system recognizing the complementary roles of consumers and providers in optimizing outcomes.

The "health of the community" report could be designed to serve as a planning document for the community, including both the public and the providers. The performance of the providers of care would be included not as a report card, but as a description of the results of previous efforts, identifying areas for future improvement work, and increasing understanding of the strengths and weaknesses of the system as a whole. Disclosure of which providers achieved which results would be important to those working on improvement, but not necessarily for the public.

Such reports would be very different from most current reports designed to inform the public. They would be less oriented to giving individual providers a grade than to guiding the public to do what is best for their own health. This could include information that would lead consumers to one provider or another. The information, however, would be specifically designed to lead to behaviors that optimize use of the community's health care resources taken as a whole. For example, rather than describing short-term outcomes for patients of individual providers performing a specific procedure (e.g., coronary artery bypass surgery mortality by surgeon), the report might indicate long-term outcomes for patients with a *condition* managed by a *team* of providers, carefully addressing case mix, severity, and statistical issues (for example, long-term functional status for patients with ischemic heart disease cared for at an institution). Providers would be viewed in their system role, rather than as individual entrepreneurs competing for the public's business. The reports might recommend that certain patient subgroups be directed to certain providers, with the goal of optimizing overall outcomes.

It is interesting that the role of reports cards in education is at times questioned, since doing the minimum to achieve the desired grade may result, rather than the foundation laid for lifelong learning. Might the creation of health care "report cards" be adopting one of the useful but flawed methods of the education system?

In the spirit of continuous improvement, the frequency of such reporting would be determined by what would best improve the system. This would not necessarily be yearly. Sample size and confidence in findings would argue for looking at long-term trends while rapid deployment would argue for frequent evaluations of the data. "Control charts" graphing results over time might be the best compromise, allowing frequent updating with the long-term trend always presented visually. Furthermore, the information and guidance included would be much more timely than most current systems that often present "stale" information that looks backward at past performance.

Learning Organization Activities

The idea of the "learning organization" is a useful concept in thinking about what health care organizations and the public could together achieve. In his book on systems thinking, Peter Senge describes this larger concept of the learning organization and how it can come about.[10] A common theme in that book, and others viewing the significant environmental changes coming in both business and health care, is that with rapid change only those organizations that can learn and adapt will thrive. Many of the concepts of systems thinking and learning organizations overlap with those of quality improvement.

In expanding on the concept of the learning organization, David Gavin, another leader in organizational quality transformation described five key activities of an effective learning organization[11] that include:

- *Promoting scientific problem solving*—This includes a number of components of quality improvement, systems thinking, and good analysis.
- *Promoting experimentation*—Increased experimentation helps organizations learn about the relative benefit of close alternatives without waiting for others to report experiments, and without following the often misleading approach of before-after comparisons, i.e., implementing an uncontrolled change and then wondering if the change itself or national trends led to the ultimate results found.
- *Learning from the organization's own experiences*—This is in part related to communication and in part to the careful measurement and monitoring of the impact of past improvements.

- *Learning from the experiences of others*—This is closely related to the concept of "benchmarking" to understand the processes, outcomes, and systems at other organizations so that your own organization can improve to (and ideally beyond) the cutting-edge performers.
- *Disseminating the knowledge*—Knowledge dissemination throughout the organization relates to the four previous activities as well as other forms of knowledge that organizations all too often allow to remain isolated.

What does this have to do with public accountability? If you think of the public at the community level, the maximal degree of accountability and improvement would be achieved if the health care system of the community or region acted like a learning organization. To achieve this, these five activities would need to occur and be performed by people from both the provider and consumer sides working together. Having the public and health care organizations at arm's length by passing reports cards and data to each other would not achieve this goal. Yet this is possible with public accountability advocates and health care organizations working together as part of the same community-level system.

Conclusions

Although this chapter is written primarily from the quality improvement perspective, it seems clear that we have the capacity to make both health care quality improvement and public accountability work. As described in preceding sections, the visions of quality improvement and public accountability are compatible. Yet the reality of both falls short of the vision in ways that create conflicts. This is exacerbated by different paradigms and relationships between the providers and consumers of health care. "Buyer beware" as a consumer perspective is not the best start to a trusting partnership focused on improvement. Undiscussables and concerns about confidentiality lead to protectiveness on the provider side that is similarly problematic.

Nevertheless, the sections describing community-level partnerships and quality reports indicate how a system incorporating both quality improvement and public accountability might work. Those communities that take on health status as a joint responsibility of all parties, including both the health care providers and the public, have the best chance to make rapid progress.

However, community models may need to stretch further to achieve the kind of integration and learning that are proposed here. They need to recognize that providers will work on improving what is measured and need to ensure that we measure what is important. Public accountability and quality improvement can coexist or be coordinated successfully. In the long term, however, integration offers the best hope of achieving the greatest improvements in health status now and in the reformed health care environment of the future.

References

1. Nolan TW: *Activities for Leaders in Building the Infrastrucure to Support Improvement.* Associates in Process Improvement. Presented at Quality Management Network meeting, Boston, 1992.

2. Scholtes PR: Total quality or performance appraisal: Choose one. *National Productivity Review* Summer 1993.

3. Cohen AB. Evaluating new ways of managing quality: An interview with Stephen M. Shortell and Jim O'Brien. *J Quality Improvement* 20:90–96, 1994.

4. Deming WE: *Out of the crisis.* Massachusetts Institute of Technology: Cambridge, 1982.

5. Reppun JI: Buy right. *Hawaii Med J* 52:4, 1993.

6. Corporate Hospital Rating Project, Phase II. Written communication from Mark Pauly, PhD, Leonard Davis Institute, University of Pennsylvania, July 26, 1991.

7. Iezzoni LI, et al: The utility of severity of illness information in assessing the quality of hospital care: The role of the clinical trajectory. *Medical Care* 30:428–44, 1992.

8. Woods P: Shopping for quality: The Greater Cleveland Health Quality Choice Project. *Nurs Econ* 8:319–21, 1990.

9. Ryan KD, Oestreich DK: *Driving Fear out of the Workplace.* Jossey-Bass Publishers: San Francisco, 1991.

10. Senge PM: *The Fifth Discipline: The Art and Practice of the Learning Organization.* Doubleday: New York, 1990.

11. Garvin D: *Learning Organization Core Activities.* Presented at the annual GOAL/QPC Total Quality Management Conference, Boston, October, 1993.

Chapter Eight

PHYSICIANS' RESPONSIBILITIES AND THE EVALUATION OF OUTCOMES OF MEDICAL CARE

Joseph S. Gonnella, MD

Daniel Z. Louis, MS

The determination of what is beneficial and affordable in medicine has always been a challenge. Given the increasing cost of medical care, this challenge is receiving attention from physicians, health services researchers, economists, government officials, and the public. The federal government and many states have published hospital specific data on costs (charges) and outcomes of care. Both Pennsylvania (voluntarily) and New York State (as a result of a court order) have published data that identify physicians by name.

Unfortunately, these data are being released without their limitations being fully understood or explained to the public. The data are too global and superficial to be interpreted. They unfairly suggest, for example, that the hospitals or physicians with the highest mortality provide marginal or poor care, but they fail to adequately consider the severity of the problems being treated. While mortality results, hospital costs (charges), and patients' satisfaction are all clues that require analyses, the premature release of this type of information creates a defensive atmosphere. Such an atmosphere precludes a thoughtful discussion of the expectations, obligations, and responsibilities for which physicians and others in the health care system should be held accountable.

In this chapter, we focus on two areas that have yet to be clearly defined. The first is a framework for defining the responsibilities of physicians in providing medical care, and the second is the need for clinical specificity when comparing outcomes. We then provide examples of how these concepts may be applied in the evaluation of quality and outcomes of care. It is our hope that this framework can help guide research on the relationship between specific processes and outcomes of care. Without clear definitions, physicians and society will be unable to establish priorities. As a result, time and money will be squandered. The long-run savings in resources is important to bear in mind because outcome studies will be costly. New personnel need to be trained to collect data and analyze information using sophisticated techniques. Also, once the data are collected, who will receive them? We may very well overwhelm the public with information that has little clinical relevance, and which is difficult to understand and use appropriately.

Utilization of medical services and quality of care are affected by many variables, including the competence of the physician and other health professionals, the environment of the institution in which the physician practices, the contribution of the patient, and the patient's social environment and support systems.[1-5] Medical care evaluation studies that fail to consider the health care status of the patient when first seen by the physician will lead to inappropriate analyses and ineffective recommendations (e.g., inappropriate educational programs or unjustified restriction of a physician's medical privileges), which will not solve the identified problems. Evaluation of care given in a hospital should document the health status of the patient before and during medical intervention, at the time of discharge, and, depending on the nature of the problem, data may need to be collected after the patient leaves the hospital. The change before and after medical intervention is a reflection of the care received by the patient, although factors beyond the physician's or hospital's control may also be responsible for the change.

The ideal quality assurance methodology should measure objectively what happens to patients; namely, the changes in their physical, emotional, and social well-being or disabilities. In addition, it should be simple and relatively inexpensive. The system should provide data that accurately document the contributions of the health professionals, patients, hospitals, and the communities.

Physicians' Responsibilities for Health Care

Physicians' patient care responsibilities require that they act as clinicians, managers, and teachers. Different measures should be used to evaluate the different aspects of physician performance and evaluation studies should clearly identify which of these roles is being evaluated.

As clinicians, irrespective of the discipline, physician responsibilities include:

- Understanding the importance of risk factors, such as obesity, smoking, hypertension, and social stress in their patients.
- Recognizing diseases at their earliest possible stages. To achieve this goal, hypotheses must be generated with regard to health problems, relevant data (for example, history, physical, laboratory) must be collected, and, based on both, medical judgments must be made. The hypotheses must be tested; new hypotheses must be formulated or new data may need to be collected.
- Recommending diagnostic and therapeutic strategies based on logical medical judgments with the participation and understanding of patients (and their families when appropriate).
- Providing appropriate, timely, and skillful treatment and monitoring its success.

- Recognizing the long-term physical, mental, and social consequences of medical problems and outlining long-term rehabilitation. For chronic diseases, information in addition to biological data should be collected to document functional well-being.

Physicians' responsibilities as managers include:

- Participating in planning activities for the optimal utilization of resources based upon documented needs.
- Properly delegating and coordinating tasks among a variety of people. Human and other resources must be mobilized to achieve the desired health care outcomes at the level of today's knowledge.
- Securing and evaluating required information.
- Maintaining records to document the previous steps.

As teachers, physicians have to combine various skills outlined for them in their roles as clinicians and as managers. Physicians' educational responsibilities include:

- Educating their patients about the dangers of risk factors and outlining a regimen that may reduce them;
- Ensuring that their patients understand their illness and the recommended treatment; and
- Considering how risk factors or medical problems of their patients affect other members of the family. Physicians assume responsibility for educating the family or communicating their findings to other physicians responsible for the care of their patients and other members of the family.

A few of the responsibilities of physicians can be best understood by outlining the problems faced by the physician and the patient who is suffering with diabetes mellitus. When seen for the first time, a patient with diabetes mellitus should have data collected regarding genetic background, stage of disease, presence of other diseases, type of work, dietary habits, and social support systems. The treatment to be used will include weight reduction, special diets, insulin administration, and other forms of interventions, depending on the presence of ocular, vascular, or renal complications. The collection of data and treatment may require expensive diagnostic tests, a variety of consultations, and repeated hospitalizations. All of these responsibilities will demand a great deal of physicians' time and will need to be discharged with sensitivity and compassion. Success will require the understanding and cooperation of the patient and the family. Biological data, information on functional well-being, and degree of satisfaction with the care received are needed to document results.

Competence (i.e., knowledge, skills, and attitudes) as well as continuity of care are needed to achieve these objectives (Table 1).[6] Physicians should know what to do, be able to collect the data needed to make the necessary decisions or judgments, and perform to their fullest capabilities with compassion and efficiency. These are physicians' responsibilities that should be measured using a variety of instruments and statistically valid approaches. The medical record has data that can document success or failure in meeting many of these responsibilities, especially those that reflect the competence of physicians as clinicians. Other methods (e.g., peer review, data collected from other health professionals and patients) must be used to document the presence of other competencies.

Personnel should be trained in the collection and analysis of data reflecting physicians' roles and competencies. The technical difficulties will be many and the cost will be high. Major efforts should be expended at all levels (hospitals, accreditation organizations, and state and federal agencies) to collect data that are relevant and necessary to perform proper analyses.[7–10] In addition, when problems are found, they should be corrected using methods that are appropriate and specific (e.g., the learning of a technical skill will require a different "educational treatment" than the learning of a knowledge or attitudinal objective).[11] It should also be understood that although physicians may display appropriate competence, some patients will develop complications or die for reasons outside of the physicians' control.

The Contribution of the Patient

The role of patients is of crucial importance in measuring outcomes. Patients play an active part, not only in the diagnostic process, but also in the outcome of care. They may fail to seek medical care, even though it is available and they are able to pay for it. Some of the reasons for this behavior may be ignorance or fear of learning the truth about their health. They may procrastinate and seek medical intervention only when they are no longer able to function at their jobs or routine tasks of life. Even after they have sought medical care and the physi-

TABLE 1

A Framework for Evaluation of Physician Roles and Competence*

Physician Competence	Physician Roles: Clinician	Patient Educator	Resource Manager
Knowledge	Knows biophysical and psychosocial factors in disease development Knows associated risk factors Knows levels of prevention for stage of disease Knows appropriate diagnostic and therapeutic procedures	Knows patients cultural values and health belief system Knows level of patient understanding of illness, the rationale for the management plan, expected outcomes and potential economic and social problems Knows effective methods to modify behavior and enhance compliance	Knows economic, legal and ethical ramifications of health behavior and medical intervention Knows efficient methods to coordinate care among disciplines Knows available resources for patient Knows methods for performing cost-benefit and cost-effective analysis
Skills	Collects relevant history data Performs manual skills appropriate to discipline Interprets lab results appropriately Makes early and accurate diagnosis Recognizes risk factors in patient Develops up-to-date therapeutic and rehabilitation plans Monitors progress appropriately	Applies principles of learning and reinforcement Teaches effectively to ensure patient and family understand rationale for management plan, expected outcomes, and potential problems Encourages compliance with therapeutic plan	Obtains essential data for decision analysis Communicates effectively with other members of health care team Uses human and other resources appropriately Refers efficiently for consultations, diagnosis tests, procedures, and therapeutic intervention
Personal Qualities	Approaches patient with sensitivity and compassion Appreciates patient's uniqueness and lifestyle Adheres to ethical and professional standards	Considers individual differences in learning styles Patiently reinforces learning for patient and family	Facilitates team approach to develop and implement preventative and therapeutic plan Involves patient and family in coordinating decisions

* From Gonnella JS, et al (eds): *Assessment Measures in Medical School, Residency and Practice.* New York: Springer Publishing Co., 1993, p 171. Used by permission.

cian has recognized the problem(s), patients may not comply with recommendations because they are unwilling to change their habits (e.g., stop smoking, or lose weight) or use their resources to correct their health problems. One of the major challenges in the area of health care is to educate patients to understand, accept, and comply with their obligations in achieving the desired results.

The Contribution of the Setting

The setting influences the performance of physicians in many ways. For instance, the facilities and equipment available within the institution, as well as the availability of well-trained health care personnel, are important variables. Hospitals that require physicians and other health personnel to participate in various kinds of educational programs based upon peer review activities foster an atmosphere of intellectual challenge.

The hospital must be able to attract qualified personnel to join the professional staff to ensure that the patient will receive the most technically competent and humanly compassionate care at a reasonable cost, or transfer the patient to another institution. Obviously, the hospital must have skillful administrators and a board of trustees who are aware of their responsibilities. The board of trustees must have effective communication with the hospital administration and with the medical staff in order to identify problems, set priorities, make effective commitments of resources, and evaluate the effectiveness of its programs. The board must also have a means of communicating its problems to the community, and, in turn, of learning the community's needs.

The board of trustees, as the unit legally responsible for the quality of care given within the institution, must be able to ensure that the administrative and professional components of the hospital have developed objectives that are known, understood, and accepted by all. It is in the area of commitment of resources that the hospital's trustees demonstrate their willingness to support the professional staff and the hospital administration to achieve their goals. They obviously cannot commit resources wisely unless they are fully informed.

The Contribution of the Social and Physical Environment

The quality of a patient's social and physical environment greatly influences the prevention and recognition of medical problems. Unfortunately, there may be some powerful institutions in the community that will exercise important influence inconsistent with good health. The negative contributions of the cigarette, food, beverage, and automobile industries are a few striking examples. Moreover, local, state, and federal governments may receive significant portions of their operating budgets from taxes imposed on the above industries. Thus, government may have conflicting interests in supporting certain behaviors, while at the same time attempting to minimize or correct health problems caused or aggravated by the products of these industries. In addition, the community plays a vital role in many areas affecting patient outcomes, including ambulance services, care for patients who live alone, financial support for health services sponsored by the hospital, and the allocation of resources for providing rehabilitation services for patients and their families in the presence of chronic health problems.

The Measurement Model: The Need for Clinical Specificity

A necessary condition for any empirical science such as health care evaluation is the development of a set of standardized measurements that will permit objective assessment. Since health has three components—physical, mental, and social well-being—there is a need to develop scales to measure each.[2,9] Ideally, an evaluation should be ongoing, involving periodic assessment throughout "the journey" through the health care system. At the very least, assessments should be made before medical intervention, or at the time of entry to the health care system, and after medical intervention, or at exit from the system.

Historically, quality assessment methodologies have been classified into three groups: structural, process, and outcome.[5] Outcome evaluation has received prominence since, from a theoretical standpoint, it is the ideal measurement. Structural and process measures are useful as they have been demonstrated to impact on outcomes. At any point in the journey through the health care system assessments may be made to measure the outcome of the preceding processes of care. The crucial link between these processes and patient outcomes may be demonstrated, in some cases, by a randomized prospective trial. In more complex situations, where intervening variables are numerous, mathematical models, such as Bayesian decision trees, Markov simulations, influence diagrams, and other techniques, may be developed to estimate the nature of the relationship between process and outcome.[12]

Regardless of which of these approaches is employed, it is critical that the scales used for measurement be clinically specific. Both expected patient outcomes and the appropriate processes of care are clearly related to a patient's clinical condition which should be specifically considered in evaluation studies.

Structural evaluation should also be based on clinically specific data. For example, structural measures of quality, such as appropriate staff expertise or adequacy of facilities, can only be evaluated in light of the particular mix of patients for which care is provided. It is necessary to develop measures to evaluate mental, functional, and social disability. While important, these will not be discussed in the following section, which focuses on an approach for documenting biological specificity.

Disease Staging

Where? Why? How serious? These are the basic questions that one must attempt to answer when a patient presents with a medical problem. The same questions must be answered to make appropriate comparisons in outcomes studies or other quality assessment measurements. The "where" is the specific organ or system of the body; the "why" is the identification of the etiology of the problem; and the "how serious" is the pathophysiologic changes that have occurred.

Historically, medical taxonomy has been related more to pathophysiologic and anatomical findings than to the identification of patient groupings useful for predicting the results of medical treatment. With goals similar to cancer staging, Disease Staging is a classification which uses diagnostic findings to group patients into clusters based on the common denominations of requiring similar procedures or treatment and having similar expected outcomes.[13]

Disease staging defines levels of biological severity, as documented by physical and/or laboratory findings, for specific medical problems, where severity is defined as the risk of organ failure or death. It classifies the severity of a medical problem into distinct stages based on the natural progression of the disease. Ideally, a diagnostic label should have explicit data about the location of the health problem (systems of the body), cause of the problem, and severity of the problem. The majority of diagnostic labels identify only the site of the disease (e.g., appendicitis, cholecystitis, diverticulitis, peptic ulcer). Some provide information about the system involved and cause of the problem (e.g., pneumococcal pneumonia, urinary tract infection caused by bacteria of a specific type). Other diagnostic labels are manifestations of problems (e.g., hypertension, anemia). A few, because of the body system involved, also convey a degree of severity (e.g., myocardial infarction, meningitis). Only in the area of cancer has the medical profession developed a diagnostic classification that includes severity. The reason for this exception has been the need to measure the efficacy of various forms of treatment, that is, the need to compare the results of experimental treatment for similar clusters of patients. Now that society is challenging the medical profession to document the quality of the medical care system, a measuring instrument such as the staging concept needs to be developed for all medical problems.

The technique defines different levels of severity as follows: Stage 1—a disease with no complications; Stage 2—a disease with local complications; and Stage 3—a disease with systemic complications. Table 2 contains examples that have been developed for bacterial pneumonia, diabetes mellitus, and cholecystitus. These scales are useful not only in assessing the health status of the patients when they are first seen by the physician, but also in measuring a change in their health and in documenting whether medical problems have been prevented, cured, or progressed into more serious stages. The results allow comparison of alternative methods of health care delivery.[9]

Evaluation of patient outcomes, such as mortality, and resource use must consider etiology and stage of disease (Tables 3 and 4). A Stage 1 complication of one disease may have different implications than a similar stage of another disease. For example, hyperglycemia (Stage 1 Diabetes Mellitus) is different from positive serological evidence of AIDS (Stage 1). Even when major pathophysiologic damage exists, such as coma, which in all diseases is a Stage 3 complication, the prognosis may be different for each disease, since for some there is treatment that may reverse the complication. Most diseases begin at Stage 1 (their earliest detectable manifestation) and continue through Stage 3. However, there are exceptions. Some self-limiting diseases, such as cataracts, do not include a Stage 3. Others begin at either Stage 2 or 3, since they are complications of other diseases (e.g., bacteremia, for which the site of bacterial entry is not evident, or bacterial meningitis, which can be a complication of sinusitis, otitis media, or bacterial pneumonia).

Examples of Evaluation of Quality of Care

The importance of clinical specificity in evaluation of both inpatient and outpatient care is made clear by the examples in Table 5.

Data are available from administrative databases that contain both diagnostic and therapeutic information derived from a large number of health care facilities. Their synthesis provides a picture of what may be considered "average

TABLE 2

Disease Staging: Sample Criteria*

Stage	Bacterial Pneumonia	Diabetes Mellitus	Cholecystitis
1	1.1 Pneumonia in one lobe 1.2 with small areas in multiple lobes or bronchopneumonia 1.3 with atelactasis	1.1 Asymptomatic diabetes mellitus/hyperglycemia 1.2 Symptomatic diabetes mellitus 1.3 Type I diabetes mellitus (insulin-dependent diabetes mellitus)	1.1 Chronic cholecystitis or cholelithiasis
2	2.1 Pneumonia with bacteremia 2.2 with empyema 2.3 with lung abscess or bronchopleural fistula or bronchopleural cutaneous fistula 2.4 with diffuse involvement of multiple lobes	2.1 Diabetes mellitus with retinopathy, or glomerulosclerosis, or neuropathy, or peripheral vascular disease, or azotemia 2.2 with retinopathy and blindness 2.3 with cellulitis or urinary tract infection 2.4 with gangrenous infection 2.5 with osteomyelitis	2.1 Cholecystitis with choledocholithiasis 2.2 Acute cholecystitis 2.3 Acute cholecystitis with choledocholithiasis 2.4 with empyema of the gallbladder 2.5 with gangrene of the gallbladder 2.6 with localized perforation of the gallbladder 2.7 acute or chronic with gallstone ileus or cholecystoduodenal fistula or cholecystoenteric fistula 2.8 with ascending cholangitis 2.9 with perforation of gallbladder and bile peritonitis
3	3.1 Pneumonia and septicemia 3.2 with septic arthritis 3.3 with acute osteomyelitis 3.4 with peritonitis or subphrenic abscess 3.5 with pericarditis or pericardial effusion 3.6 with endocarditis or meningitis 3.7 with acute respiratory failure 3.8 with septic shock	3.1 Diabetes mellitus with hyperosmolar state 3.2 with ketoacidosis 3.3 with necrotizing papillitis 3.4 with renal failure 3.5 with septicemia 3.6 with coma 3.7 with hyperosmolar coma 3.8 with septic shock	3.1 Cholecystitis and pancreatitis 3.2 with septicemia 3.3 with septic shock

* From Gonnella JS (ed): *Clinical Criteria for Disease Staging by SysteMetrics*, ed 4. Ann Arbor, MI: Medstat Systems, 1994. Used by permission.

TABLE 3

Death Rates for Bacterial Pneumonia Hospitalizations*

	In-Hospital Deaths (%)			
Cause of Pneumonia	**Stage 1**	**Stage 2**	**Stage 3**	**Total**
H. influenzae	3.1	**	7.1	3.5
Klebsiella pneumoniae	7.1	**	25.4	11.0
Pseudomonas	14.5	**	42.3	21.2
Staphylococcus	17.2	**	37.8	24.0
Streptococcus	2.8	5.3	12.2	4.0
Other bacteria	9.0	38.3	44.2	14.1
Unspecified organism	5.0	2.8	35.2	7.8
TOTAL	5.6	9.5	33.1	8.7

**Sample sizes in these categories were too small.

* From the National Hospital Discharge Survey (1987). Published in Markson LE, et al: *Evaluation and the Health Professions,* vol 14, no 2. Thousand Oaks, CA: Sage Publications, 1991, p 205. Used by permission.

clinical practice." Indicators such as those listed in Table 5, derived from Medicare claims or hospital discharge abstracts, have been used to design and carry out nonrandomized retrospective studies of comparative outcomes of care.[14]

Of the examples of indicators listed in Table 5, hospital mortality figures have received the most public attention in recent years following the public release of Medicare hospital mortality data by the Health Care Financing Administration (HCFA).[15–20] Raw mortality data, however, do not provide a meaningful and objective indicator in the absence of such important comparative adjustments among hospitals as: case mix, severity mix of cases, expectancy of adverse outcome by diagnostic group, patients' use of resources, and sample size per hospital, among others. The significance of unadjusted hospital mortality data as direct indicators of quality of care have been challenged, particularly with regard to the absence of adjustments for the differences in severity mix of cases among various hospitals.[21]

TABLE 4

Average Length of Hospital Stay for Bacterial Pneumonia Hospitalizations*

	Mean Length of Stay (Days)			
Cause of Pneumonia	**Stage 1**	**Stage 2**	**Stage 3**	**Total**
H. influenzae	7.7	**	16.4	8.7
Klebsiella pneumoniae	8.8	**	22.9	10.7
Pseudomonas	12.9	**	23.3	14.8
Staphylococcus	10.2	**	17.0	11.9
Streptococcus	7.3	7.4	14.5	8.1
Other bacteria	7.8	13.1	14.2	8.4
Unspecified organism	7.3	9.5	11.4	7.6
TOTAL	7.5	9.4	13.6	8.1

**Sample sizes in these categories were too small.

* From the National Hospital Discharge Survey (1987). Published in Markson LE, et al: *Evaluation and the Health Professions,* vol 14, no 2. Thousand Oaks, CA: Sage Publications, 1991, p 205. Used by permission.

The duration of hospital stay is also an indicator that should not be assessed comparatively across institutions, even within samples of the same diagnostic group, without adjustments for severity of disease. Resource use by patients is known to differ significantly depending on the severity of their disease.[22,23] The importance of disease staging data in making objective outcome comparisons of this type has been demonstrated in the case of diabetes mellitus, whose hospital stay was found to be three times longer for Stage 3 compared to Stage 1 patients.[24]

Comparative outcome evaluation remains a useful tool for identifying statistical outliers whose practice results appear to deviate significantly from the norm. Caution must be used, however, in interpreting these findings as actual differences in quality of care for several reasons. First, as previously stated, the case mix adjustment may provide the explanation for the different outcomes.[25] Second, since adverse outcomes may be relatively rare events, small sample sizes can make observed differences difficult to interpret.

TABLE 5

Administrative Data and Quality Assessment

Examples of indicators of the quality of medical care that are used in evaluating outcomes:

- Hospital mortality
- Duration of hospital stay
- Hospital readmission rates
- Nosocomial infection rates
- Unexpected need for repeated surgical intervention
- Hospital admissions originating from short procedure units
- Severity of illness at hospitalization/timeliness of hospital admission

Finally, it is important to keep in mind that even when all adjustments have been made, those outcomes defined as "outliers" do not necessarily deviate from a "gold standard," but rather from a current norm that should itself be subject to continuing scrutiny.[26]

Evaluation of Changes in Severity as an Outcome Measure

Changes in severity of illness over time can be measured in the defined segment between admission and discharge as a measure of patient outcome.[27] The measurement in change of disease severity across this segment, termed "clinical trajectory" by Iezzoni,[28] can be used to establish measures of expected length of stay and the related costs associated with obtaining a given change in the stage of a specific disease. Averaging this measurement over cases in multiple institutions allows for interprovider comparisons.

Meaningful comparative assessments of this type require analysis of data from multiple intermediary points of measurement during an illness episode. For example, patient evaluation within the first 24 hours following admission may be compared with patient condition later in the hospital stay. To obtain this level of clinical detail and specificity, diagnostic data from the hospital discharge summaries and claims databases must be supplemented by additional data from chart reviews, laboratory results, and other records.

In some diseases the objective of care in a given episode may not be to change the disease stage but to extend the duration of the current stage, and thus delay progression to late stage, for which limited treatment is available, as is the case with AIDS. Measurements of change in the disease stage in such cases are not revealing when applied to a given hospital stay; instead, data from longitudinal databases, which encompass larger portions of the disease course, should be used.

In the future, enhanced data-collection systems will allow the clinical trajectories' approach, with multiple-point measurements based on detailed clinical data and longitudinal data when appropriate, to provide more meaningful analysis of outcomes and more accurate definition of practice patterns.

Reviews of Practice Profiles and Medical Staff's Clinical Experience

Resource consumption and the cost efficiency of clinical decision making have become important dimensions in the context of the prospective payment system, as instituted by Medicare, and increasingly by other payers. The resource consumption resulting from the clinical decisions made by every individual physician has a direct and immediate financial impact on their respective institutions.

As a consequence, many hospitals and managed care organizations produce and review detailed practice profiles of individual physicians. As an assessment tool, practice profiles of individual physicians based on the analysis of financial impact by diagnostic related groupings (DRGs) must incorporate detailed clinical data to be objective.

Even when adjustments for severity of illness have been made to qualify cost versus DRG data, results must be analyzed and interpreted with care. A practice profile showing, for example, higher in-hospital laboratory costs may indicate excess laboratory utilization or inadequate diagnostic work-up prior to admission. To determine whether changes in practice behavior are called for to streamline and standardize care, the administration must seek the cooperation of the physicians whose practice patterns are being analyzed. The physicians must participate in the process of refining the practice profiles as an assessment tool of cost efficiency of clinical decision making.

It is difficult to change behavior.[26] Nevertheless, practice profiles, when appropriately used, may be a highly effective administrative tool to effect practice changes. Physicians are more responsive when a perceived clinical leader presents them, on a one-on-one basis, with individual practice-profile data within the framework of the performance of their peers, and solicits their input in a nonpunitive, nonconfrontational approach. Physicians should be encouraged to describe current processes of care and suggest streamlining improvements.

The concept of using clinical profiles as an assessment tool is also important for evaluating the scope and depth of training of medical students. The quality of the clinical training obtained by medical students depends in part on the mix of patients seen during their clinical clerkships, which in turn depends on the type of setting where the training was obtained. An academic medical center is likely to have a higher proportion of advanced-stage patients than other affiliated institutions. An in-depth evaluation of clinical training should include information on the mix of cases and disease stages, describing the organ systems involved, and causes as well as severity of diseases.

Guidelines

Developing guidelines and incorporating them into a target-oriented clinical practice may serve to diminish clinical uncertainty and lead to an overall improvement in the practice of medicine.[29] To be effective, such guidelines must have some well-defined characteristics.[30] The guidelines must be:

- Comprehensive (encompassing the whole spectrum of clinical practice);
- Specific (clearly describing each condition to which they are applicable);
- Detailed (allowing clear distinction between indications);
- Contextual (describing all circumstances under which a given procedure is indicated); and
- Manageable.

The critical importance of clinical specificity as a major feature of the guidelines is made evident by the fact that many procedures are known to have clinical value for more than one condition.

For example, pulmonary conditions ranging from bronchitis to emphysema and asthma, or cardiac conditions such as heart failure are all indications for performing blood gas analysis. Yet the American College of Physicians' Guidelines for blood gas analysis describe the analysis as "indicated for acutely ill asthmatic patients" or for "chronically ill patient when a change in clinical status occurs."[31] In fact, the term "acutely ill" may describe asthmatic patients who have bronchial asthma with dyspnea and inspiratory wheezing (Stage 2.1) as well as more seriously ill patients with severe bronchial asthma with hypoxemia (Stage 3.1). The guidelines do not make it clear whether arterial blood gas analysis is appropriate in both cases, whereas in clinical practice the analysis is likely to be used for Stage 3.1 asthma but not for Stage 2.1. A similar distinction by disease stage can be made for patients with bronchitis and emphysema.

Enhanced clinical specificity, along with comprehensiveness, is clearly needed in guidelines to cover low versus high stages of specific diseases. It is sometimes difficult to state unambiguously whether a given test or procedure is appropriate for a certain disease state. Nevertheless, the very process of establishing guidelines that aim at such fine distinctions serves to identify areas of practice where clinical efficacy needs to be determined.

An additional benefit of guidelines related to specific disease stage is their value in educating clinicians as well as physicians in training on existing standards of practice and in evaluating patient charts for utilization review. While physician acceptance of guidelines may not always be optimal,[32] physicians' willingness to adopt and use such guidelines, noted by others,[33] can only be strengthened by the enhancement of the guidelines' clinical specificity.

Clinical Privileges

Accurate assessment of a practitioner's clinical competence is one of the cornerstones of effective hospital quality assurance.[34] The delineation of clinical privileges validates and codifies this assessment of competence. With the advent of more sophisticated cost allocation and tracking systems, hospitals can develop profiles that reflect a physician's resource consumption. When these cost–based profiles are merged with better clinical descriptors of each patient encounter, a powerful new descriptive tool emerges.

Currently, the delineation of clinical privileges is typically focused on a list of specialty specific procedures. For example, an internist or primary care physician might be restricted to a list of specific "procedures" such as arterial puncture, thoracentesis, lumbar puncture, and electrocardiography.

However the privilege delineation checklist is an inadequate reflection of the complexity of clinical practice. The procedural skills necessary to perform an arterial puncture or to interpret an electrocardiogram reveal very little about the intellectual skills necessary to treat the complications of diabetes or hypertension, or other common primary care diagnoses.

We believe there is a place for a stage-specific practice profile which could be tied to the credentialing process.[35] The chairman of a clinical department could accurately define "who can do what" in this department. Once privileges have been approved by the medical staff, data such as complication rates can be collected prospectively to document whether the physician is qualified in specific areas. The profiles which are accumulated would allow the physician, department chairman, and medical staff committees to decide whether correction of problems found on the analysis of data requires continuing medical education activity, the acquisition of new skills, or restriction of privileges.

Evaluation of Ambulatory Care

Clinical condition at time of hospitalization can be used as an indicator of the outcome of ambulatory care by classifying the "timing of hospital care." For some diseases, such as appendicitis, hospitalization is clearly appropriate at the earliest stage of the disease. Other diseases, such as essential hypertension, rarely require hospitalization at the early stages, and hospitalization is only required if the disease progresses to more advanced stages.[36]

The distinction between a "timely" and a "preventable" admission is important when assessing timing of hospital care. The admission of a patient with Stage 1 appendicitis is timely and unpreventable, while that of a patient with Stage 2.3 diabetes mellitus and facial cellulitis is timely but preventable. The distinction is that the former does not raise doubts about the appropriateness of care prior to hospitalization, whereas the latter raises the question of appropriate outpatient care, which could have averted the progression of the disease to this stage. Similarly, a patient admitted with acute cholecystitis and gangrene of the gallbladder clearly has a severe complication that might have been avoided with earlier treatment. These advanced-stage admissions should be reviewed to evaluate whether they resulted from physician-related problems (e.g., delayed or incorrect diagnosis), patient-related problems (e.g., failure to seek timely care), community problems (e.g., lack of geographical or financial access to care), or whether they were unpreventable (e.g., resulting from rapid disease progression).[37–39]

As these examples illustrate, the stage of the disease at the time of admission may provide an indicator of the quality of care received prior to hospitalization.[40–42] In such cases, this may implicate problems in outpatient care as the defaulting process responsible for hospital admissions of patients in advanced stages of disease. Even though some of these admissions are not preventable, the reasons for late care should be analyzed in the utilization review process. Utilization review programs in hospitals as well as peer review organizations should incorporate definitions of "late" versus "timely" care in their ongoing reviews.

Discussion

Physicians have many obligations, and to discharge them they must acquire a variety of competencies during medical education and postgraduate training. They are expected to recognize such health-risk factors as hypertension, obesity, and alcoholism and to educate patients as to their implications. Physicians should be able to recognize diseases early, a skill indicative of clinical efficiency. Having recognized a disease or problem, they should treat each patient appropriately, including providing educational support to increase the patient's likelihood of compliance, and monitoring the effectiveness of the treatment. Physicians should also plan for the rehabilitation of patients with chronic health problems and should look for similar health problems in other members of the family and community. While these are some of the legitimate responsibilities of physicians, all of them can be discharged well without significantly improving the health of patients if the other elements of the health care system are not fulfilling their obligations.

The physician's competence in treating a patient is based on medical knowledge; clinical, pedagogical, and managerial skills acquired in medical school and thereafter; technical abilities; interpersonal skills; and personal qualities. Nevertheless, institutional and environmental elements, resources, and expectations, as well as the patient's knowledge, attitudes, and social support system, also affect the quality of the patient's outcome.

The appropriateness of diagnostic and therapeutic services ordered by physicians is being evaluated by a number of methods. Unfortunately, the methods often fail to distinguish specific skills or behavior that are solely or largely under the control of an individual physician from those that are influenced by nonphysician factors. What is needed is a clear definition of the circumstances under which a measurement should be used and the number of physicians being involved in a particular case. This is especially true when medical record reviews or morbidity and mortality analysis are done.

Whether some physicians order more diagnostic tests or use more expensive therapeutic agents than others may depend not only on their knowledge or competence but also on other variables such as the severity of the patient's disease, the patient's expectations, the availability of health service resources, and the reward system. As the medical profession and others in society begin to develop methods that measure utilization of resources, careful attention needs to be paid to variables that are not under the control of physicians.

While researchers need to be encouraged to develop new tools, they also need to be required to specify the limitations of their methods. The complexity of measuring the competencies of physicians as clinicians, patient educators, and resource managers needs to be clearly understood when physicians are being assessed using peer ratings, medical record reviews, and morbidity and mortality data. Measurement of health care results is essential, but the contributions of both physician and nonphysician determinants should be considered.

While changes in death rates, infant mortality, and the incidence and prevalence of disease are valuable indices of health, additional measures are needed to evaluate conditions that are disabling but do not lead to immediate death. Measurements that assess physical, functional, and emotional disability are needed. Each will require its own methods of data collection that will combine objective evaluation by health professionals with the individuals' perceptions of their well–being. In most situations, several measures should be used, since no single indicator will document quality, satisfaction, or cost of the health care services.[14]

In this chapter, we have proposed a framework for defining physician's responsibilities, described a clinically specific method for classifying patents for evaluation studies, and provided some examples of how these may be applied in evaluation of quality and outcomes of care. Of course, assessment is only the first step, analogous to making a diagnosis. To correct the problem, treatment must be initiated. If the etiology of the problem includes inadequate physician performance then the treatment must include changing physician behavior. In their review in the *New England Journal of Medicine*, Greco and Eisenberg classify efforts to change physician's practices into six general methods: education, feedback, participation by physicians in efforts to bring about change, administrative rules, and financial penalties.[43] Each of these methods has demonstrated some success, and many failures, in changing physician behavior. They conclude that no specific type of intervention is inherently effective, particularly when used in isolation. We suggest that physicians implicitly play three roles in patient care: clinician, patient educator, and resource manager. Performance in each of these roles is based on knowledge, skills, and personal qualities that we have described in a taxonomy of physician roles and factors in patient care. It is our hope that this framework may be a step toward a more specific diagnosis of the nature and etiology of the problem that can be of value in designing more effective methods for changing performance.

Finally, we should understand that in the process of educating the public regarding the quality of health care, we may overwhelm the public with information which may confuse rather than clarify. Should patients choose physicians on the basis of diagnostic and therapeutic skills, or on the physicians' abilities to use resources appropriately, give instructions which are understood, and provide care which minimizes waiting time? While we should strive for perfection, which deficiencies are more acceptable before professional privileges are restricted? When comparisons are made, are they done after severity of illness is controlled, and are they based on statistically valid results? Thoughtful debate will be required to answer these questions. In addition, the costs will be high since highly trained personnel will be needed, and collection and analyses of data will be expensive.

References

1. Gonnella JS, Zeleznik C: Factors involved in comprehensive patient care evaluation. *Medical Care* 12:928, 1974.

2. Starfield B: Health services research: A working model. *N Engl J Med* 289:132, 1973.

3. Gonnella JS, et al: Evaluation of patient care. *JAMA* 214:2040, 1970.

4. Herman MW: The poor: Their medical needs and the health services available to them. *Ann Am Acad Pol Soc Sci* 399:12, 1972.

5. Donabedian A: Evaluating the quality of medical care. *Milbank Mem Fund Quart* 44:Part 2, 1966.

6. Gonnella JS, et al: What have we learned and where do we go from here? In Gonnella JS, et al (eds): *Assessment Measures in Medical School, Residency, and Practice: The Connections*. New York, NY: Springer Publishing Co., Inc., 1993, pp 155–73.

7. Kravitz RL, et al: Differences in the mix of patients among medical specialties and systems of care: Results from the Medical Outcomes Study. *JAMA* 267:1617–23, 1992.

8. Greenfield S, et al: Variations in resource utilization among medical specialties and systems of care: Results from the Medical Outcomes Study. *JAMA* 267:1624–30, 1992.

9. Markson LE, et al: Clinical Outcomes Management and Disease Staging. *Eval Health Professions* 14:201–27, 1991.

10. Louis DZ, Gonnella JS: Letter to the editor. *JAMA* 269:43–44, 1993.

11. Hatlie MJ: Climbing the learning curve: New technologies, emerging obligations. *JAMA* 270:1364–65, 1993.

12. Owens DK, Nease RF: Development of outcomes-based guidelines: A method for structuring problems and synthesizing evidence. *The Joint Commission Journal on Quality Improvement* 19:248–63, 1993.

13. Gonnella JS (ed), Louis DZ, Gozum ME (assoc eds): *Disease Staging Clinical Criteria*. Ann Arbor, MI: The MEDSTAT Group, 4th ed, 1994.

14. Epstein AM: The outcomes movement: Will it get us where we want to go? *N Engl J Med* 323, 266–70, 1990.

15. Baldwin MF: Hospital industry leaders criticize publication of hospital death rates. *Modern Healthcare* 26–27, March 28, 1986.

16. Blumberg M: Comments on HCFA hospital death rate outliers. *Health Services Research* 21:715–39, 1987.

17. Brinkley J: U.S. releasing lists of hospitals with abnormal mortality rates. *New York Times* A1, A22, March 12, 1986.

18. Dubois RW: Hospital mortality as an indicator of quality. In Goldfield N, Nash DB (eds): *Providing Quality Care: The Challenge to Clinicians*. Philadelphia, PA: American College of Physicians, 1989, Ch 4.

19. Eggers PW: Prospective payment system and quality: Early results and research strategy. *Health Care Financing Review* (Annual Suppl.) 29–37, 1987.

20. Rosen HM: The HCFA excess mortality lists: A methodological critique. *Hospital and Health Services Administration* 119–27, February 1987.

21. Berwick DM, Wald DL: Hospital leaders' opinions of the HCFA mortality data. *JAMA* 263, 247–49, 1990.

22. Conklin JE, et al: Disease staging: Implications for hospital reimbursement and management. *Health Care Financing Review* (Annual Suppl.) 13–22, 1984.

23. Gonnella JS, Hornbrook MC, Louis DZ: Staging of disease: A case–mix measurement. *JAMA* 251:637–44, 1984.

24. Gonnella JS, Louis DZ: Severity of illness in the assessment of quality: Disease staging. In Hughes EFX (ed): *Perspectives on Quality in American Health Care*. Washington, DC: McGraw-Hill, 1988, pp 69–84.

25. Jencks SF, Dobson A: Refining the case-mix adjustment. *N Engl J Med* 317:679–86, 1987.

26. Eisenberg JM: *Doctors' Decisions and the Cost of Medical Care.* Ann Arbor, MI: Health Administration Press Perspectives, 1986, p 11.

27. Gonnella JS, Goran MJ: Quality of patient care—a measurement of change: The staging concept. *Medical Care* 13:467–73, 1975.

28. Iezzoni LI: Measuring the severity of illness and case mix. In Goldfield N, Nash DB (eds): *Providing Quality of Care: The Challenge to Clinicians.* Philadelphia, PA: American College of Physicians, 1989, Ch 4.

29. White LJ, Ball JR : Integrating practice guidelines with financial incentives. *Quart Rev Bull* 16:50–53, 1990.

30. Leape LL: Practice guidelines and standards: An overview. *Quart Rev Bull* 16:42–49, 1990.

31. Sox HC (ed): Assessment of medical outcomes: New opportunities for achieving a long sought-after objective. *International Journal of Technology Assessment in Health Care* 6:333–39, 1990.

32. Lomas JA, et al: Do practice guidelines guide practice: The effect of a consensus statement on the practice of physicians. *N Engl J Med* 321:1306–11, 1989.

33. Myers SA, Gleicher N: A successful program to lower cesarean-section rates. *N Engl J Med* 319:1511–16, 1989.

34. Roberts JR, Radany MH, Nash DB: Privilege delineation in a demanding new environment. *Ann Intern Med* 108:880–86, 1988.

35. Nash DB, Louis DZ, Gonnella JS: Improved practice profiles called key to better care. *QA Review* 2(7):1–4, September 1990.

36. Gonnella JS, et al: The problem of late hospitalization: A quality and cost issue. *Academic Medicine* 65:314–19, 1990.

37. Gonnella JS, Louis DZ: Evaluation of ambulatory care. *Journal of Ambulatory Care Management* 11(3): 68–83, 1988.

38. Gonnella JS, Louis DZ: Severity of illness in the assessment of quality: Disease staging. In Hughes EFX (ed): *Perspectives on Quality in American Health Care*. Washington, DC: McGraw-Hill, 1988, pp 69–84.

39. Louis DZ, Gonnella JS: Disease staging: Application for utilization review and quality assurance. *Quality Assurance and Utilization Review* 1:13–18, 1986.

40. Gonnella JS et al: Use of outcome measures in ambulatory care evaluation. In Giebink GA, White NH (eds): *Ambulatory Medical Care Quality Assurance*. La Jolla, CA: La Jolla Health Science Publications, 1977.

41. Gonnella JS, Louis DZ, McCord JJ: The staging concept: An approach of the assessment of outcome of ambulatory care. *Medical Care* 14:13–21, 1976

42. Louis DZ, Gonnella JS, Zeleznik C: *An Approach to the Prevention of Late Hospital Admissions in Stemming the Rising Costs of Medical Care: Answers and Antidotes*. Battle Creek, MI: W.K. Kellogg Foundation, 1988, pp 147–157.

43. Greco PJ, Eisenberg JM: Changing physician's practices. *N Engl J Med* 329:1271–73, 1993.

Chapter Nine

FOR WHAT SHOULD HOSPITALS BE ACCOUNTABLE?

Haya R. Rubin, MD, PHD

An underlying assumption in discussing what hospitals should be accountable for is that the public trusts that hospitals will act in patients' best interests. Therefore, hospitals must be accountable to demonstrate that they deliver high-quality care. They must also demonstrate that they are doing so as efficiently as possible for the patients of public payers (and others).

Current mechanisms for public accountability are neither comprehensive nor do they incorporate a systematic approach for ensuring that hospitals deliver high-quality care. Current efforts to establish which information is helpful for monitoring the quality of hospital care are duplicative and incomplete. In addition, many current approaches are not reliable or valid; there is no routine mechanism for evaluating reliability and validity of data released to the public.

To answer the question stated in this chapter's title, I will make some necessary assumptions and then delineate criteria for judging which levels of accountability are appropriate. Next, I will review the current status of public accountability and recommend what hospitals should be accountable to provide to public agencies, what information should be released to the public, and what hospitals should be required to do to follow up on possible problems. Finally, I will discuss changes in public policy that would help achieve public accountability.

Background

For what should hospitals be publicly accountable? Answering this question requires a philosophical and ethical perspective about the role of hospitals in society. Freidson has argued that doctors are licensed to act with professional autonomy based on the assumption that they are public servants who act in their patients' best interest.[1] Similarly, the public perceives that hospitals are also acting in their patients' best interests. Certainly most Americans believe that someone besides them is, and should be, regulating and monitoring the quality of hospital care. Yet most states and municipalities have fewer mechanisms for monitoring and preventing threats to public health due to poor hospital care than for threats to public health from poor quality food in restaurants.

The following discussion assumes that the reader accepts that hospitals should be accountable to deliver high-quality care.

Answering the question, "for what should hospitals be accountable?" also implies that we treat all hospitals alike, including public, proprietary, not-for-profit, and teaching hospitals. The perception that hospitals act in the public interest regardless of payment provides a common basis for making recommendations concerning public accountability. Accountability to deliver care as efficiently as possible becomes important for the patients of public payers such as Medicare, Medicaid or local programs for indigent patients, and public hospitals. Other payers also insist that hospitals be accountable for cost-effective care, but that is beyond the scope of this chapter.

We assume, then, that all hospitals should be publicly accountable to deliver high-quality care for all patients and efficient care for patients of public payers. High-quality care is defined, for purposes of this discussion, as care in accordance with information known about effectiveness of care, as well as agreed upon standards for care.

Critique of Existing Approaches

Currently, there is no ongoing program to ensure public accountability for quality of care in all hospitals. It is duplicative and wasteful for many hospitals, hospital consortia, payers, and so on, to invest independently in developing systems to ensure hospital accountability for quality of care. Standard mechanisms are needed and must be developed efficiently and unbiased under public, and preferably federal, auspices.

Only recently have explicit state and federal legislation included independent oversight of the quality of hospital care. Most states' hospital licensing authorities permit the hospital industry to police itself, allowing accreditation by the Joint Commission (an industry-based independent monitoring agency) to replace state licensure requirements for hospitals. Until the 1980s, this was virtually the only organization that monitored the quality of hospital care on the public's behalf. In the last 15 years, greater public accountability has been explicitly legislated for hospitals treating Medicare and Medicaid patients whose care is paid for by the public. Legislation first created the federal PSRO (professional standards review organization), then the PRO (peer review organization) program to oversee the quality of care delivered to Medicare patients.[2] Although this legislation addressed the quality of care delivered by physicians, only recently, in the Health Care Financing Administration's (HCFA) Fourth Scope of Work for PROs, have quality problems with hospitals been identified separately from those attributed to the attending physician.

Thus, current public mechanisms are limited to those instituted by public payers, particularly HCFA. Some of these mechanisms may not be optimally serving the public interest because they are not comprehensive and/or lack reliability and validity. Nevertheless, some of the resultant data have been released to the public or given to state licensure boards, who then decide whether or not to impose sanctions on physicians.

With respect to comprehensiveness, efforts to measure quality of care have been limited to mortality rate monitoring, contracts to PROs for screening, peer review hospital records, and pre-authorization for some surgical procedures. Little or no data have been collected on hospital-specific rates of adverse events with appropriate patient classification and risk adjustment, or other outcomes such as patient health-related quality of life or patient evaluations of their care. Comprehensiveness is also limited because there are currently few mechanisms of public accountability for quality of care for non-Medicare patients, and other payers determine the extent to which they wish to police hospitals. Currently, these payers are more concerned with expending funds efficiently than with quality of care.

With respect to reliability and validity, there is no public regulation that ensures that quality-of-care measures used by public agencies such as HCFA or the PROs are evaluated on a continuing basis for reliability, validity, and comprehensiveness, and that their performance is made known to the public and the health care industry. Studies have demonstrated that screening and peer review methods, such as the HCFA generic screens used until recently by PROs, have been unreliable and inaccurate.[3]

There are good reasons for thinking that too much data have been released to the public, and that publicly accountable mechanisms without release of data to the general public would be more constructive. Currently, data delivered to public agencies can be obtained by the press or other members of the public under the Freedom of Information Act. For example, hospitals provide discharge abstracts to many states and HCFA, and their mortality data are released to the public. Judged from the goal of improving the quality of care for the greatest number of persons, the hospital industry is correct to object to the release of mortality data in its current state-of-the-art, on the grounds that the data unfairly identify many good or average hospitals as poor. Similarly, to the extent that unreliable PRO judgments were made part of state licensure for physicians, they may not always serve the public interest.

On the other hand, recent changes in the PRO contracts and scope of work are spurring the development of quality-improvement programs designed to give feedback to hospitals. This change offers more promise for working together constructively with hospitals. These are better models for the kind of public accountability that should be required under new health care legislation given the current state of the art of measuring the quality of care. Such programs can still meet standards for public accountability by requiring hospitals to provide information to public agencies. These agencies would then be charged with making sure that hospitals actually improve their quality of care and are also acting in the public interest.

These criticisms are not meant to militate against providing publicly available information to enforcement agencies. Public agencies need enforcement authority separate from payment incentives and mechanisms. Public agencies that are monitoring should be responsible for helping hospitals improve, should have the authority to limit the hospital's scope of services, and should release data to the public about a hospital that has consistently and repeatedly had severe and widespread problems. Public agencies themselves, however, must be independently evaluated and held accountable for their own performance. If their methods are not accurate and reliable, they should not be releasing their data to enforcement agencies. It is important to determine which method of handling data is most cost-effective, i.e., "how much" quality improvement is achieved at what cost.

Recommendations for Public Accountability of Hospitals

There should be at least three levels of public accountability: (1) monitoring by public agencies; (2) release of performance information to the public at large; and (3) follow-up of possible problems detected by public agencies. At a minimum, hospitals might be required to have systems in place to monitor and improve their own care, alone or in conjunction with other hospitals. These systems could be approved and audited by public agencies. Secondly, hospitals might be required to collect some common data elements to allow comparative quality assessment, subject to audit by public agencies. Third, hospitals might be asked to deliver data to public agencies for processing and feedback about quality of care, and evaluating whether improvements have been made (without release to the general public). Fourth, hospitals might be required to deliver data to public agencies for release in forums that reach beyond the staff of these agencies, such as the news media. Finally, maximum accountability might entail hospitals demonstrating to public agencies that problems detected through comparative profiling of standard data have been addressed, and where neces-

TABLE 1

Levels of Accountability

Minimum ▲	Internal monitoring programs approved by public agencies
	Collection of standardized data subject to audit
	Provision of standardized data to public agencies to allow comparative profiling for feedback to providers to guide quality improvement efforts
	Release of comparative data to public for purchasing decisions
▼ Maximum	Demonstration that problems detected by public agencies have been corrected

sary, improved. For example, hospitals might be required to demonstrate that poor risk-adjusted outcomes relative to other centers are due to differing patient risk in a way not measured by the standard data, and that poor processes of care have been improved.

What Level of Accountability?

Public discussion is needed to determine what level of accountability is desirable, as some levels cost more than others and increase the costs of care (Table 1). What criteria could be used to determine which level of accountability is appropriate? One criterion might be that mechanisms for accountability should be those that achieve the greatest improvement in the public's ability to obtain high-quality care. Judgments of quality of care on which these mechanisms are built must be reliable and valid. For example, they must be comprehensive, incorporating both public standards as well as expert judgments of what is appropriate care. Additionally, onerous accountability requirements for hospitals are unfair to the public because the costs are passed on to consumers. Therefore, the cost-effectiveness of mechanisms of public accountability for improving the quality of care needs to be considered.

Recommendations for Accountability

Information to Be Monitored by Public Agencies

Hospitals should be required to deliver data to public agencies (Table 2). These agencies can then aggregate and screen the data to identify hospitals with opportunities to improve the quality of their care, as well as those hospitals that can set examples for others. Public agencies can either directly analyze the data, or perhaps contract this work to research organizations with expertise in the analytical tasks involved. The resulting data analysis can be used to supply hospitals comparative data about quality of care, and make sure that hospitals with possible quality of care problems conduct further studies and correct identified problems. At the current state of the art of quality assessment in hospital care, this information could contain the following elements to be reported back to hospitals, including a comparison of their performance to that of other hospitals:

Volume of procedures and diagnoses—Hospitals should report by physician and for the hospital as a whole, their volumes for common procedures and diagnoses so that the public can identify hospitals in terms of their experience in treating specialized problems.

Mortality rates by principal diagnosis and procedure—Reporting of risk-adjusted in-hospital and 30-day mortality should continue. To improve this reporting, clinically sensible ways must be developed to group International Classification of Disease (ICD-9-CM) codes into standard clinical patient cohorts. This should be one of the first tasks of a federal agency producing standard quality measures. In addition, separate risk models need to be developed for each common clinical condition. Mortality figures are best reported within condition or condition/procedure groups. Because hospitals' mix of patients vary widely, hospitalwide or other cross-diagnostic group mortality figures are meaningless without weights for each condition's risk.

Complication rates by principal diagnosis and procedure—A set of adverse events can be defined that are relevant across many diagnoses (for example, nosocomial pneumonia, pulmonary embolism, myocardial infarction, stroke, or acute renal failure). Complications of specific diagnoses and procedures can be added to this list for the appropriate patients (for example, those patients with sternal wound infection for coronary artery bypass graft [CABG] surgery). Such data must be reported within clinically similar groups.

TABLE 2

Standard Quality Measures to Be Monitored by Public Agencies

Quality Measure	Recommended Data Groupings
Volume	Of procedures or patients treated in a diagnostic cohort, by hospital and by physician
Mortality rates In-hospital and 30-day	By hospital, for diagnostic or procedure cohorts; Risk-adjusted for generic comorbidity and physiologic severity of illness; adjusted for specific risk factors for that diagnosis or procedure as they become better understood
Complication or "adverse event" rates	Same as for mortality rates
Health-related quality of life (from patients)	By diagnostic or procedure cohort
Patient evaluations of hospital care	By diagnostic or procedure cohort, hospital service, or "product line;" Risk adjusted for age, educational level, self-reported health and depression
Adherence to criteria: Explicit review criteria guideline-based algorithms	By principal diagnostic cohort or procedure, condition-specific

Patient surveys of health-related quality of life—For most conditions, death is rare, and how patients function and feel is the most important outcome affected by hospital care. Again, these data are most meaningful when reported within clinically similar groups. Developing risk models for the outcomes of each clinical condition should be a high priority.

Patient evaluations of hospital care—Standard instruments such as the Patient Judgments of Hospital Quality questionnaire[4] are available to survey patients after discharge about how they evaluate their hospital care. Hospitals should be required to report such data and should receive comparative feedback. For data analysis, patients should be grouped (for example, as medical, surgical, or obstetric patients), although diagnostic specificity is not as important for risk adjustment with this outcome. Risk adjustment within such groups does require questions on patient age, educational level, and self-reported health status, especially depression and mental health in general.

Adherence to criteria—Condition-specific explicit review criteria and algorithms based on rigorously developed guidelines for care should be applied by hospitals to medical records for high-volume conditions. This type of quality measure is the most difficult to develop and update; as more effectiveness studies and clinical trials are performed, changes are yielded in care guidelines and standards of medical practice. It is also labor intensive, requiring many data elements. On the other hand, it is very informative about what hospitals can do to improve the quality of care. An example of this type of assessment is New York State's review of the appropriateness of coronary artery bypass surgery by hospital based on the American College of Cardiology/American Heart Association guidelines and appropriateness criteria developed by RAND.[5]

In summary, the state of the art allows for hospitals to report data on patient volume for all diagnoses and procedures, mortality for a few selected procedures or diagnoses with well-developed risk models, and patient evaluations of hospital care. In the future, a more comprehensive list of generic adverse events could be identified. A concerted two- to three-year effort would improve diagnostic groupings and identification of clinical risk variables for each high-volume condition. Standard postdischarge health status measures could be adopted easily, although a three- to five-year research effort would be required to determine the needed risk adjustments. Comprehensive criteria based on evidence pose the greatest challenge, and their development and maintenance are the most costly part of these efforts.

Information for Public Release

Today it seems that almost any data developed to assess quality of care is subject to public release. It is important to consider whether legislation can be developed to protect data from the Freedom of Information Act until they meet standards for public release. The goal should be to publicly release data about volume and comparative outcomes for conditions and hospitals that have enough volume to allow this type of analysis at the hospital level. A much higher level of development of risk-adjusted outcome measures and higher predictive value of poor-performance indicators is necessary for public release, as consumers will act on these data not as screens but as definitive indicators of quality of care. In my judgment, data should not be released to the public if more than 1% or 2% of good or average hospitals are misclassified as poor.

Data on volume of procedures could be released immediately. Improvement in diagnostic classification is important, especially for nonsurgical conditions. No other currently collected and aggregated data are ready for public release. Data nearest to readiness are mortality figures with risk adjustment, by hospital and surgeon, for the most common surgical procedures, especially CABG surgery. Nevertheless, we need better risk data than are now collected by states such as New York and Pennsylvania, which are releasing CABG mortality rates to the public. An appropriate risk model for CABG surgery, based on patients' symptoms, stage of disease, coronary anatomy, left ventricular function, and comorbid disease, has been developed. For example, the Northern New England Cardiovascular Study Group[6] compared hospitals in terms of risk-adjusted CABG outcomes. By involving surgeons assessed in deciding which risk data should be collected, the process promoted fairness, validity, and behavior change. This study is a model for how to provide information that is valid enough for public release while improving the quality of care that the public receives. State agencies should also make the processes open to providers. Their risk models should bear clinical and methodologic scrutiny, and until they do so, data should not be released to the public.

Much work remains to prepare other outcomes, such as adverse events and health-related quality of life after discharge, for public release. Details of compliance with explicit criteria that constantly change are not helpful to the public. Nevertheless, if a comprehensive set of explicit criteria was maintained and performance measured, an overall performance score for compliance with all criteria measured would be useful to include in public information.

Accountability to Investigate and Address Problems

What should hospitals be required to do when, in screening the hospital, a state agency finds that a significant quality problem exists? This might be manifested as an outlier rate, or a rate higher than a prespecified standard. The hospital should be accountable to perform a complete investigation, including more specific studies to determine if there is need for improvement, and to deliver these data to the regulatory agency. The regulatory agency should have the needed resources to determine if these data are valid or to perform its own investigation—to which hospitals should be required to submit. If problems are apparent, the hospital should be required to develop a plan with the agency to fix them, although the system should also encourage self-regulation so that hospitals are not entirely dependent upon outside agencies to detect quality of care problems. The agency should then conduct a reevaluation to determine if significant improvement is sustained.

What Is Needed to Improve Public Accountability for Quality of Care?

Development of Measures and Improvement Tools by a Federal Agency

A standard, national effort to develop quality measures and improvement strategies should be undertaken. This should be done with input from the health care industry under the auspices of one or more relevant federal agencies such as the Agency for Health Care Policy and Research (AHCPR), or HCFA's Office of Research and Demonstrations. Industry groups may develop their own products and provide them as inputs to public agencies, but these need to be evaluated independently by the public agencies for comprehensiveness, reliability, and validity. Hospital and health care industry personnel should be required to participate in these developmental efforts but should not be primarily responsible for these activities. This is not only because of inherent bias, but because it is a prodigious waste of money for each hospital or hospital consortia to spend enormous funds, ultimately public funds, to develop duplicative systems of measurement. This will result only in unique systems that the public cannot compare to one another when choosing health plans and hospitals. To maximize the quality of care for all residents of the United States, this should be a task undertaken by public, preferably federal, agencies.

To facilitate this development, research is needed on:

- how to measure desired outcomes;
- how to risk-adjust for each outcome;
- how to determine the effectiveness of various strategies for managing health problems;
- how to measure provider adherence to treatment guidelines that are effective at improving outcomes; and
- how to help providers follow effective strategies.

Federal Research Policy

Funding must be directed to the research needs just described. Allocating money, however, is not enough. Funding policy is also important to make sure that research is done efficiently. Funding mechanisms should encourage collaborative research and eschew competition, and should be developed in conjunction with the federal agency or board developing standard quality measurement and improvement tools. A set of specific requests for applications (RFAs) should be designed to develop a comprehensive set of quality measures and tools, like a smaller-scale Human Genome Project (which has allocated the tasks of sequencing the entire human genome across a large number of centers in the United States to accomplish the goal as quickly as possible).

These RFAs should specify research questions, although creativity will be enhanced if investigators are asked to propose the design of the research as investigator-initiated or cooperative agreements. Agency staff should work with researchers to make sure that proposals are not duplicative, and reviewers should help make research designs effective and efficient. Funding agencies should ensure that research includes plans for effective dissemination to health care purchasers and regulators. Similar policies should govern the development of standard health care quality measures and improvement tools.

Public Regulatory Policy

The most important change in public policy needed to facilitate public accountability is legislation identifying a federal agency to develop standard measures of quality of care. Also, government bodies should be responsible for using standard measures to monitor quality, making sure that hospitals improve it, and disseminating quality of care data to the public. Regulatory policy should build in checks and balances, as well as regular evaluation of such agencies to ensure that they operate in the public interest.

The political environment should reward high-quality care and its improvement, and discourage policies that reduce the quality of care even if they save money. The regulatory environment of public accountability is subject to multiple forms of influence from within the health care industry. Government regulatory agencies must use the expertise of health care professionals to develop quality of care measures and improvement systems. Ideally, government regulatory staff should come from the health care industry to ensure relevant expertise. This means, however, that regulatory agencies are subject to subtle industry influences that may cause the systems developed to be insensitive to true differences in quality of care. For example, staff who have previously worked at hospitals may understand the hospital staff's needs better than patients' needs and may be reluctant to demand changes and put hospitals under pressure to provide more information. There may be fewer people thinking about the public interest.

It is difficult to guard against these political factors. To help ensure accurate data, rewards need to be established for full disclosure and for detecting opportunities for improvement.

Reward of delivery of accurate data to federal agencies and punishment for inaccuracy could be done in conjunction with public payer reimbursement policy. For example, discounts could be given for complete data and/or fines applied for inaccuracy. Routine random and indicator-driven audits by the public agency should be conducted. Special mechanisms may be needed to help quality measurement and improvement efforts in public hospitals, which may be penalized when municipalities and electorates fail to fund quality assessment and improvement. Municipalities could be encouraged to allocate funds for this purpose through incentives such as eligibility requirements for receipt of federal funds or through federal payer reimbursement policies.

Finally, regulatory policy can both prevent release to the public of inaccurate data by regional or state agencies and protect data from Freedom of Information Act release until there is an extremely low rate of misclassification.

Reimbursement and Contracting Policy

Reimbursement and contracting incentives will promote the public interest if they are based on accurate measures of quality of care. This can be achieved in a competitive environment only if accurate information about the quality of care is available and if enough options exist so that quality of care can be a true determinant in choice of provider. Currently there is little incentive for health care providers to supply accurate information about quality of care. With cost of care being the major concern, there is little incentive for any health care reform legislation to include meaningful quality measurement. In fact, participating in quality-of-care measurement and improvement efforts will add cost, certainly in the short term. It would be important to study whether and how reimbursement policy can be designed to improve the quality of care and public accountability for it.

TABLE 3

Accountability Goals: Monitoring by Public Agencies to Facilitate Quality Improvement

Current Year Goals	Future Goals
Define diagnostic cohorts for nonsurgical or nonprocedure admissions based on groupings of principal ICD codes	Require hospitals to collect data on pre-admission health status using a standardized brief measure for all patients admitted (1 year)
Define standard list of generic complications and require hospitals to collect these on all patients	Require hospitals to collect data on risk factors for patients with conditions and procedures for which these have been identified (1 year)
Define specific list of complications for high-volume procedure and medical cohorts; require hospitals to collect and report these on all patients	Choose postdischarge health status measure appropriate to specific conditions and procedures as well as a generic one for all other patients (1 year)
Choose public-domain generic comorbidity measure based on secondary diagnoses on the day of hospital admission; require hospitals to collect and report data to calculate this for all patients	Require hospitals to collect standardized patient judgment measure on sample of all patients and sample of patients with specific conditions and procedures (1 year)
Define generic physiologic data on hospital admission that have been demonstrated to predict mortality in at least one patient cohort; require hospitals to report these for patients who receive these lab tests	Require hospitals to collect postdischarge health status data on samples of patients with specific conditions and procedures (2 years)
For coronary revascularization procedures, require hospitals to collect standard data on all known clinical risk factors	
Choose brief generic patient-reported health status tool to be administered at admission or as soon as patient is able to complete it about health status prior to admission	
Define risk factors for various outcomes for several other specific procedures and conditions	
Choose generic measure to evaluate patient judgments of their care	

Table 4

Accountability Goals: Information for Public Release to Guide Consumer and Purchaser Choice

Current Year Goals	Future Goals
Release volume data for procedures	Use new data collection to develop refined risk model for coronary revascularization (1 year)
Define diagnostic cohorts for medical conditions and release volume data for these	Release risk-adjusted mortality and complication rates for coronary revascularization (2 years)
	Release comparative patient judgement data for all patient cohorts (2 years)
	Develop risk models for mortality rates and complications for other procedures based on data collected for monitoring (2 years)
	Release risk-adjusted mortality and complication rates for other procedures (3 years)
	Develop models for post-discharge health status and long-term outcomes of coronary revascularization (3 years)
	Develop models for post-discharge health status for other conditions and procedures (4 years)
	Release risk-adjusted health status outcome data for coronary revascularization (4 years)
	Release risk-adjusted health status outcome data for other conditions and procedures (5 years)

Public payers could make hospitals eligible for a higher rate of reimbursement if they deliver complete, timely, and accurate data to public agencies. As discussed, federal payment policy could encourage municipalities to operate their hospitals in a publicly accountable way.

Table 3 lists the short- and long-term goals that public agencies should strive for in facilitating quality improvement, and Table 4 lists those short- and long-term goals that are pertinent to the appropriate release of information to the public.

Conclusion

Based on social assumptions and the public's trust, all hospitals should be publicly accountable for delivering high-quality care and for efficiently treating the patients of public payers. The long-term goal should be for state or regional agencies to collect complete information about the quality of care—such as hospital volumes and risk-adjusted outcomes for high-volume patient groups—for public release and to feed back both process and outcome measures to hospitals. We need a federal effort to identify standard quality measures. We also need federal legislation to identify and fund state or regional organizations charged with monitoring and ensuring the improvement of quality of care for all hospitals in that area using these standard measures. If public regulatory policy, research funding policy, and reimbursement policy are changed to facilitate these efforts and identify these organizations, then routine measurement, reporting of meaningful comparative data to providers, and improvement of the quality of care can become integral to health care delivery.

References

1. Friedson E: *Profession of Medicine: A Study of the Sociology of Applied Knowledge.* New York: Harper and Row, 1970.

2. Lohr K (ed): *Medicare: A Strategy for Quality Assurance,* Vol I. Washington, DC: National Academy Press, 1990.

3. Rubin HR, et al: Watching the doctor watchers: How well do peer review organization methods detect hospital care quality problems? *JAMA* 267:2349–54, 1992.

4. Rubin HR, et al: The patient judgments of hospital quality (PJHQ) questionnaire. In Meterko M, et al (eds): Patient judgments of hospital quality: Report of a pilot study. *Medical Care* 28(9):S17–S18, 1990.

5. Leape L, et al: *Coronary Artery Bypass Graft: A Literature Review and Ratings of Appropriateness and Necessity*. Santa Monica, CA: Rand Corp., 1991.

6. O'Connor GT, et al: A regional prospective study of in-hospital mortality associated with coronary artery bypass grafting. *JAMA* 266(6):803–09, 1991.

GLOSSARY

Glossary

Accountability

The obligation to disclose periodically, in adequate detail and consistent form, to all directly and indirectly responsible or properly interested parties, the purposes, principles, procedures, relationships, results, incomes, and expenditures involved in any activity, enterprise, or assignment so that they can be evaluated by the interested parties

AHA

American Hospital Association

AHCA

American Health Care Association

AHCPR

Agency for Health Care Policy and Research

AHIMA

American Health Information Management Association

AMI

Acute myocardial infarction

ASC

Ancillary service category

ASHRM

American Society for Healthcare Risk Management

AWP

Any willing provider (laws)

BBGH

Bay Area Business Group on Health

CABG
Coronary artery bypass graft (procedure)

Case-based review
Evaluation of quality of care based on review of individual medical records by health professionals who make judgments as to whether the care delivered was of acceptable quality

CCU
Critical care unit

CHC
Coalitions for Health Care

CHMIS
Community Health Management Information System

CHOICE
Cleveland Hospital Outcomes Indicators of Care Evaluations

CPRI
Computer-Based Patient Record Institute

CQI
Continuous quality improvement

DRG
Diagnosis-related group

DNR
Do not resuscitate (orders)

EDI
Electronic Data Interchange

EPIQual
Employers Purchasing Initiative for Quality

Gatekeeper
Individual who monitors and/or oversees the actions of other persons, as in a physician who determines health services to be provided to a patient and coordinates provision of the services by other persons

HCFA
Health Care Financing Administration

HCHP
Harvard Community Health Plan

HCPA
Health Care Purchasers Association

HCQIP
Healthcare Quality Improvement Program

Health Security Act
Health reform bill introduced to Congress in 1993 that ensures individual and family security through health coverage for all Americans in a manner that contains the rate or growth in health care costs and promotes responsible health insurance practices, to promote choice in health care, and to insure and protect the health care of all Americans

HEDIS
Health Plan Employer Data and Information Set

HEP
Hospital Experimental Payment Program (Rochester, New York)

HMO
Health maintenance organization

HPCI
Health Policy Corporation of Iowa

HRSA
Health Resources and Services Administration

HSAC
Health Services Advisory Committee

ICU
Intensive care unit

IMS
Indicator Measurement System

JCAHO
Joint Commission on Accreditation of Healthcare Organizations

Lithotripsy
Noninvasive pulverization of urinary tract stones by means of a lithotripter

MBGH
Midwest Business Group on Health

NAHDO
National Association of Health Data Organizations

NCQA
National Committee for Quality Assurance

NBCH
National Business Coalition on Health

NCHS
National Center for Health Statistics

Nosocomial
Pertaining to or originating in a hospital

OABGH
Ozarks Area Business Group on Health

OSHPD
California Office of Statewide Health Planning and Development

OTA
Office of Technology and Assessment

Outcomes measurement
A measurement of what does or does not happen after a process(es), service(s), or activity(ies) is or is not performed, or a structural component (such as technology or a medical specialist) exists or does not exist; the measurement quantifies an organization's, a practitioner's, or a community's actual results in providing services the organization is capable of providing

Pattern of care
The distribution of rates of performance among members of a group of practitioners, health care organizations, or communities

PCP
Primary care physician

PHO
Physician Hospital Organization

PPO
Preferred provider organization

PPRC
Physician Payment Review Commission

PRO
Peer review organization

PSRO
Professional standards review organization

PTCA
Percutaneous transluminal coronary angioplasty

RFA
Request for application (i.e., for federal funds for research)

Risk adjustment
The use of severity of illness measures, such as age, to estimate the risk (the measurable or predictable chance of loss, injury, or death) to which a patient is subject before receiving some health care intervention

Risk management
The function of planning, organizing, and directing a comprehensive program of activities to identify, evaluate, and take corrective action against risks that may lead to patient inury, employee injury, and property loss or damage with resulting institutional financial loss or legal liability

SAT
Scholastic Aptitude Test

SDO
State data organization

Severity adjustment
The process of classifying patients by severity-of-illness data so that performance and quality across organizations and practitioners can be more meaningfully compared

Small-area analysis
Method used to compare utilization and charges among population groupings or geographic areas

Stakeholders

Providers and purchasers of care in a system of healthcare

Total quality management

A continuous quality improvement management system directed from the top, but empowering employees and focusing on systemic, not individual, employee problems

Validation

The process of establishing that a given method, procedure, or process is sound

Value

Worth (of health care) times efficacy over cost

VROAM

Valid risk-adjusted outcome monitoring

WBGH

Washington Business Group on Health

WEDI

Workgroup for Electronic Data Interchange

INDEX

INDEX

A

B

C

D

E

F

G

H

I

J

K

L

M

N

O

P

Q

R

S

T